THE OTHER EIGHTIES

THE OTHER EIGHTIES

A Secret History of America

in the Age of Reagan

BRADFORD MARTIN

Hill and Wang

A division of Farrar, Straus and Giroux

New York

Hill and Wang
A division of Farrar, Straus and Giroux
18 West 18th Street, New York 10011

Grateful acknowledgment is made for permission to reprint lyrics from "Themselves,"
by the Minutemen, written by Dennes Boon, copyright © New Alliance Music (BMI) /
Administered by BUG. All rights reserved. Used by permission.

Library of Congress Cataloging-in-Publication Data
Martin, Bradford D., 1966–
    The other eighties : a secret history of America in the age of Reagan / Bradford
    Martin.— 1st ed.
        p.   cm.
    Includes bibliographical references and index.
    ISBN 978-0-8090-7461-7 (alk. paper)
        1. United States—Politics and government—1981–1989.   2. United States—
    Politics and government—1989–1993.   3. Reagan, Ronald—Adversaries.
    I. Title.

    E876 .M3626 2010
    973.927—dc22

                                                                    2010022830

Designed by Jonathan D. Lippincott

www.fsgbooks.com

10   9   8   7   6   5   4   3   2   1

For Jackson, Hazel, Harry, and Charlie

CONTENTS

PREFACE

This book started with a challenge. Discussing the as yet modest output of historical literature on the 1980s, an editor friend announced, "Any book on the 1980s inevitably turns into a Reagan book." A substantial portion of his assertion rang true. In many ways, the singular figure of Ronald Wilson Reagan, the most popular president in a generation, dominated national life during the decade. The president's advocates credited him with monumental accomplishments, no less than restoring prosperity, regaining national pride, and spearheading Cold War victory. The beaming accounts of his presidency and achievements only intensified after his death in 2004, generating a wave of affectionate tributes in the popular media. Still, a look at the vicissitudes of presidential popularity during Reagan's two terms reveals that a sizable swath of the American public disapproved of the way he handled his job, even at moments of his greatest triumph.[1] This suggests that there was more to the story, that there was another 1980s, its history buried under the celebratory narrative of Reagan and conservative ascendancy. The gauntlet thrown down at my feet, I picked it up, determined to craft the untold account of the decade's opposition.

The task was more daunting than I had imagined. Indeed, a growing raft of scholarship illuminates the decade's complexities with greater sophistication than both popular accounts and much of the earliest scholarship on the period. This scholarship offers provocative revelations, sometimes fraught with irony, occasionally contradictory. These accounts argue, variously, that Reagan was smarter than he appeared; that he was "the single most important political figure of his age"; that he was the key figure in the "Great Reconciliation" between 1960s liberalism and 1980s conservatism; that he decisively inspired and presided over a rightward shift in the nation's political economy and political culture, somehow managing to leave room for a more tolerant and diverse society than existed at the decade's outset; that he effectively marshaled an unapologetic patriotism and nationalism in world affairs that John F. Kennedy and Franklin D. Roosevelt also tapped into, albeit one that pointed the nation in a profoundly different ideological direction; and that Republican electoral triumphs were more a function of the personal popularity that Reagan's warmth, humor, and reassuring leadership style engendered than any fundamental realignment of the American electorate in a more conservative direction.[2] Substantial elements of truth resound through these claims, and this book, far from rejecting them, seeks to acknowledge its intellectual indebtedness en route to sifting through and building upon these interpretations. What these accounts do have in common, however, and what my own study embarks on a quest to move beyond, is a profound Reaganocentrism. The foregrounding of Reagan in historical interpretations of the 1980s, though partially justified, displaces many important actors, events, and movements whose stories deserve telling.

Historical memory renders Reagan's electoral victories in 1980 and 1984 veritable avalanches, from the rejection of the embattled Jimmy Carter and embrace of a new direction in American politics in 1980 to the 1984 reelection, which is often viewed as the "culmination" of more than a decade of ferment for conservative ideas—from lower taxes and smaller government to renewed Cold War vitality and family values.[3] Indeed, the results of these national referenda were clear-cut and decisive, particularly in the electoral college. Yet a look at the popular vote reveals that more than 40 percent of American voters demurred from sanctioning this movement, not to mention the roughly 50 percent of voting-age Americans who declined to exercise their right altogether.[4] These figures suggest Reagan's status as a polarizing figure for a sizable but less-trumpeted group of Americans in the 1980s who remained unenchanted by his vision of "Morning in America." This book examines the less-told story of Americans who opposed the decade's prevailing political tides. In doing so, it relies on several key questions as guideposts for constructing an alternative perspective: What was the nature of opposition to Reagan conservatism in the 1980s? What recurring themes, ideas, and sensibilities infused it? What were its accomplishments, limitations, and downright failures? Why has this opposition been so overshadowed in the decade's dominant narrative?

The search for answers to these questions reveals a handful of salient ideas and discernible patterns. First and foremost, accurately telling the story of the opposition during the 1980s requires moving beyond mainstream politics. The Democratic Party opened the decade reeling, its traditional constituencies ravaged by the emergent phenomenon of Reagan Democrats, and finished the decade enmeshed in the headlong pursuit of regaining the political center by moving farther to the right. By Walter Mondale's 1984 campaign, political liberalism had reoriented itself, away from the New Deal vision of benign governmental promotion of the public well-being that dominated the mid-twentieth century and toward a program founded on private-sector-driven economic growth that modestly promised to maintain most existing government services with a new focus on frugal management. To this, Mondale added the candid but politically fatal admission that he would be forced to raise taxes to offset the burgeoning Reagan deficit. In 1988 the Democratic presidential candidate found himself on the defensive against the very word "liberal." Michael Dukakis shriveled as George H. W. Bush attacked him as a liberal and a "card-carrying member of the ACLU." As the campaign wore on, those epithets became conflated in the popular parlance, rendering Dukakis a "card-carrying liberal." The candidate spent much of the remainder of the campaign trying to avoid the label by running on a promise of efficient government management and economic growth, while trying to avoid Mondale's mistake of addressing the possibility of tax hikes. In the meantime, his opponent hammered him by exploiting a series of Democratic wedge issues, most notably with the infamous Willie Horton political ad, which profiled a convicted murderer who raped a woman while on prison furlough under Dukakis's watch as Massachusetts governor.[5] Two weak presidential candidates and their disastrous campaigns represented only the most visible symbol of a Democratic futility and disunity whose roots ran much deeper. Mondale and Dukakis embodied the defining trait of the 1980s dunderheaded Democrats that undermined the party throughout the decade—the abandonment of full-throated progressive idealism, articulated in the

New Deal and the Great Society, in favor of a pragmatic, if quixotic, shift to the center. As Democrats came more and more to resemble the Republicans they putatively opposed, the resulting political identity crisis left many of the most exciting and animated adversaries of conservative Reagan-Bush-era policy outside of mainstream national politics.

For this reason, *The Other Eighties* focuses on the opposition to Reagan conservatism, broadly construed. This encompasses a range of voices and expressions—those who pursued claims in traditional politics, lobbying Congress to support a nuclear freeze and celebrating Geraldine Ferraro as the first woman on a major party presidential ticket, and those who fought their battles in the cultural realm, from Bruce Springsteen's humanizing portraits of the decade's dispossessed to the angry artists of Gran Fury and their expressions of rage at inadequate government response to the AIDS epidemic. My central argument is that despite the decade's reputation for conservative ascendancy and Reagan's personal popularity, there was another 1980s, one in which the opposition played a key role. Often this role involved playing defense, engaging in a tactical struggle to preserve the liberal and progressive gains of the 1960s and 1970s. Black mayors' initiatives to make municipal government more responsive to their constituencies and pro-choice women's efforts to protect abortion rights against an ever more conservative federal judiciary and a virulent pro-life countermovement exemplify this struggle for field position. Responding to Reagan foreign policy, 1980s activists tamed, tempered, and constrained the most bellicose and ambitious aspects of the administration's designs. It is a notable outcome of this era, for instance, that Americans do not speak of a "Nicaragua War."

At times, the decade's opposition recorded accomplishments that exceeded the preservation of the hard-won gains of previous eras, tallying progressive advances. Many activist organizations and individuals and their counterparts in the cultural sphere demonstrated an outward-looking transnational sensibility, showing heightened awareness of the international implications of national issues, anticipating the global interconnectedness of the early twenty-first century. Against the Right's hard-nosed emphasis on personal responsibility over structural injustice, the decade witnessed a reawakening of social conscience in popular culture, led by rock stars and movie stars. Black and white musical subcultures developed with an oppositional attitude, and frequently with confrontational content, boldly challenging the political and economic status quo, carving inroads into mainstream culture by decade's end. Countering media imagery of an apathetic youth, the divestment movement on American college campuses led an underpublicized resurgence of student activism. Doggedly fighting back the diatribes of conservative intellectuals and their allies in national politics, progressives in higher education not only defended the strides that women, minority, homosexual, and non-Western cultures had made toward representation in the curriculum, they furthered diversity and multiculturalism as institutional goals.

The opposition was far from a unified movement. Those who participated in the political activism, social transformation, and cultural strivings this book describes hailed from a variety of backgrounds and agitated for wide-ranging agendas, using disparate methods and tactics that covered the full spectrum of strategies for change, from direct action protest, to electoral solutions, to making political poster art. Moreover, the 1980s opposition displayed surprising geographic diversity—this was not simply a story of the progressive coasts versus the conservative heartland. On the contrary, the decade's activist movements enjoyed consistent representation in areas generally regarded as conservative strongholds.

From this diversity, though, clear patterns emerge. Broad coalitions jelled around key issues such as the nuclear freeze movement, then dissolved to reassert themselves elsewhere, the massive prochoice mobilizations of the late 1980s and early 1990s standing as a prominent example. Often, the personnel involved in such initiatives overlapped, with Central America solidarity activists proceeding seamlessly to South African divestment protests, post-punkers and rappers who railed against Reagan militarism testifying against music industry censorship, a skirmish embedded in the decade's larger culture wars. Ordinary Americans, distressed by the nation's direction and mood, increasingly rose to penetrate fortresses of technical and bureaucratic expertise—from antinuclear activists who challenged the high priesthood of the defense establishment to AIDS activists' quest to expedite the Food and Drug Administration's testing protocols. Their efforts re-enchanted the political arena for those disheartened by conservative dominance and resulted in activist leaders gaining substantial and sometimes unparalleled levels of self-taught expertise.

In turn, these individuals often professionalized these new proficiencies, creating new fields of employment, from services for AIDS victims to rape crisis centers.[6]

The point of this book is not to minimize the impact of conservatism and Reaganism in the 1980s. To do so would be foolish and would fail to acknowledge the decade's dramatic political realignment, characterized by such important phenomena as the Republicans' strengthened grip on the South and the legions of working-class Americans compelled by Reagan's magnetism and attracted by his positions on a range of social issues. But most of conservatism's biggest gains remained on the highly visible stage of national political life. Away from this white-hot spotlight, conservatives advanced their influence to be sure—evangelical Christianity's expanding reach into public life represents a conspicuous example—but in the more nebulous realm of social and cultural change, progressives enjoyed discernible and often unheralded victories.[7] The national media's emphasis on a clear narrative of restored patriotic pride, a return to traditional values after the permissiveness of the 1960s and 1970s, and a love affair with a telegenic, charismatic president obscured a more complex story, a "secret history" of how the threads of the decade's progressive impulses were woven together.

This broad oppositional movement quietly consolidated, ratified, and even extended many of the salient changes of the 1960s and 1970s. The influence and experiences of 1960s activists, acknowledged and otherwise, hang heavy over the 1980s' attempts for change. The younger Americans examined here frequently downplayed or denied the influence of 1960s movements—from civil rights to the antiwar movement to feminism—even as they uncannily mimicked their tactics. Alternatively, other activists coming of age in the 1980s displayed a profound longing for a sense of community and togetherness linked to their historical image of the 1960s. Older voices on the left, now graying and entering (if not ensconced in) middle age, cut their political teeth in the 1960s movements and sought to use the lessons of their failures, and successes, to their advantage.

That said, the 1980s were no 1960s. New tactical innovations arose to supplement 1960s-style direct action. Unlike their 1960s forebears, 1980s activists were as likely to try to influence established institutions as to undermine the foundations of their authority. Where the social and political movements of the 1960s took exploratory steps toward connecting with like-minded activists and oppressed peoples in other corners of the globe, 1980s activists did so with far greater sophistication, pursuing such connections more consistently and actively. Telling differences in the style of opposition existed between the generations as well. Though both opposed militarism, it is difficult to imagine 1980s post-punks, with their acerbic irony and skepticism, taking off their clothes in the sincere celebration of peace and love their countercultural parents experienced at Woodstock. Although the civil rights and antiwar movement strategies had harnessed the power of television to their causes to highlight authoritarian violence, ACT UP videographers took technological savvy to a new level, consciously and powerfully documenting their movement in a wide-ranging alternative media enterprise.

The first three chapters of this book examine three grassroots activist movements pursuing global visions of social justice and self-determination that sought to influence the policies of large institutions from the federal government to American colleges and universities. Chapter 1 focuses on the early 1980s nuclear freeze movement, which called for halting the production of new weaponry and drew American antinuclear forces closer to their European brethren. Though Reagan avoided appearing vulnerable to public pressure and even upped the ante by introducing his ambitious if fanciful "Star Wars" idea, the freeze movement made a valuable contribution to the public dialogue on peace and national defense and nudged the president toward arms reduction talks. Chapter 2 explores the Central America solidarity movement, highlighting how both its secular and religious wings shone a light on the Reagan administration's activities in the region and their devastating effects on local populations regardless of whether they were involved with leftist politics. Chapter 3 explores the reawakening of student activism on American college campuses as young people tried to address the injustices of apartheid by focusing on its nearest expression: college and university investments in corporations that did business in South Africa. In the long run, movement pressure encouraged a wave of partial or total divestments that played a role in the erosion of the American policy of constructive engagement and ultimately hastened the demise of the South African system of racial supremacy.

Chapters 4 and 5 feature contrasting case studies of opposition from the decade's cultural life. Chapter 4 reveals how 1980s popular culture, though laden with glitzy materialism and reflections of the new conservatism, nevertheless witnessed a reawakening of social conscience after the hedonistic 1970s. From Live Aid to *Platoon*, from Bruce Springsteen's deepening social engagement at the zenith of his popular appeal to the Hollywood Women's Political Committee's efforts at electoral impact, the decade's pop culture was not as bereft of left, liberal, or progressive impulses as one might think. The chapter also examines the "culture wars" that began in the late 1980s and extended into the 1990s, arguing that relentless attacks from "traditionalists" demonstrated how thoroughly the social and cultural transformations of the 1960s and 1970s were woven into the fabric of American life. Chapter 5 focuses on the margins of cultural life rather than its center, showing how "post-punk"—or "alternative"—music forged an oppositional voice, opposing corporate dominance of American life, criticizing Reagan-era militarism, and promoting shared identity and community among fans. The momentum generated by this community and its music proved substantial enough to propel it into the mainstream, led by Nirvana's 1991 breakthrough album, *Nevermind*.

The last three chapters look at the political and cultural strivings of three sectors of the American public that used group identity as a basis for mobilization. Chapter 6 observes black politics in the 1980s, from the growing ranks of big-city black mayors, to Jesse Jackson's two presidential campaigns, to the cultural politics of rap music's Ice T and Public Enemy. Whether the tactics pursued were those of accommodation, inclusion, pressure, or confrontation, these African American voices rejected the pervasive media stereotype of a passive underclass pathology and exhibited a vigorous desire to reshape conditions in their communities. Chapter 7 investigates the fate of feminist mobilization after its heyday in the 1970s. Though weathering the storm of the much-touted media and political backlash, feminism survived in the 1980s as women gained increased legitimacy and visibility in national politics and deepened their inroads into institutions of national life, from enhanced anti–sexual harassment provisions in the workplace, to the mainstreaming of 1960s and 1970s alternative institutions like rape crisis centers and battered women's shelters, to the growing ubiquity of women's studies in college curricula. Chapter 8 looks at the radical disruptions of the AIDS Coalition to Unleash Power (ACT UP), the shock troops of AIDS activism, which aimed to challenge individuals and institutions hostile or unresponsive to a health crisis that wrought particularly devastating effects on the gay community. Despite ACT UP's provocative approach, much of its most effective work came on a quieter level of pursuing research designed to justify expedited development and testing of promising new AIDS drugs, and of promoting a sense of politically mobilized community among those who participated in its diverse activities.

The story outlined in these chapters does not aspire to provide a comprehensive history of the 1980s, nor do the individuals and groups featured here amount to an exhaustive account of the decade's opposition. There are some noticeable omissions. For instance, environmental activism expanded against conservative pushback in the 1980s, most strikingly with Greenpeace and the radical Earth First!, but claiming important institutional gains as well. The trajectory of this movement would have lent itself to this book's arguments and purposes, but alas, it remains beyond the scope of what is manageable to present here. The battle against nuclear power in the late 1970s—which reached its crescendo with the militant protests of the Clamshell Alliance and the No Nukes! concerts in the aftermath of the 1979 Three Mile Island incident—shares many of the same personnel that figure in the movements I discuss, particularly the nuclear freeze movement. But this cluster of activity took place during the Carter years and lacked the same sense of focused opposition against the conservative tide. What I have tried to do here, therefore, is to provide a provocative selection of highlights of 1980s opposition that collectively suggest the range of groups, organizations, and individuals that confronted the decade's conservative forces.

Though most of the events this book chronicles transpired in the 1980s, historical "decades" frequently fail to sort themselves into tidy numeric packages ending in zero. Just as often, they are alternatively defined by critical thematic elements rather than mere chronology. Thus my definition of the 1980s encompasses the years of the Reagan and George H. W. Bush presidencies. The period begins with Reagan's effort to dissipate the Carter malaise and ends with the election of William Jefferson Clinton. Aside from those obvious guideposts from the marquee of national politics, another set of developments suggests

1992 as an appropriate endpoint for this era. The 1991 Persian Gulf War reflected a different model of warfare than the largely covert Cold War by proxy interventions in Central America and the Caribbean Basin in the 1980s. Despite saturating mainstream media coverage celebrating the "awe and wonder" of Operation Desert Storm, war strategy was restrained by the street-level presence of an underpublicized but growing antiwar movement in the late winter months of 1991. The end of the Cold War and the breakup of the Soviet Union ushered in a new era of American foreign policy, eradicating a common anticommunist thread to conservatives' criticism of many of the movements profiled here. Domestically, President Bush's approval rating, which skyrocketed in the aftermath of the Gulf War, dropped precipitously with the recession of 1991–92 and Americans' growing disdain for a patrician leader exposed as hopelessly unfamiliar with workaday realities such as electronic grocery scanners. The arrival of centrist Democrat Bill Clinton's presidency muddied the waters of opposition, making it difficult for progressives to tell if a friend or merely an adversary in different clothing resided at 1600 Pennsylvania Avenue. Alternative music's breakthrough to the mainstream in 1991 and the contemporaneous transition from gangsta rap as a niche genre to hip-hop as the default sound track for American youth regardless of racial background seemed to signal the arrival of a new set of cultural sensibilities.

Writing the history of the recent past carries its special rewards and pitfalls. The exhilaration of breaking new historical ground, of logging an early interpretation of events that lie within lived memory, is counterbalanced by the sobering thought that most enterprises of historical interpretation live to be modified, revised, rejected, or even mocked. Complicating matters further is the issue of one's personal relationship with the material. It is my contention that whether examining the foundations of democracy in ancient Greece, the social practices of the nobility in late medieval Europe, or very recent U.S. history, a "politics of selection" exists in historians' choice of subject matter. That is, historians tend to gravitate to topics with which they feel some personal affinity. With this in mind, a bit of housekeeping in the way of my own personal connections to the "other 1980s" is in order. I came of age in the Reagan 1980s, living out my high school years during his first term and my college years during his second. In my early twenties I was a marginal participant in some of the events and activities described in this book. I attended a couple of pro-divestment rallies on my college campus, marched in a few ACT UP demonstrations, and played music in a short-lived post-punk band. Though I never played a leadership role, I will admit to sharing certain sympathies.

Now, almost two decades later, I do not believe that any of this renders me unfit to tell the story of these movements and expressions of opposition. On the contrary, I view caring about the individuals and groups profiled here as a prerequisite for evaluating their history accurately, since doing so requires accepting historical actors' own observations about their intentions and motivations, without being dismissive, as a starting point of scholarly inquiry. This is particularly important when dealing with voices of change operating in the cultural realm, which many historians ignore as frivolous and unimportant, focusing instead on the more "serious" arena of political economy. During these intervening years I have acquired the training and methods of the historical profession, which compel me to hold the protagonists in the 1980s "secret history" up to exacting scrutiny. Just as a European medievalist would, I must now try to stand back and read the historical record with the scholarly detachment that is a core principle of that training and let the sources speak. In writing this book and listening to these sources, I have discovered many surprises and contradictions along the way that have profoundly altered my view of the period. Accordingly, I have tried to describe and evaluate them as honestly as possible. Whether I have done so successfully, I leave to the reader's judgment.

THE OTHER EIGHTIES

1

CALLING TO HALT
The Nuclear Freeze Campaign

On June 12, 1982, children and octogenerians were on the march. So were World War II veterans and Tibetans for World Peace. Coretta Scott King and the Bread and Puppet Theater. College students and trade unionists. Movie stars and rock stars. Quakers and Roman Catholic bishops. International pilgrims hailing from such far corners of the globe as Japan, Europe, the Soviet Union, Zambia, and Bangladesh. The total tallied somewhere around three-quarters of a million souls, all making the trek from the United Nations to the Great Lawn of New York City's Central Park, where the march concluded with a rally for nuclear disarmament. The gathering marked a high point of popular support for the disarmament movement, the largest protest rally in United States history to date. Contemporary observers repeatedly noted its diversity. Phrases like "kaleidoscope of humanity," "rainbow spectrum," and "largest, most diverse gathering for a single cause" redounded through media accounts of the event.[1] Within that diversity, discernible patterns appeared. The usual suspects on the political left were well represented. Established peace and disarmament groups, from Mobilization for Survival to the Committee for a Sane Nuclear Policy (SANE), organized the event to coincide with the United Nations second special session on disarmament. Peace-oriented religious groups, including the American Friends Service Committee, Pax Christi USA, the Fellowship of Reconciliation, and the Southern Christian Leadership Conference, loomed prominently among the sponsors. Professional organizations from Physicians for Social Responsibility, to the Union of Concerned Scientists, to the National Lawyers Guild all lent support. Jackson Browne, James Taylor, Bruce Springsteen, Joan Baez, and Linda Ronstadt, musicians with long track records of support for peace and antinuclear causes, all performed.

But though the usual suspects organized the rally, its vast, broad-based assemblage made the Central Park gathering different. The Nuclear Weapons Freeze Campaign, as the central organization's official title ran, struck upon a simple and galvanizing idea—for the United States and the Soviet Union to enter a mutual and verifiable freeze on the testing, production, and deployment of all nuclear weapons—and through widespread grassroots activity delivered that message to mainstream America. The campaign drew from all socioeconomic groups in almost every geographic region—and even garnered support from Republicans.

The campaign rode this wave of enthusiasm through the 1982 midterm elections, which saw a number of freeze resolutions around the country succeed in state referenda. After that, the movement declined, failing to translate popular momentum into concrete policy measures and faltering badly with the advent of President Reagan's Star Wars plan and his 1984 reelection.[2] But along the way, the movement wielded more influence than popular accounts suggest, reshaping the foreign policy landscape in which the Reagan administration operated. The saber-rattling Cold Warrior rhetoric of Reagan during his candidacy and the early part of his first administration asked the American public to envision fighting and winning a nuclear war and to commit the necessary resources to building nuclear arsenals to achieve superiority over the Soviets. The freeze campaign pressured the administration to tone down its foreign policy ambitions and encouraged a move toward arms reduction negotiations. It eroded the authority of the high priesthood of defense intellectuals, a group that developed a self-reinforcing idea that nuclear weapons policy ought to remain the exclusive domain of expert insiders who had mastered the highly technical intricacies of ICBMs and MX and Pershing II missiles. It re-energized public discussion about national security by making it more accessible. Most Americans, whether or not they agreed with the idea, could wrap their minds around the concept of stopping the creation of more nuclear weapons as a logical first step to eliminating them altogether. Finally, the movement succeeded in orienting many Americans toward a more internationalist and global peace perspective and away from fixation on the bipolar superpower conflict by exploring common ground between the interests of American citizens and those of people around the world.

The freeze movement combined veteran activist leadership at the national level with a tremendous vitality at the grass roots. From the local pressure of Vermont town meetings passing resolutions to the populist statement of half a million Californians signing a petition, the campaign empowered ordinary people to challenge the national security establishment. It fostered greater awareness of Americans' interconnectedness with European "neighbors" threatened by the specter of nuclear war, and it represented genuine ferment at the grass roots that surfaced at the level of national politics. Despite the simplicity of its appeal, it failed to achieve its targeted results of stopping nuclear weapons testing, production, and deployment. Though it mobilized new activists by the thousands, its lack of a militant wing, capable of direct action when necessary, encouraged co-optation and discouraged more substantive concessions from national leaders. Priding itself on being a more reasonable, tempered kind of movement that eschewed the excesses of 1960s activism, the freeze movement reflected the resurgence of a consensus-oriented, anti-dissent mood that pervaded the dominant culture of the 1980s. This attitude set limits on the movement's potency. But against the backdrop of the early Reagan administration's militant tone and actions, freeze supporters elevated public awareness of peace and disarmament issues, reshaped the dialogue about nuclear weapons, and forced national policymakers to adopt a subtler, less frontal approach to waging the Cold War.

Calling to Halt: Randall Forsberg and the Idea of the Freeze

Though mass movements frequently downplay the importance of individual leaders, Randall Forsberg was the freeze's most identifiable figure. Forsberg's arms control career took her from the Stockholm International Peace Research Institute (SIPRI), to a political science doctorate at the Massachusetts Institute of Technology, to founding the

Institute for Defense and Disarmament Studies in 1980. Her experience at SIPRI, an institution dedicated to independent analysis of U.S.-Soviet rivalry, loomed large. There, originally working as a typist, Forsberg discovered that superpower talks over a 1963 test ban treaty had broken down over U.S. insistence on seven inspections a year, while the Russians held the line at three. The experience made her wonder, "Why not compromise on five?"[3] This evenhanded, commonsense approach to the Cold War pervaded Forsberg's intellectual outlook and shaped the freeze's bilateral approach. It also guided her willingness to confront the arms control establishment's insular technocracy.

Forsberg crafted the freeze's seminal statement, "A Call to Halt the Nuclear Arms Race," to penetrate the nuclear elite's intimidating culture of expertise. The 1980 document built on the work of groups such as Mobilization for Survival, the American Friends Service Committee (AFSC), and the Fellowship of Reconciliation, which had also called for a moratorium on constructing and deploying nuclear weapons. In 1979 the AFSC sponsored a delegation to the Soviet Union, which included Forsberg, to explore the feasibility of this plan. Upon her return, Forsberg revised the freeze idea to maximize its potential to attract support from mainstream America. She conceived of the proposed freeze as a manageable first small step toward further, more comprehensive disarmament initiatives—one that could unify diverse groups of activists and citizens on the way to something much bigger that would ultimately produce a more peaceful world.

Yet against the backdrop of the arms race, a total freeze was no mere baby step. Halting the testing, production, and deployment of nuclear weapons would mean that neither the United States nor the Soviets could add to their stockpiles or improve nuclear technologies to newly lethal levels. Seductively simple, Forsberg's plan transcended previous arms control proposals by promising first to stop the arms race in its tracks, then to pursue further reductions.[4] Proponents of a mutual and verifiable freeze cleverly provided an accessible goal that a broad cross section of the American public could rally behind.

Moreover, the clear language of "Call to Halt" gave activists the confidence to enter the national policymaking debate on nuclear weapons. Contending that "the horror of a nuclear holocaust is universally acknowledged," the freeze proposal cast the issue as simple common sense. It claimed that the two superpowers possessed upward of fifty thousand nuclear weapons, a stockpile that could wipe out "all cities in the northern hemisphere" in half an hour. With these facts simply stated, "Call to Halt" underscored the excessive nature of plans for the United States and the U.S.S.R. to build twenty thousand more nuclear warheads, along with new missiles and aircraft. Echoing Albert Einstein's maxim about the impossibility of simultaneously preparing for and preventing war, the freeze proposal claimed that burgeoning weapons programs would "pull the nuclear tripwire tighter," creating "hairtrigger readiness for a massive nuclear exchange." Rejecting the logic of deterrence that underpinned three decades of arms race escalation, the freeze idea posited that more nuclear weapons made the world more dangerous rather than safer. "Call to Halt" also invoked the mammoth fiscal savings a freeze would entail, sketching out numerous domestic spending alternatives and a range of attendant social and economic benefits. Finally, the proposal pointed to further steps toward a lasting peace that could be addressed after achieving a U.S.-Soviet freeze, including extending the freeze to other nations and reducing existing nuclear arsenals.

An inspiring document with populist appeal, "Call to Halt" was quickly endorsed by a laundry list of prominent activists, intellectuals, and leaders, including the former undersecretary of state George Ball, the most prominent of President Lyndon Johnson's advisers to oppose escalation in Vietnam; the former secretary of defense Clark Clifford; the former CIA director William Colby; the former ambassador to the Soviet Union Averell Harriman; and the U.S. Cold War policy architect George Kennan. Scientific community supporters included the two-time Nobel laureate Linus Pauling, the former MIT president Jerome Wiesner, the *Bulletin of the Atomic Scientists* editor Bernard Feld, Jonas Salk, and the *Cosmos* host Carl Sagan. With these and other illustrious names behind it, the movement swiftly gained legitimacy.[5]

But just as the freeze movement gained popular support, it was forced to grapple with an event that posed a grave threat to its goals: the election of Ronald Reagan. The complex public sentiment that could simultaneously produce a potent statement against nuclear weapons and install a hard-line Cold Warrior in the highest office reflected a transitional moment in national politics. Americans wrestled in a psychic tug-of-war between fear of nuclear annihilation and desire for renewed military might. One *New York Times*/CBS poll showed 72 percent support for a freeze but hastened to point out that the numbers roughly flipped if such a moratorium froze a Soviet weapons advantage in place.[6]

Sensing this ambivalence, peace activists recognized the need to develop a systematic approach to organizing, educating, and wielding political influence, and in March 1981 they convened in Washington, D.C., to formulate the game plan. Though excitement pervaded the conference, a set of conflicts emerged among the attendees. Some activists viewed the nuclear freeze as an end in itself, an important and legitimate arms control goal worth striving for; others, including Forsberg, saw it as a discrete, winnable battle that could open up the policymaking terrain for confronting broader issues of militarism. Further, they contended that such a freeze might ultimately transform international relations, especially U.S.-Soviet animosity and suspicion. The competing goals and visions for the freeze raised complex questions for movement strategy as well. If freeze activists wished to use the proposal to confront the arms race and militarism more broadly, this suggested a more militant approach that could educate about the connections, for instance, between the bipolar weapons race and Cold War interventionism in the Third World. On the other hand, if the vision of the freeze as its own prize prevailed, this suggested avoiding larger, more ideologically charged issues, since these risked alienating mainstream supporters who bristled at leftist critiques of militarism that flowed from the ranks of the more radical peace activists.

Ultimately, the conference committed to a tight focus on the main issue and a strategy that emphasized slow, steady education and building grassroots support. Restricting the agenda was a conscious choice, contrary to the wishes of supporters who also wanted a movement that indicted Cold War militarism generally. Though most organizers agreed that the freeze was a legitimate goal, it also represented a lowest common denominator strategy. Steering clear of controversy enough to attract support from mainstream Americans with no previous activist experience, it was "small enough to be achievable, and large enough to be inspiring." The residue of distaste for the excesses of 1960s-era radical protest, increasingly excoriated and discredited by 1980s media and intelligentsia, hung heavy. Accordingly, the conference's resolution—a four-phase strategy of demonstrating the concept's potential, building public support, leveraging policymakers and provoking national debate, and making the freeze a national policy objective—sought to maximize mainstream participation at the grass roots. Freeze organizers wanted to avoid creating a movement where veteran radical peace activists played the central role. As Forsberg remarked, she wanted the movement "very middle class."[7] As it turned out, this strategy succeeded, for better and for worse.

Grass Roots

Independently of Forsberg's efforts, Massachusetts peace activists led by Randy Kehler of the Traprock Peace Center had been collecting signatures at supermarkets and shopping centers for a state ballot measure calling on the president to propose a bilateral nuclear weapons moratorium. In November 1980, after a summer and fall educational campaign about the arms race and its social and economic impact that included house meetings, study groups, film showings, and school presentations, voters in three western Massachusetts state senatorial districts endorsed the freeze measure by a 3:2 ratio. Kehler, later the freeze campaign's national coordinator, touted its potential: "The nuclear race transcends party division and conservative-liberal divisions, and this proves that the American public is indeed ready to see the nuclear arms race ended." Kehler waxed enthusiastic about the possibilities for broad-based support and predicted that the Massachusetts victory would catalyze similar campaigns elsewhere. This proved prophetic when, in March 1981, sixteen towns in neighboring Vermont and New Hampshire passed freeze measures, calling on their state congressional delegations to sponsor a resolution in Congress. The scenes of these victories, in time-honored New England town meetings, were not completely without controversy. Traditionally held on the second Tuesday of March, these meetings embodied American democratic traditions at their best, but nevertheless the freeze issue inspired debate about whether the forum was appropriate. Echoing the view that matters of national security and nuclear weapons policy ought to be the exclusive terrain of expert federal policymakers, one opponent cried, "There's no place in town meeting for politics!" Of course, what this New Hampshirite meant was that nuclear policy—as part of national politics, and a highly technical area within national politics at that—did not appropriately deserve consideration alongside other town affairs he regarded as more direct and legitimate.[8] Yet the majority of voters in these sixteen Yankee towns staked their claim that ordinary citizens merited a role in a national discussion of how to avoid nuclear peril. The wide margin of these victories suggests the issue's immediacy at the dawn of the Reagan presidency.

On the other coast, the Massachusetts news energized the Southern Californian Nick Seidita, who remembered, "I jumped from my chair exclaiming to myself, 'If they could put the Freeze on the ballot in Massachusetts, we can put it on the ballot in California.'" Along with his wife, Jo, a veteran of the antiwar Democratic candidate Eugene McCarthy's 1968 campaign, Seidita engineered California Proposition 12, jump-starting the freeze movement on the West Coast. The Seiditas also initially encountered skepticism about whether a state referendum was an appropriate forum for a measure aimed to halt the arms race that was the centerpiece of national Cold War strategy. Told that California law would not permit a national policy issue on the state ballot, the Seiditas got some help from a lawyer friend and tweaked the future Proposition 12 to require the governor to write to the president to notify him that a majority of the state's electorate voted for a nuclear freeze.[9]

The California freeze campaign spawned feverish political organizing and educational efforts in the quest to secure the more than three hundred thousand signatures necessary to get the initiative on the ballot. These included showings for high school, college, and community groups of *The Last Epidemic*, a documentary film that enshrined itself as a movement staple. The film, distributed by Physicians for Social Responsibility, detailed the horrific effects of a hypothetical nuclear detonation on the San Francisco area. But this same fear of atomic conflagration that freeze proponents used to stir up legions at the grass roots also attracted another element to the movement—establishment arms control advocates. In California, the millionaire businessman and former anti–Vietnam War activist Harold Willens infused the campaign with copious cash and new tactics, hiring media consultants and mobilizing direct mail marketers to sway public opinion, leverage endorsements, raise money, and get Californians to sign the petition. As it would prove in the freeze campaign as a whole, this influx of professionalism in California was a mixed blessing. On the one hand, the California freeze rustled up more than seven hundred thousand signatures to gain a spot on the November ballot. On the other hand, to secure such broad-based support, Willens pushed to add language assuring Californians that the proposal mandated U.S. verification of Soviet compliance, thus erasing any potential qualms about unilateralism. Willens also prevailed in deleting language calling for redirecting funds slated for nuclear arms toward social uses, a measure that polls suggested might cost Proposition 12 close to 10 percent of voters. The strategy of maximizing support by making the ballot language as "inoffensive" and "free from peace rally rhetoric" as possible undermined its moral critique of militarism. The quest to make the freeze palatable to the mainstream both encouraged its great vitality at the grass roots and ultimately weakened its impact as national policy.

Willens's involvement in the successful California campaign also signified a sea change in the style of mass democratic activism in the 1980s. Kehler, the freeze's national coordinator and also a veteran of 1960s anti–Vietnam War activism, recalled Willens's advice when the two first met: if the movement was to succeed, it needed to "scrap the 1960s retreads."[10] This comment spoke to the perceived need amid the more conservative 1980s political terrain to mute the roles of veteran activists like Kehler, who had cut their teeth on the previous generation's activist movements—in a play for a more professionalized, clean-cut middle-class sensibility to maximize mainstream appeal. Though the strategic experience of 1960s veterans was vital to the freeze campaign, Willens's advice was largely heeded in the movement's public presentation.

The movement's public influence peaked in 1982. In March, the Vermont town meetings were once again the site of democratic ferment and national media attention. Of the state's 180 towns, 159 passed resolutions calling on their senators and representatives to urge the president to propose to the Soviets a mutual and verifiable freeze on nuclear weapons testing, production, and deployment.[11] Once again at issue in the Vermont deliberations was the legitimacy of small-town politics as a forum for national security matters. In Cornwall, Vermont, the proposed article appeared on the town meeting agenda between measures calling for a new furnace in the firehouse and the purchase of land to make a parking lot for the town hall.[12] One resident claimed that the freeze resolution was his best chance as "one citizen" to "send a message to our elected officials" for the United States and the Soviets to cease adding to nuclear stockpiles that are "set on triggers, ready to go off." Others dissented. One retired army colonel argued, "It is pretty silly for us to be advising the country on foreign policy," though he conceded the freeze's appeal. In Northfield, Vermont, where the measure lost by a single vote, one opponent contended that "it is very presumptuous for people to send a message to the President suggesting how we should conduct the foreign policy of this country." Yet a Newfane businessman, in a flourish of political metaphysics, eloquently elucidated a counterargument: "To reverse the trend toward nuclear warfare is a voyage of a million miles. Like all voyages, it starts with a single step. This town meeting is a place to take that first step." Patty Seubert, nuclear freeze coordinator for Addison County, Vermont, concurred, citing the long-standing tradition of the petition as an "effective force" for addressing national issues "even when it's operating at the very bottom rung of the political ladder."[13]

This latter position won out as momentum at the grass roots surged through 1982. Though freeze support found a heavy concentration in New England, the mid-Atlantic states, and the West Coast—the "usual suspects" of left/liberal activism—the movement gained traction with Americans of all ages and social classes, with additional pockets of support in the Midwest, Colorado, and even the South. Indeed, freeze support had a knack for cropping up in unusual places.[14] In Nebraska, the state with the third-highest percentage supporting Reagan's 1984 reelection, the Omaha freeze chapter conducted petition campaigns against the MX missile, organized freeze walks, ran freeze voter workshops, and sponsored an array of pro-freeze speakers. In Lincoln, a highly active chapter addressed the arms crisis from a decidedly Nebraskan perspective. It appealed to locals by linking increased military spending under Reagan with cuts to agricultural programs, and it argued that with money freed from the arms race to help American farmers, the resulting increased production of U.S. food exports could relieve hunger and promote security around the globe, concluding, "What a boon for American agriculture!" The Oklahoma freeze introduced educational and electoral strategies that reflected local politics as well, arranging screenings of *The Day After*, leafleting the Billy Graham Crusade, and holding a freeze walk that was praised as a "pioneer effort in fundraising for disarmament in a conservative state."[15]

The campaign even generated a respectable level of support in the traditionally conservative and pro-military South. This support was strongest in the economically depressed states of the border south such as West Virginia and Arkansas, where Pentagon spending was minimal. Invoking Dwight Eisenhower's eloquent warning that national security is the "total product" of economic, intellectual, moral, and military strengths, and that while "absolute security" can never be attained, a nation can easily become "bankrupt" in "attempting to reach that goal through arms alone," the West Virginia freeze campaign prepared a Jobs with Peace Budget, delivered in a well-crafted pamphlet that connected the state's dire economic predicament to Reagan administration defense spending gone amok. Rejecting the pursuit of defense largesse to bolster the Mountain State's vitality, the pamphlet affirmed, "Our future lies in a strong civilian economy" and not in "Star Wars schemes of laser weapons and particle beams." Even in the heart of the former Confederacy, where post–World War II Dixie politicians built careers on luring military bases and contracts to the region, the freeze managed to scare up a modicum of support. In North Carolina, home to Fort Bragg and Camp Lejeune, freeze petitions gathered forty thousand signatures and won approval from seven cities. A statewide resolution passed the North Carolina house but was defeated by a single vote in the senate. Perhaps its most important symbolic victory came when the North Carolina freeze won the support of the Tarheels' legendary basketball coach, Dean Smith, who filmed a series of television messages on its behalf. Even in the Deep South, three different Alabama freeze groups labored to spread the word, invoking the arms race's threat to planetary security, the increasing likelihood of a nuclear accident, and the economic drain on the state's citizenry caused by runaway defense spending and its accompanying high tax burden.[16]

Of course, pockets of ardent support in the heartland and in the South did not change the fact that these areas remained fundamentally conservative and in many ways reflected movement leaders' perception of public support as "a mile wide and an inch deep." But this widely scattered support also gave the freeze movement widespread visibility and conveyed that it was not limited to bleeding heart liberals in the North. Geographic diversity at the grass roots enhanced its legitimacy as a national movement with the strength to put freeze referenda on the ballot in nine states in November 1982. One organizer pointed out how even in a small state—where putting such a measure on a statewide ballot would have cost many hundreds of thousands of dollars—hearty volunteer support at the grass roots "substituted human labor and energy for a lack of financial capital." Door-to-door canvassing campaigns allowed a level of coverage and pro-freeze educational activity that a "couple of peace bureaucrats sitting alone in an office" never could have done.[17] As grassroots ferment crested at home, it was paralleled and fueled by a fervent movement across the pond.

European Peace Activism

Americans who joined the freeze movement were not the only ones alarmed at Ronald Reagan's saber rattling in the early 1980s. Europeans voiced concern early and acted quickly, since Europe loomed as the most likely battleground for a prospective U.S.-Soviet nuclear confrontation that many forecast as World War III. Europeans' uneasiness with their security had roots in the Carter administration's 1979 decision, with the lukewarm assent of NATO's European members, to deploy hundreds of intermediate-range nuclear missiles, including the notorious Pershing II's, in five European countries. But with Reagan's more strident Cold Warrior rhetoric, the chance of nuclear war appeared much larger to the United States's Western European allies. While Carter played both ends against the middle, simultaneously deploying Euromissiles and negotiating with the Soviets for reductions, Reagan casually discussed the possibility of a limited exchange of tactical weapons "without it bringing either one of the major powers to pushing the button." His secretary of state, Alexander Haig, remarked that NATO contingency plans for deterring a Soviet incursion on Western Europe included the option of exploding a nuclear warhead as a "demonstration."[18] Though administration officials swiftly backtracked from these provocative comments, their tone nevertheless alarmed European ears; the West German chancellor Helmut Schmidt dubbed American foreign policy makers "nuclear cowboys."[19] In response to the perceived threat, grassroots peace movements sprang up throughout

Europe. These movements mobilized great masses of Europeans for demonstrations against the dangers of nuclear weapons, and in 1981 and 1982 hundreds of thousands turned out for rallies in Bonn, London, Paris, Rome, and Amsterdam as Europeans were energized, or frightened, into disarmament activism.[20]

Across Europe, mass rallies were accompanied by sustained activism. The leading British disarmament group, the Campaign for Nuclear Disarmament (CND) saw its membership flourish from nine thousand in 1980 to more than a hundred thousand in 1985. Like Americans, British peace activists reacted to the rise of a stalwart Cold Warrior—the "Iron Lady," Margaret Thatcher. Britain's first woman prime minister, Thatcher steadfastly opposed Soviet Communism and supported the Euromissile deployment. CND members, when surveyed about why they joined the movement, often responded with one of two replies: "Thatcher" or "Reagan." British disarmament forces resembled their American cousins demographically as well, receiving disproportionate support from the educated, professional sector of society.[21] Though students and young Britons played a greater role in the U.K. movement than their U.S. counterparts, the political Left and women played an important role in both, with blue-collar workers notably absent. Like freeze activists in the United States, CND supporters focused on the dangers of nuclear arms, avoiding divisive distractions and partisan rancor by embracing single-issue coalition politics. Unlike the freeze proposal, which called for "mutual, verifiable" action by the United States and the Soviets, the CND hoped unilateral action by the West would catalyze Soviet disarmament through the court of world public opinion, yet it embraced bilateralism as well when strategy dictated.

Closely linked to the CND, European Nuclear Disarmament (END) strove to coordinate the wide-ranging disarmament activities throughout Europe and took inspiration from the philosophical and intellectual guidance of E. P. Thompson. The renowned author of the seminal history *The Making of the English Working Class*, Thompson, a fifty-four-year-old scholar and Left activist at the time of END's creation, emblematized the professional intelligentsia's leadership role in European disarmament. Thompson, a former Communist Party member after World War II and a pioneering Marxist historian, left the party in the 1950s and sought a resolution to the Cold War that eschewed the perspective of both superpowers. He proved a trenchant critic of both Communist repression—arguing that peace and liberty must go hand in hand—and U.S. militarism. His "Appeal for European Nuclear Disarmament," which launched END in 1980, highlighted this equal opportunity for ladling out blame. "Guilt lies squarely on both parties," END's founding statement contended, underscoring that both the United States and the Soviets "have adopted menacing postures and committed aggressive actions in different parts of the world."[22] Thompson and END argued that rather than waiting for these two nuclear giants to either disarm themselves or actually use the bombs in a "limited" nuclear war that seemed "increasingly likely," Europeans needed to launch a "third path to peace," independent of the two superpowers. Thompson galvanized an aggressive, well-coordinated, and nonaligned peace movement across the continent to wage "détente from below."[23] To END, this meant energizing an independent grassroots movement, led by professionals and citizens with specialized disarmament expertise, that would bridge Eastern and Western Europe, and calling for the removal of nuclear weapons from the continent in the most expedient way possible, either unilaterally or bilaterally. Thompson and END left wide latitude for groups representing a range of goals, tactics, and strategies to get involved, suggesting, "We do not wish to impose any uniformity on the movement."[24] Accordingly, an eclectic array of European groups joined the cause.

The Greenham Common women were among the most memorable. In September 1981 a group of thirty-six women called Women for Life on Earth marched from Cardiff, Wales, to Greenham Common, in Berkshire, England, home to an air force base where ninety-six cruise missiles were slated for deployment. Demonstrating great urgency, the Greenham Common women intervened using direct action tactics, launching a protest that ultimately lasted nineteen years. The women's immediate demand—a television debate on nuclear weapons with the British government—suggested a larger desire to educate and publicize the cause of disarmament. When this demand failed, several women remained at the base, importing tents, cooking utensils, and bedding, until they established a "permanent peace camp." With the peace camp established, the women stepped up efforts to disrupt business as usual. Nonviolent resistance was common beginning in March 1982, when 250 women blockaded the base, resulting in thirty-four arrests. As though in reprisal for the heightened civil disobedience, local police commenced efforts to evict the women, initiating a "cat and mouse" game with the local district council that lasted more than a decade. The Greenham Common women proved resilient, however, and the original peace camp sprouted into several decentralized encampments around the base. In December 1982, thirty thousand women showed up to "Embrace the Base," linking arms to surround the nine-mile perimeter fence and create a consummately media-friendly event.

Though many of the Greenham Common women were linked to the CND, the women's protest broached larger cultural issues than the technical and practical considerations that often dominated disarmament activism. The protest at Greenham Common reflected an awareness of women's traditionally strong role in peace movements and also incorporated ideas of contemporary feminism. This was evident in its February 1982 decision to become a female-only peace camp. A press release announcing the move cited women's initiative in conceiving the project and the desire to safeguard women's roles as its primary leaders and decision makers. Though the organizers carefully sought to preserve an off-site role for sympathetic men, the decision to make the peace camp women-only resonated with the feminist movement's ideal of self-determination and its critique of power relations between the sexes. "We said we want to achieve something for ourselves and by ourselves," the activist Sarah Hopkins contended. "If men are at the camp it will be assumed they did it all."[25] These remarks demonstrated the Greenham women's concern with how their protest would "play" to the media.

Their deft approach to public relations indicated that they could do more than simply oppose the siting of a bevy of cruise missiles in rural England. Rather, through its numerous symbolic actions at the Greenham air base, the group succeeded in dramatizing larger ideas about how to achieve a peaceful society and women's role in that transformation. In the Embrace the Base action, the women not only encircled the fence, they adorned it with "gifts" designed to "symbolize life"—from flowers and paintings to pictures of babies and embroidery and newly planted daffodil bulbs. Other symbolic statements at Greenham Common included two hundred women dressed as furry animals and teddy bears, trespassing on military grounds for a protest picnic, and a 1983 reprise of encircling the base, this time holding up mirrors to reflect the image of nuclear peril and militarism back at the base it-self. Though the Greenham Common women represented a level of direct action and symbolic politics that was largely absent from the American freeze and disarmament movements, they were aware of developments on the other side of the Atlantic. Embrace the Base, for instance, had been adapted from a similar women's action at the Pentagon. At one point the Greenham Common women, along with two U.S. congressmen, actually sued President Reagan, arguing that the deployment of cruise missiles on British soil was unconstitutional. Though the suit proved unsuccessful, its existence demonstrated how, during the early 1980s, the Greenham women and European disarmament activists intertwined with freeze representatives and American pro-disarmament forces transatlantically, creating an atmosphere of ferment in opposition to nuclear weapons.

The U.S. freeze movement was in close contact with END and with European groups focused on eliminating the Euromissiles. Though the American movement was more domestically oriented than its European counterpart, and sometimes Europeans registered frustration with the Yanks for insufficient focus on eradicating the Euromissiles that imperiled European life and limb, there was considerable connection and collaboration. European and American speakers ventured back and forth across the Atlantic continuously, sharing reports of their respective movements' activities and inspiring globally minded disarmament activism in the locales they visited. Whenever possible, specific rallies and demonstrations were coordinated between the American and European movements. There were structural connections through the International Peace Communication and Coordination Center—which met four times annually in various European cities—and representatives from disarmament organizations in the United States and Europe. Though both movements viewed the state-sponsored Soviet-aligned peace movements of Eastern Europe warily, preferring to parcel out blame for the Cold War's nuclear escalation in equal measures to both superpowers, the European movement proved able to fashion a more thoroughgoing critique of the militarism on both sides, while the American freeze hewed to a tight policy agenda, hoping for incremental progress.[26] The sheer presence of this growing international coalition figured among the factors propelling the issue to the forefront of American domestic politics. It wasn't long before national politicians began regarding the freeze proposal opportunistically.

The Freeze on the National Stage

In February 1982 the Massachusetts representative Edward Markey, a Democrat, sensing political advantage from allying with the freeze movement, introduced a resolution to the House. Shortly thereafter, Ted Kennedy, already eyeing the 1984 Democratic presidential nomination, introduced a similar measure in the Senate, gaining bipartisan sponsorship from the Republican senator Marc Hatfield of Oregon. Deliberations and debate, jockeying and lobbying proceeded apace in Congress as popular momentum for the proposal surged. The June Central Park rally generated a largely positive wave of national media coverage. Reports noted its broad-based support among the 750,000 participants and praised its "orderlinesss" and good manners. Favorable comparisons with 1960s-era protests abounded, with observers applauding the lack of animosity among the protesters and the spirit of antinuclear consensus: "It's not just the hippies and crazies anymore," a demonstrator told *The New York Times.* "It's everybody." On the other coast, in Pasadena, California, 85,000 music-loving antinukers jammed the Rose Bowl for a "Peace Sunday: We Have a Dream" benefit that, like the Central Park rally, was timed to coincide with the U.N. special session on disarmament. Peace Sunday was the largest benefit to that point, and it anticipated mid-1980s "mega-events" from Live Aid to Band Aid to Farm Aid. Graham Nash assembled the performers, who ranged from musicians with prior antinuclear credentials such as Jackson Browne, Bonnie Raitt, and Dan Fogelberg to 1960s protest music veterans Bob Dylan and Joan Baez. While singing familiar peace anthems such as "Teach Your Children" and "Give Peace a Chance," together they raised a quarter of a million dollars. Even the macho ironic posturing of Van Halen's David Lee Roth—who stood on the sidelines and quipped, "I'd agree to a freeze, but I'd tell our guys to stash a few on our side"—could not derail the day's buoyed spirits and heady optimism.[27]

That November the broad-based support was evident at the polls as voters in Massachusetts, Michigan, Montana, New Jersey, North

Dakota, Oregon, and Rhode Island approved freeze resolutions by substantial margins. Even in California, where Reagan administration officials went on a speaking tour to oppose the freeze referendum and a shoestring citizens group called Californians for a Strong America mobilized the Federal Communications Commissions' fairness doctrine to air an anti-freeze ad starring Charlton Heston, the freeze campaign still eked out a 52 percent to 48 percent victory. Nationwide, a total of eighteen million Americans weighed in on the question, with freeze resolutions garnering 60 percent support. In Congress, pro-freeze forces picked up twenty-six votes, a development that allowed a freeze resolution to pass overwhelmingly in May 1983, erasing the narrow failure of an earlier version the previous August. With political pundits stressing that the Reagan administration now faced the choice of whether to "exploit this strong popular tide" or to ignore it at its own peril,[28] freeze proponents might have basked in their own elation. But far from ushering in a new era of enhanced impact on weapons policy, this success only portended the beginning of the end.

So how did such an auspicious victory lead to a quick demise? The answer lies in the late Cold War politics that permeated the rhetoric of freeze opponents. One key anti-freeze argument was that a halt to weapons testing, production, and deployment would leave the Soviets in a position of advantage. Echoing 1950s anticommunist invective, critics from the arms control establishment and outside commentators lambasted freeze proponents for their naïveté. The prominent conservative William F. Buckley ridiculed freeze supporters as Communist dupes and speculated that Soviet propagandists conjured support for the freeze in much the same way as ad execs hyped consumer baubles. Reagan himself went so far as to blame the freeze on "foreign agents," who, desiring "the weakening of America," manipulated unwitting activists, though in a conciliatory gesture the president conceded that a majority of pro-freeze Americans were "sincere and well-intentioned."[29]

Just as the freeze neared its apex, it suffered a number of ironic disappointments. Simplicity had won the movement its widespread following and generated considerable bipartisan support in Congress. By the middle of 1982 many legislators scrambled to get behind a freeze proposal for their own political advantage. Yet they were also mindful that though polls demonstrated that a majority of the public supported a freeze, the same polls also revealed that most Americans did not want to freeze a Soviet advantage in place. Competing attempts to find politically palatable resolution language proliferated. Conservatives introduced their own version of a "freeze," which would occur only after both sides completed major reductions to achieve parity. This approach co-opted the politically popular term "freeze" but reversed its original intent as a first step toward nuclear disarmament, earning it the sobriquet "phony freeze" from movement activists. Another version made the freeze conditional upon first catching up to the Soviets from a presumed weapons deficit. Such nuances allowed politicians to reap the benefits of the politically "hot" freeze label while maintaining a loophole allowing for military modernization and the development of new weapons systems that left their credentials as Cold Warriors intact. The eventual result was that in May 1983 Congress passed a watered-down resolution fraught with contingencies and compromise. The resolution was not binding: only weapons for which both superpowers could agree to verification terms would be frozen, and even then it was revocable if negotiated arms reductions failed to follow within a specified time limit. To the activist community that had launched the campaign with hopes of spawning a larger movement against militarism and nuclear peril, this "freeze" amounted to small recompense. Adding insult to injury, within a few weeks after this vote, which observers claimed "reflected less the strength of support for the freeze than the ambiguity of the resolution," the House and Senate decisively approved funding for Reagan's controversial MX missile, underscoring the impotence of the measure's final incarnation.[30]

After the state resolution victories in November 1982, one observer had predicted that as a "canny" politician, Reagan would not turn a political tin ear toward the growing din, but rather would work toward more effective arms control to counter the movement's popular appeal. This forecast proved accurate, if in unexpected ways. In a March 1983 televised address, the president outlined his case for increased defense spending, arguing that defense was "not about spending arithmetic," but rather about seeking security through preparedness to meet all threats. Reagan mocked the freeze idea, citing the Soviets' ongoing deployment of SS-20 missiles despite Premier Leonid Brezhnev's pledge to cease and desist. With characteristic movie star aplomb, Reagan quipped, "Some freeze!," scorning the idea of taking Soviet promises to disarm at face value. Reagan did acknowledge the sincerity and breadth of the movement: "I know too that many of you seriously believe that a nuclear freeze would further the cause of peace." Yet after giving the freeze its due, he quickly underscored the shortcomings that he believed prohibited its adoption, citing problems with verification and arguing that it would reward the Soviets for their military buildup and hamper U.S. military modernization. Then Reagan unveiled the evening's major surprise. Lamenting the Cold War–era ideology of national security based on deterrence, massive retaliation, and mutually assured destruction as "a sad commentary on the human condition," he speculated, "What if free people could live secure in the knowledge that their security did not rest upon the threat of instant U.S. retaliation to deter a Soviet attack?" Reagan proceeded to sketch out plans for a Strategic Defense Initiative (SDI) that, through massive mobilization of technology and resources, would produce the capability to intercept and destroy strategic ballistic missiles before they reached American soil. The immense technical challenges of such a program, acknowledged by the president himself, caused opponents and proponents alike to dub the project "Star Wars," evoking a greater connection to science fantasy than to reality.

Despite a tenuous relationship with the landscape of possibility, Star Wars dealt a serious blow to the freeze movement. Like the diluted congressional resolutions, Star Wars managed to steal the movement's thunder by addressing and redirecting some of its key concerns. Where the freeze campaign had gained popularity by stressing the danger of nuclear weapons, suddenly Reagan was offering a space shield that would make such weapons obsolete. The SDI idea allowed Reagan to claim the moral high ground by using language indicating that he too was looking forward to a world without nuclear weapons and to the end of the Cold War. This bit of turnabout let the wind out of the movement's sails as the Reagan administration seized the initiative in matters of defense and disarmament.[31]

Yet from another angle, even if its momentum had ebbed, the freeze movement had achieved a discernible impact. The grassroots coalition spearheaded the disarmament activism that created the political climate that encouraged Reagan to sign the Intermediate-Range Nuclear Forces Treaty, removing the provocative cruise and Pershing II missiles from Europe. Its meteoric rise energized the broader public climate and ultimately pressured Reagan—who boasted of his opposition to every arms control agreement before the freeze movement—to weigh in with proposals for reductions of his own. That these proposals were motivated by a desire to assuage domestic critics rather than a genuine wish for international rapprochement proved less relevant than the reality that it opened the door for the new Soviet leader, Mikhail Gorbachev, to pursue reductions and a reawakening of détente. The freeze debate successfully eroded the nuclear priesthood's aura of expertise and opened up national discourse on disarmament and national security policy. Furthermore, it set limits on the aggression and scope of the Reagan administration's Cold War rhetoric and ambition, and it restored an environment of bipartisan consensus on arms control in national politics. Though the arms control establishment and the Reagan administration viewed the end of the Cold War as a testament to "peace through strength" caused by an arms race that created debilitating financial pressures on the Soviet Union, it is equally true that the freeze campaign coalesced at the center of a growing popular call to end nuclear escalation in the 1980s, facilitating international cooperation and negotiations and diffusing hostilities. Finally, the freeze emerged as a tremendous recruiting effort, bringing thousands of new people into lifelong activism on behalf of what one movement leader called "a safer, saner, more just and peaceful world."[32]

That said, it would be a mistake to paint too rosy a picture of the movement's achievements. After all, nuclear weapons production and deployment were not halted, and in fact, several new weapons systems were introduced after the movement fizzled in the wake of Reagan's 1984 reelection. Despite its potency at the grass roots, a lack of militancy undermined the cause. This was most evident in the movement's reluctance to use direct action tactics at strategic moments in conjunction with its legislative agenda. Though the national media was quick to congratulate freeze activists for their lack of 1960s-style rancor, this very politeness left a gaping hole in anything that might have resembled a radical wing of the movement. There was no one left to pressure national politicians into making concessions to movement moderates. Furthermore, the narrow focus on the freeze as a simple first step toward an eventual larger disarmament campaign jettisoned much of the larger philosophical and ideological rationale in public discussion. Ultimately this left the substance behind the freeze vulnerable to the machinations of national politicians in Congress for whom nuclear disarmament played

second fiddle to their own political advancement. Though a high proportion of freeze supporters were critical of U.S. foreign and military
policy as a whole, the movement avoided engaging larger questions
regarding the connections between the arms race, Reagan administration militarism, and Cold War interventionism. It was left to a smaller
and more radical Central America solidarity movement to address
those issues.

2

THE CENTRAL AMERICA SOLIDARITY MOVEMENT
Opposing Secret Wars in the Backyard

Collapsed in smoking ruins near the Nicaraguan town of Jalapa, the tobacco farm marked a scene of human misery. Civilian casualties included an infant, two toddlers, and a grandmother, victims of attacks by Nicaraguan counterrevolutionaries, or "contras." The contras set up bases in Honduras to launch cross-border offensives to destabilize the leftist Sandinista government and reverse the 1979 revolution that ousted Anastasio Somoza Debayle, ending a repressive U.S.-backed family dynasty that dated back to the 1930s. The tobacco farm targeted in this 1983 attack was no accident. The contras systematically wreaked havoc on signs of economic activity, fledgling social institutions, and community development that the Sandinistas might claim as successes to buttress their legitimacy. By the time of the attack, U.S. support, sponsorship, and training of the contras was a secret kept poorly enough for *Newsweek* to have run a cover story on America's "Secret War for Nicaragua."

News of the contras' distressingly routine deeds of terror, torture, and murder reached the ears of many American citizens who were disinclined to trust their purportedly benign purposes. Ronald Reagan referred to the contras as "freedom fighters," and characterized them as heroic combatants in a vital Cold War struggle to eradicate the Soviet Union's pernicious influence from America's backyard. Delegations of the skeptical, many of whom believed that the Sandinistas' intentions had more to do with ending oligarchic rule and leveling the playing field of Nicaraguan society, felt sufficiently compelled to journey down to Central America to see for themselves. One group investigated the tobacco farm shortly after the attack. Scanning the carnage and rubble lining the mountainous terrain, they noticed a contra command post just over the Honduran border and wondered why the firing had ceased. A young Nicaraguan soldier floated the idea that the Americans' presence acted as a deterrent to further contra attacks. There was a logic to this. If the Reagan administration was funding the contras, it made sense that attacks would stop with the risk of spilling American blood, since the public outrage this would spark in the United States might threaten further contra aid. In a lightbulb moment, Jefferson Boyer, an anthropologist from North Carolina who had worked for the Peace Corps in Honduras in the 1960s, piped up, "If all it takes to stop this killing is to get a bunch of Americans down here, then let's do it," and called for fifteen hundred gringo volunteers to stop the fighting.[1]

This insight gave birth to Witness for Peace, a group of committed volunteers who set up a long-term vigil that offered their bodies and presence as a "shield of love" to deter contra offensives. Shorter-term volunteers journeyed to Central America to observe the contras in action, witness the atrocities and misery caused with the complicity of covert U.S. training and economic aid, and then report what they had seen stateside to pressure the Reagan administration to modify its interventionist policies. Though Witness for Peace represented high-stakes direct action politics to the hilt—a willingness and even a desire to "share the danger" with the Nicaraguan people threatened by contra attacks—it also embodied many of the ideas, ideals, and tactics of the larger Central America solidarity movement that comprised the cutting edge of opposition to Reagan administration policies in the region.

Witness for Peace's activities shed light on how Central Americans helped shape the response to U.S. policy. The close interplay between Central and North Americans epitomized the movement goal of solidarity. The tenacity of Witness for Peace also illustrated the willingness of ordinary citizens to take on the difficult and often unpopular task of opposing a popular president in a foreign policy area he repeatedly stressed as central to national interests. In Nicaragua, this meant contesting activities that were part of covert rather than official U.S.

foreign policy, which necessitated waging a battle for legitimacy in American public discussion of Central America. Witness for Peace also symbolized one of the Central America movement's unique attributes: the role of religion and faith in a struggle for social justice at a time when Christianity was typically harnessed to more conservative social purposes.

Compared with the Nuclear Weapons Freeze Campaign or Greenpeace activism, the Central America movement was relatively small, consisting of a core of about twenty thousand people. Despite this, the movement compiled an impressive record of accomplishment under often adverse circumstances. Though poverty and violence still exist in the region, the solidarity movement profoundly altered the course of events in Central America during the 1980s. For one thing, it helped to prevent a full-scale war in Nicaragua that loomed as a real possibility despite the national wariness of avoiding another costly and divisive war—that is, "another Vietnam." Though this "Vietnam syndrome" hung heavy, the historian Van Gosse has argued for an alternative meaning of the phrase, suggesting that the real Vietnam syndrome was the establishment of a durable foreign policy opposition that began in the 1960s, its roots in the Vietnam antiwar movement, and that solidified with activism opposing the U.S. role in the 1973 Chilean coup, enduring in a potent anti-interventionist force that contested U.S. attempts to wage the Cold War in an array of Third World outposts. The Central America movement drew from this anti-interventionist tradition. It forged allegiances with Democratic members of Congress that were fraught with compromise, but nevertheless it created a robust coalition that forced the Reagan administration to fight through proxies, underwrite covert military training and economic support, and align itself with forces on the wrong side of human rights abuses. This led to the politically crippling Iran-Contra Affair, which sounded the death knell for the ardent Central American interventionism the Reagan administration foreign policy had foregrounded. North Americans' visits to Central America, in delegations such as those sponsored by Witness for Peace, paved the way for the revelations of Iran-Contra by providing alternate accounts of events on the ground in El Salvador, Nicaragua, and Guatemala. The movement used mainstream and leftist media to plant a seed of doubt with the American public about official praise for the contras as national liberators and the labeling of the Salvadoran death squads as "counterterrorists." Further, the movement ameliorated the damage caused to Central American civilians by the contras and the death squads, with their well-demonstrated record of human rights abuses. By the end of the decade, the movement had generated a plethora of Central America solidarity organizations that provided a model of transnational cooperation with the United States's southern neighbors.[2]

"Inevitable" Revolutions?

During the 1980s, Cold War rhetoric tinted U.S. involvement in Central America, but heavy-handed Yankee activity there was nothing new. The first major statement of U.S. foreign policy in the region, the 1823 Monroe Doctrine, implied future American dominance even as its ostensible purpose was to warn European powers not to meddle in the Western Hemisphere. In the early twentieth century, Theodore Roosevelt, emboldened by burgeoning U.S. industrial and economic power, tacked on an amendment to the Monroe Doctrine. The 1904 Roosevelt Corollary upped the ante for U.S. influence and power in Latin America by providing an explicit rationale for American intervention in the region. Seeking to codify the dominant relationship that had already emerged and to secure operations in the area of the Panama Canal then under construction, Roosevelt reasoned that the United States was the natural protector of the other geographically, economically, and militarily smaller and less powerful nations in the region. Appropriating the language of Progressive Era reformers, Roosevelt argued that the frequent revolutions that beset Latin America were "inefficient" and potentially threatening to American interests, and thus should be subject to American power. Subtly reversing the meaning of the Monroe Doctrine, which discouraged European intervention in the Western Hemisphere, Roosevelt's Corollary provided a rationale for the United States to intervene in Latin America.[3] Armed with this "Big Stick," the United States took this opening time and time again throughout the twentieth century.

Sometimes this involved flexing military muscles, such as the occupation of Nicaragua from the 1910s to the 1930s, multiple troop mobilizations in Honduras during the 1920s, and, most notoriously, the CIA-aided Guatemala coup in 1954 in which U.S. planes heavily bombed Guatemala City. Yet underlying these military actions was a fundamental economic interconnectedness between the United States and Central America, a relationship of dependency that kept the region perpetually impoverished, weak, and subject to the whims of landed oligarchies and U.S.-backed dictators. This was not accidental. Rather, it represented a highly evolved system in which American economic, business, and strategic interests dominated Central American life without the hassle of imposing direct imperial or administrative control. In this system, the region's diminutive nations became "banana republics," their economies dependent on one or two key export crops, such as coffee, sugar, or—fittingly—bananas. The industries based on these crops were typically controlled by major U.S. corporate players—the behemoth United Fruit Company, for example—and by local elites, leaving the Central American masses perennially vulnerable to the vicissitudes of foreign markets. The historian Walter LaFeber has argued that under these conditions, the outbreak of discontent and revolutionary sentiment among the poverty-stricken Central American masses was all but inevitable. Over the course of the twentieth century, whenever revolutionary ferment cropped up, imperiling the bonds of economic dependency, it marked the tipping point for the United States to use military force.[4]

Though the 1954 Guatemala coup epitomizes this formula for applying military force in Central America, the landscape in which these decisions were made took on a different cast in the post-Vietnam era. By the 1980s, national squeamishness about fighting the Cold War in Third World venues or spilling American blood for debatable purposes still weighed heavily on the populace. The Reagan administration pursued its goal of restoring national power in an environment where public opinion urged avoiding direct interventions abroad and their concomitant casualties. In this context, the doctrine of "low-intensity warfare" emerged as a way to counter insurgencies, promote American interests, and wage the Cold War in Central America. One fundamental tenet of this school of thought was to pay attention to the politics of Central American conflicts rather than strictly to the military situation. Tactics included generous economic aid to shore up "friendly" (i.e., non-leftist) regimes. United States policy also sought to isolate political regimes that were "unfriendly"—the Sandinistas in Nicaragua and opposition groups such as the Farabundo Martí National Liberation Front (FMLN) in El Salvador—while supporting allies such as the contras and El Salvador's Duarte government. One U.S. military official called it "total war at the grassroots level." The strategy comprised a mélange of psychological warfare, harassment and intimidation of key opposition sympathizers at the local level, and sabotage of economic activity and social reform. This was especially evident in Nicaragua, where the fledgling leftist Sandinista government sought to remake the country after decades of the Somoza regime's repression. Low-intensity warfare aimed to force the Central American people to arrive at a cost-benefit conclusion that supporting local opponents of U.S. policy was too painful to remain an option.

The signal feature of low-intensity warfare was its use of proxies to carry out a range of nefarious missions that avoided full-fledged attacks, evaded international media scrutiny, and sidestepped the politically and emotionally unpalatable possibility of American casualties. Thus "low-intensity" referred to the idea that U.S. policy in Central America would be carried out without full military engagement, and with minimized cost in terms of American bloodshed. From the standpoint of Central American civilians, however, there was nothing low-intensity about it. Indeed, the impact on civilians was central to the strategy. Bombings, burnings of villages, forced evacuations, and scorched-earth crop destruction of designated areas sought to separate Sandinistas and Salvadoran guerrillas from their bases of civilian support. The Guatemalan military, banned from aid during the Carter years owing to an abysmal human rights record, nevertheless used loopholes to draw contracts and arms transfers under Reagan and precipitated the massacres of hundreds of thousands of indigenous people. Death squads targeted local figures suspected of cooperation with the guerrillas, leaving dismembered corpses on public display for a terrorized civilian population to consider.[5] Mothers of the disappeared searched through spiral binders crammed with photos of mutilated casualties of political murders.

Despite grinding poverty and merciless repression, Central Americans on the wrong end of these assaults often transcended a stereotypical role as wretched victims. Faced with a limited range of choices, many Central Americans managed to mobilize what few resources were available to influence their northern neighbors to pressure their political leaders to stop the violence. The most powerful tactic was to tell their stories about experiences and conditions in their home countries to appeal to potentially sympathetic U.S. citizens who might in turn seek to change Reagan administration policy.[6] These stories galvanized the Central America solidarity movement.

Sanctuary and the Faith-Based Movement

In 1981, Jim Corbett, a Quaker goat rancher from Arizona, encountered tales of civil war, abduction, torture, and harrowing journeys across the Mexican border from Salvadoran refugees in the American Southwest. These refugees were desperately trying to avoid deportation at the hands of the U.S. Immigration and Naturalization Service (INS) and the Border Patrol, since such a fate meant almost certain death squad assassination upon returning home to El Salvador. Central American refugees presented U.S. authorities with a sticky issue. Granting them political refugee status risked acknowledging that the U.S.-funded right-wing governments of El Salvador and Guatemala were sufficiently repressive to necessitate asylum for citizens on the wrong side of authority. This would undermine the image of benevolent U.S. aid. Instead, the INS routinely designated thousands of Central Americans as "economic refugees," condemning them to deportation, violent reprisal, and often gruesome executions for having fled their home countries in the first place. Many Central Americans were not even made aware of their right to petition for asylum. The majority of those who pursued a legal route to immigration through political refugee status were denied and ultimately deported despite their efforts, forfeiting hefty bond payments in the process. John Fife, a Tucson clergyman, remarked that the legal defense efforts were "neither effective nor moral" and therefore it made no sense to continue them.[7]

Faced with what they viewed as a moral imperative to help Central American refugees, Corbett, Fife, and others drew upon their religious backgrounds and activated the time-honored ideal of sanctuary. The moral outlook that enabled these clergy to harbor refugees illegally—a felony—galvanized what became the Sanctuary Movement, and culled from many sources. One minister felt reluctant to break the law yet found conviction when he recalled how Jewish refugees during World War II were turned away from American shores and returned to the Nazis. The activist past of the 1960s also loomed large among the founders of Sanctuary. Fife was a veteran of civil rights–era marches for desegregation and voting rights, and Corbett had counseled conscientious objectors. During the Vietnam War, dozens of American churches sheltered GI deserters who had concluded that further participation in the war contradicted their deepest values. Most immediately, American clergy were acquainted with the Salvadoran regime's brutality, especially the 1980 assassination of Archbishop Oscar Romero and the vicious rapes and murders later that year of four American churchwomen who were administering food, clothing, and medical aid to the country's poor. These killings not only sparked popular resistance in El Salvador, they also enlisted many in the American religious community who were shocked by the violence and inspired by the message of the victims, whom they revered as martyrs.[8]

For Corbett, the die was cast. In violation of federal immigration law, he personally provided temporary shelter for Central American refugees on an ad hoc basis, leaving them with his friends and relatives, an act of civil disobedience energized by moral conscience. When Corbett exhausted these possibilities, he approached Fife, who persuaded his congregation to make available the Southside Presbyterian Church. This reprised the Vietnam-era practice of churches providing safe haven for conscientious objectors. Later in 1982, when the numbers of refugees exceeded the Tucson church community's capacity, Corbett convinced the Chicago Religious Task Force (CRTF) on Central America to coordinate a national sanctuary movement. With the CRTF's guidance, a new "underground railroad" movement for the twentieth century flourished, now no longer conducting runaway southern slaves across the Mason-Dixon line, but rather shepherding Salvadoran and Guatemalan refugees to the safety of communities of worship. Ultimately, the network grew to more than three hundred congregations nationally, with thousands more endorsing and supporting the enterprise.[9]

Sanctuaries sprang up in a wide geographic scatterplot. From its beginnings in Tucson, the idea spread quickly over the next two years—to Chicago's Wellington Avenue United Church of Christ; to more than two dozen congregations in the Berkeley, California, area; to Racine,

Wisconsin; to New York City's Riverside Church and its legendary peace activist pastor, William Sloane Coffin; and to more than three dozen Jewish synagogues across the country. At least a dozen cities, from Seattle to Santa Fe and from Los Angeles to Cambridge, Massachusetts, declared sanctuary, symbolizing solidarity with Central American refugees. More tangibly, these municipal sanctuaries offered the advantage of assuring that local police would not be mobilized to assist the INS in enforcing immigration law. An order of Benedictine monks from Weston Priory in Vermont welcomed a family of seven masked Guatemalans traveling under assumed names. Invoking the legacy of the Underground Railroad, and linking the historical struggle of African Americans in solidarity with the plight of Central Americans in the 1980s, the national headquarters of Jesse Jackson's Operation PUSH (People United to Serve Humanity) declared itself a sanctuary for a Salvadoran family of five. Justifying this action, Jackson hinted at the political undertones of this humanitarian act, speculating that if Americans had begun protesting the Vietnam War earlier, the country might have been spared the worst of that conflict's costs.[10]

In each of these locales, the Sanctuary Movement disseminated information about the miserable conditions the refugees faced in their home countries and the role of Reagan administration policy in their creation. In what was a standard ritual and strategy of this movement, the refugees retold their stories of danger and abuse, torture, mutilation, and death. At Chicago's Wellington Avenue Church, Juan, a Salvadoran refugee, recounted his apprehension and torture by the country's police while he was a student at the University of El Salvador. Juan enumerated the police's nefarious methods of torment. He insisted that his treatment was not due to his participation in student activism, but rather stemmed from the special knowledge he had gained during his previous career as a truck driver, during which he had come across scores of mutilated bodies on the roads of El Salvador and Guatemala. He contended that these bodies had been placed so that cars and trucks would run over them and disguise the evidence of torture, making the deaths appear accidental. To persuade the Chicago parishioners that extending sanctuary to fleeing Central Americans was the right thing to do, Juan recalled a history of privation and suffering. But this was not solely a narrative of victimization. Rather, Juan's story, along with those of legions of Central Americans in the movement, functioned as a kind of "signal flare" to inform their northern neighbors about the effects of Reagan administration support for repressive regimes in El Salvador and Guatemala and the contras in Nicaragua, and to motivate them to agitate for an end to U.S. aid and intervention.

Adopting this strategy to frame their struggle as sympathetically as possible, Central Americans mobilized a language of symbolic politics through personal stories, religious testimony, and artistic and literary expressions, encouraging North Americans to visit Central America and see for themselves what conditions were like on the ground. The height of these efforts—the 1983 publication of the Quiche Indian Rigoberta Menchú's memoir—broadcast a gruesome history of oppression of indigenous Guatemalans and resistance internationally, attained a wide audience in American college classrooms, and propelled its author to the 1992 Nobel Peace Prize. These accounts of injustice, upon reaching the United States, appealed to Americans' sense of moral high ground and national identity as a people who would not stand for egregious human rights abuses. As Juan put it, "That's part of why I'm here, to demonstrate that all of us must be willing, not just one person, to stop this suffering. It's a call."[11]

CISPES and the Secular Movement

Though religiously oriented groups such as Sanctuary best illustrated Juan's call to exemplary moral action, the secular Committee in Solidarity with the People of El Salvador (CISPES) functioned as the El Salvador solidarity movement's center throughout the 1980s. CISPES emerged at roughly the same time that the FMLN—a coalition of five opposition groups in El Salvador—was formed. From the beginning, there was an exchange of ideas and information between North American activists, FMLN rebels, and the Salvadoran exile community in the United States. Though stopping short of exercising direct control, as the State Department claimed, the FMLN did help initiate a national network of solidarity organizations (with CISPES as the most significant), update U.S. activists on the Salvadoran war, and facilitate visits and "accompaniments" to El Salvador through SHARE, the Salvadoran Humanitarian Aid, Relief, and Education Foundation, which aimed at the religious community and the more secular New El Salvador Today. These accompaniments were designed to repopulate areas in which the death squads had systematically eradicated civilians who might side with the rebels. In return, CISPES, which by 1988 had grown to 525 chapters and affiliates representing all fifty states, reciprocated with solidarity to the rebel cause in El Salvador.[12]

Given the leftist tendencies of the rebels, only American activists of a certain cast gravitated to CISPES. The "solidarity" in its title meant something more than mere nonintervention, which moderate activists could and did pursue through traditional politics, lobbying their congressional representatives to vote against aid to the Salvadoran regime. Indeed, CISPES was heir to the Vietnam-era New Left's critique not only of interventionist foreign policy but also of American imperialism. For instance, a CISPES informational brochure cited disingenuous elections "devised and imposed" to "legitimize the repressive Salvadoran junta and thus justify U.S. intervention"; phony land reform wherein "more peasants were assassinated than were receiving titles to land"; and "trumped up allegations" of "Soviet/Cuban/Nicaraguan interference" as uncanny parallels to the kinds of pretenses the United States proffered to justify escalation in Vietnam.[13] This El Salvador-as-Vietnam critique resonated powerfully in a country still ravaged by the physical and psychic scars of its longest and most unpopular war, and CISPES exploited these sentiments skillfully with the popular slogan "El Salvador Is Spanish for Vietnam."

Embracing direct action tactics, CISPES mounted its first large-scale demonstration in 1982 as part of a coalition of dozens of activist groups that marched on the White House to protest the Reagan administration's Salvadoran policy. A CISPES pamphlet for the protest, timed to coincide with elections for the Salvadoran assembly, invoked a classic leftist critique of American imperialism. The pamphlet noted that the elections were to be "supervised by the same Armed Forces responsible for 30,000 murders in the last two years" and claimed that the "entire electoral scheme was devised and imposed by the U.S. in an attempt to legitimize the repressive Salvadoran junta and thus justify U.S. intervention." On the front lines, the demonstrators abbreviated this formulation to the chant "No Draft, No War, U.S. Out of El Salvador." If the president's El Salvador policy provided the immediate catalyst for this event, at least one student protestor perceived Reagan's galvanizing effect on oppositional politics, quipping, "Ronald Reagan is the best organizer we have." The protestors, who totaled twenty-three thousand by official tallies and significantly more by organizers' reckoning, represented a range of organizations and thus bought into the anti-imperialist argument with varying degrees of conviction. But they embraced the common tactic of invoking Vietnam, citing fears of large-scale escalation and sons getting drafted. Media coverage proved quick to pick up on this theme, interviewing older demonstrators about the connections to Vietnam and asking leading questions about similarities between that day's El Salvador protest and those of the Vietnam era.[14]

Though direct action remained a staple of CISPES activism throughout the decade, the organization doggedly pursued other, less rabble-rousing forms of solidarity. CISPES raised money for medical aid under the banner "Healing the Wounds of War" and promoted the development of alternative health care in rural areas abandoned by the Salvadoran government. Over the course of the decade, CISPES distributed more than one million dollars in humanitarian aid, including money for tools and agricultural seeds, as well as earthquake relief. Repudiating the Reagan administration's version of its El Salvador policy in publications like its monthly newsletter, *El Salvador Alert!*, remained a main point of emphasis. Beginning in 1986, a major focus was enhancing direct forms of solidarity that immediately impacted El Salvador, helping the popular movement survive and grow. To this end, CISPES organized numerous walkathons and many "other 'thons," as one movement veteran remembered, to raise money for material aid. CISPES also marshaled comprehensive "rapid-response alert networks" to mobilize quickly on human rights issues, and it sent thousands of pre-authorized telexes to Salvadoran authorities and the U.S. embassy to protest the almost daily attacks against, arrests, and disappearances of Salvadoran students, peasant leaders, and trade unionists—in addition to sending constant delegations to El Salvador to provide in-person protection. The Salvadoran immigrant and refugee community played a critical role in these efforts. Through the CISPES People to People Exchange Program, refugees toured the country, speaking to labor unions, church groups, and college students at "coffee klatches" about life under the "democratically elected" Duarte regime and their desire for peace. The central thrust of the passionate personal revelations at these venues was to deliver realistic human rights information to counter the Reagan administration's rosier picture, which was designed to leverage positive public relations from the election of the more moderate Duarte. Salvadoran refugees and CISPES coordinated accompaniment visits that furnished American El Salvador activists with an opportunity to gather firsthand information while serving as protection for their Central American comrades, much as Witness for Peace did in Nicaragua.[15] The primary objective of all these activities, from material, medical, and humanitarian aid, to direct action protest, to the educational campaign, was to support a Salvadoran opposition that the movement believed rightfully represented the country's popular spirit.

This involved attempts to forge alliances and influence decision making in mainstream politics as well. CISPES used grassroots pressure politics to influence key members of Congress, especially Democrats, to break the bipartisan consensus on Central American policy for which Reagan quested. CISPES advised its organizers to "bear down on the warmakers" by motivating constituents to pressure their congressional representatives to oppose administration policy. This strategy involved tried-and-true tactics of traditional politics—letter writing and phone calls to members of Congress—and resulted in some successes. A Maryland CISPES chapter churned out more than 250 personal letters to persuade its congressman to hold hearings investigating the veracity of the president's 1986 report on human rights in Central America. Simultaneously, the House Ways and Means Committee chair Dan Rostenkowski, with the fervent urging of CISPES, voiced opposition to key colleagues on an administration request for $54 million for police training in El Salvador, which was subsequently voted down. While CISPES engaged in the grinding incremental work of legislative pressure politics, a handful of lawmakers embraced its efforts more unabashedly. The California liberal stalwarts Ron Dellums and Mervyn Dymally penned CISPES fund-raising appeals on their letterhead, detailed the atrocities to Salvadoran civilians, cautioned against "the bitter prospect of another Vietnam-style war in Central America," and urged American citizens to aid the CISPES Stop the Bombing campaign to thwart the Salvadoran government's high-casualty offensives aimed at depopulating guerrilla-controlled regions.[16] Though this painstaking battle for field position in mainstream politics contrasted with the more radical ideals of many in CISPES, one episode suggests that these efforts struck a chord.

Throughout the decade, the Federal Bureau of Investigation conducted a wide-ranging investigation of and campaign of harassment against CISPES. Initially this investigation attempted to establish that CISPES, which did support the Salvadoran opposition and enjoyed a close relationship with the refugee community, was indeed under the direct control of the Salvadoran rebels, in violation of the Foreign Agents Registration Act. Although it was possible that gray areas existed between sincere, idealistic engagement in a transnational solidarity movement and violation of federal law, the FBI failed to unearth evidence of criminality. The Bureau then took a new tack, by 1983 transforming the investigation into an international counterterrorism probe, which allowed a range of surveillance techniques not permitted in purely domestic investigations. Documents released under the Freedom of Information Act revealed a comprehensive operation that employed such provocative harassments as photographing participants in demonstrations, spying on activists, infiltrating meetings with undercover agents, scrutinizing telephone records, and running police checks on cars parked outside of CISPES meetings. A Kansas State graduate student described walking home from a CISPES meeting with friends and having a car pull up and photograph them with a strobe light—apparently to "let us know we were under surveillance." Subsequently, the student learned of similar occurrences at other CISPES chapters in Kansas and decried what he saw as "federally funded political intimidation." The former FBI agent Frank Varelli, a naturalized Salvadoran who was a key informant in the probe, resigned from his post after concluding that the Bureau's chief goal was undermining the Central America movement rather than legitimate counterterrorism. For his efforts, Varelli, testifying in front of the Senate Intelligence Committee and a House Judiciary subcommittee about FBI abuses in the CISPES investigation, found himself the target of a campaign to impugn his credibility that included falsifying results from a polygraph exam he had passed three years earlier. Ultimately, an FBI internal report called for disciplinary action against six mid-level officials for mishandling the investigation.

Though the Senate Intelligence Committee conceded "excesses" and recommended that the files representing three years of FBI surveillance of CISPES be expunged or transferred to the National Archives, it also acceded to the director William Sessions's assurance that the probe's misdeeds were an aberration. Yet the sheer breadth of the investigation, which involved all fifty-nine of the FBI's field offices and led to 178 different spin-off investigations of sympathetic individuals and organizations—ranging from the Southern Christian Leadership Conference to the United Auto Workers, the American Federation of Teachers, and the U.S. Conference of Catholic Bishops—suggests that this was a comprehensive, deliberately orchestrated probe. Even institutions as well established and mainstream as the Presbyterian Church were not spared. The extent of the FBI investigation also signified CISPES's success in spreading the word and educating the public about "the real situation in El Salvador."[17] As the decade progressed, fellow Central America activists labored toward a similar end regarding the mounting crisis in Nicaragua.

Resisting America's Not-So-Secret War

The United States's October 1983 invasion of Grenada quickly squelched leftist forces there, allowing Reagan to claim a relatively neat and bloodless victory in his project of restoring national prestige from its distressing recent lows in Vietnam and the Iran hostage crisis. But Grenada also catalyzed a new chapter of Central America solidarity activity. Many Americans suspicious of Reagan's policy in the region worried that Grenada was merely an appetizer, with the main course, a full-scale invasion of Nicaragua, yet to come. Less than a month after Grenada, key figures from the Christian peace movement convened at a Pennsylvania retreat and penned a letter to distribute to churches and government authorities. The letter, "A Promise of Resistance," cited the Grenada invasion, U.S. sanctions against the Sandinista government, and the militarization of the region as developments pointing to an imminent offensive against Nicaragua. It promised to oppose such an intervention with nonviolent direct action tactics. The letter's language conveyed the faith-based background of its thirty-two signees. It framed the promise as a "covenant" and spoke of resisting with "minds, hearts, and bodies" and standing unarmed as a "loving barrier" to impede any attempted invasion of Nicaragua. Appearing in *Sojourners* magazine, the letter highlighted its authors' connection to another recently created cog in the Central America solidarity movement, Witness for Peace, expressly offering its full support and appearing next to a sidebar calling for prayer for Witness's first delegation, then freshly deployed to the Nicaragua-Honduras borderlands. Over the next several months, numerous religious and peace organizations, including the American Friends Service Committee, the Presbyterian Church, the InterReligious Task Force on Central America, SANE, and the Nuclear Weapons Freeze Campaign endorsed the letter, disseminated its ideas, and helped organize the means by which the promise could be fulfilled.[18]

This document reemerged the next summer as a "Pledge of Resistance." It now articulated a carefully orchestrated array of strategies and tactics designed to address a range of contingencies. The core strategy of the Pledge's backers was to broadcast the idea that any significant military action in Nicaragua would meet with "a credible and coordinated plan of massive public resistance," thus pressuring Congress to demand a stop to the invasion and a withdrawal of American troops. Echoing the logic of Vietnam-era antiwar forces, the pledge sought to use civil unrest to make the cost of intervention politically unpalatable. To accomplish this, it developed a clear protocol and a range of tactics. Because of the increasingly covert nature of U.S. intervention in Nicaragua, determining exactly what constituted a significant military action loomed potentially tricky. To address this, an analyst group, consisting of a dozen members with knowledge and experience in Central America, convened, representing various policymaking institutions, peace institutions, and academia. Upon the analyst group's warning of impending military action—for instance, a threatened naval blockade or quarantine—the Pledge campaign relayed this information to a signal group that was in turn charged with deciding whether to activate its national network, which alerted potential demonstrators organized through the approximately four hundred congressional districts they represented.[19]

With this carefully designed and innovative protocol in place, the Pledge also capitalized on a variety of organizing possibilities. Ken Butigan popularized the movement, pioneering the practice of mass signings of the Pledge of Resistance in front of the San Francisco Federal Building. This "sign-in" deployed the traditional organizing tool of petition signing to also create a theatricalized direct action event. Butigan also played a large role in developing and disseminating a comprehensive handbook that covered such topics as the history and background of Central American countries and their relations with the United States, the structure of decision making in the Pledge, organizing local campaigns, the history of nonviolent mass action, a nonviolence training curriculum, event planning and media kits, and fund-raising. This handbook, *Basta! No Mandate for War*, though reflecting foreign policy opposition specific to the 1980s, was steeped in the lessons of the 1960s generation of activists. The manual described the effects of tear gas and offered encouragement and advice on how to minimize its discomfort. It provided a detailed overview of the benefits and mechanics of consensus decision making, followed by a section on "overcoming masculine oppression" in group settings. Most strikingly, however, the civil rights movement and the ideology of Martin Luther King, Jr., served as *Basta's* central, recurring historical example of nonviolent direct action's potential and efficacy. Quotes from King pepper the handbook, concluding with the epigraph to the afterword, in which the civil rights icon underscored that nonviolence's efficacy depends on "a sustained, direct-action movement of civil disobedience on a national scale." Though the pledge campaign successfully broadened its base of support by adding a legal protest option to its menu of oppositional tactics, King's thought offered a revealing window into its larger aspirations.[20]

By the end of 1984 more than forty-two thousand people had taken the Pledge of Resistance, with activists sending the collected signatures off to the State Department to register their opposition. The signatures, which eventually amounted to close to eighty thousand names, represented a wide geographical distribution with more than a thousand signatures each from states as diverse as California, Massachusetts, Colorado, New Jersey, Wisconsin, Florida, Virginia, North Carolina, and Texas. Representing the "direct action arm" of the larger Central America movement, the Pledge of Resistance perpetrated numerous acts of civil disobedience. The numerous congressional contra aid votes were a recurring flash point of organizing and protest, as witnessed in the October 1986 blockade of rush-hour traffic by the Seattle Pledge of Resistance, which resulted in 103 arrests. In California, several groups organized a fast in front of the Orange County courthouse to draw attention to the "increasing militarization of Central America" and, rhetorically linking their struggle to the American Revolution's Boston Tea Party, held a "coffee party" to protest the 1988 U.S. trade embargo against Nicaragua. These actions often echoed the 1960s antiwar movement's tactics of "confronting the warmakers on their own turf." For instance, after a 1987 mass march for peace and justice in Central America, more than five hundred protestors took the additional step of marching to CIA headquarters and getting arrested. Similarly, demonstrators from seven midwestern states attempted to scale the fences of the Arlington Heights Army Reserve Center—site of training for much of the psychological and Special Forces operations prevalent in the low-intensity warfare featured in Central America— resulting in sixty-seven arrests. Other tactics—such as staging mock funeral processions and "die-ins," unfurling giant canvas banners in St. Louis's Union Station, and rappelling from beams at dizzying heights to hang anti-interventionist placards in the National Press Building in Washington, D.C.—recalled the politicized public performances of 1960s-era guerrilla theater collectives like the Diggers, the Yippies, and the Living Theatre.[21]

As the 1980s wore on and the indirect nature of Reagan administration strategy in Nicaragua became more evident, the Pledge expanded its scope to oppose a broader range of interventions and include a wider geographic focus on the entire region. In 1989, public concern with the El Salvadoran situation resurfaced after the election of the right-wing ARENA party's Alfredo Cristiani. Toward the end of the year, the FMLN launched a long-awaited offensive designed to convince government forces to reopen stalemated talks to find a political settlement to the country's civil war. In panicked response to the offensive, the Salvadoran army indiscriminately bombed sections of San Salvador that were rebel strongholds and perpetrated the brutal murders of six Jesuit priests and their housekeepers. The Pledge organized or participated in multiple actions protesting these killings. With its religious roots, the organization played a galvanizing role in the solidarity movement as a whole by encouraging the movement's faith-based and secular wings to unite in direct action opposition to administration policy. The Pledge and CISPES often cosponsored rallies and actions in the late 1980s. One such action, a protest in front of the White House commemorating the tenth anniversary of Archbishop Romero's assassination, featured fifteen thousand demonstrators and more than five hundred arrests.[22] Though its activities subsided after this event, which followed closely upon the Sandinistas' 1990 electoral defeat, the

Pledge, like the larger Central America solidarity movement, left behind a palette of tactics and a legacy of experience for future activists.

The Legacy of Solidarity

Although many of the conditions that underlay Central American strife and revolution in the 1980s remain—poverty, an uphill struggle for economic development, and the periodic recurrence of devastating earthquakes and hurricanes—there has been improvement. Even though the sides supported by the solidarity movement in Nicaragua and El Salvador—the Sandinistas and the Salvadoran rebels—never managed to sustain a left-wing revolution, a longer view suggests that both prompted reforms toward a more egalitarian and less violent social and political order. So, too, both have been woven into the fabric of their nations' political life, most obviously through the recent electoral victories of the at times distressingly antidemocratic former Sandinista leader Daniel Ortega in Nicaragua and the hopeful triumph of the FMLN's progressive standard-bearer Mauricio Funes in El Salvador, extending down to the level of municipal politics as well. Likewise, assessing the Central America solidarity movement's role in the narrowest and most literal way might result in a verdict of failure. After all, the movement never forced the Reagan administration to abandon its role in the region's wars, nor did it remove the heavy-handed dominance of the United States. Yet a wider view illuminates the myriad ways in which the movement contributed to a process of transformation that still resonates.

At the level of national politics, the solidarity movement illuminated the Central America situation, stirring the moral outrage of Americans on the left and occasioning popular culture expressions of indignation from figures ranging from the musicians Jackson Browne, U2, and the Clash to the filmmaker Oliver Stone. Even a Republican congressman from Nebraska who backed the administration's policies appreciated the clout of the movement's faith-based wing, citing the "enormous impact when organized religion decides to get involved in political issues." The president's own indefatigable communications director, Patrick Buchanan, concurred, conceding, "They have helped energize the left to an extent that it has not been energized since the Vietnam War." The swelling movement compelled Democratic members of Congress to challenge the Central American policies of a popular president, enmeshing them in a seemingly endless series of skirmishes over contra aid that hindered the administration's agenda. From these debates, in which reports from movement sources such as Witness for Peace shaped congressional testimony, the Boland Amendment emerged as a critical restraint on the president's aims. Congressional constraints forced Reagan and his point men, led by the irrepressible Oliver North, to go the covert route. This ultimately produced the embarrassing Iran-Contra Affair, which diminished the president's popularity, albeit temporarily, and, more important, discredited contra aid with the American public. Similarly, the sustained protest and activism following the murders of the Jesuit priests swayed the context of decision making that dramatically cut Salvadoran aid, hastening the military stalemate that ultimately forced its government to the bargaining table, ending the twelve-year civil war.

The ideologies and tactics of the solidarity movement and its participants did not simply vanish with the mitigation of tensions in the region from the 1990s onward. Many activists and organizations who cut their teeth in the movement have used the enhanced Central America expertise to take on more professional, less confrontational forms of solidarity, such as participating in international teams of elections supervisors and creating educational projects and initiatives to promote economic development. Witness for Peace still exists and still organizes and sponsors short-term delegations that bring North Americans into firsthand confrontation with issues of peace and economic and social justice in Latin America and the Caribbean. The Pledge of Resistance idea, to provide an organizing mechanism for large-scale civil disobedience and legal protest to respond to U.S. military intervention abroad, has been harnessed to opposition to the Iraq War and to a prospective attack on Iran. CISPES continues as a presence in El Salvador, working for "economic democracy and social justice" and sending delegations to observe human rights and electoral conditions.[23] Though the Central American playing field and the challenges it presents have changed since the early 1990s, the movement left behind a model of effective transnational solidarity that tapped an impulse shared by 1980s activists in a variety of movements.

3

"UNSIGHTLY HUTS"
Shanties and the Divestment Movement

In the chilly predawn hours of January 21, 1986, unusual turbulence in-
terrupted the wintry stillness of the Dartmouth College campus. Twelve
members of an organization called Dartmouth Committee to Beautify
the Green Before Winter Carnival (DCBGBWC), wielding sledgeham-
mers, demolished four crudely constructed shanties that had stood on
Dartmouth's Green since November, when the Dartmouth Community
for Divestment (DCD) erected them to protest the college's investments
in apartheid-era South African corporations. Though pro-divestment
activism at Dartmouth dated back to the late 1970s, and divestment protests at other American college campuses had garnered media attention
since the previous spring, the destruction of the Dartmouth shanties
brought the divestment movement national exposure.

At campuses across the country—from elite eastern institutions like
Dartmouth, Columbia, and Cornell, to large public universities with a
tradition of radicalism such as the University of California at Berkeley
and the University of Wisconsin, to seemingly unlikely locales such as
the University of Utah, Purdue University, and the University of Illinois Urbana-Champaign—students built shantytowns to symbolize the
oppressive conditions faced by black South Africans under apartheid.
The shanties became the defining feature of the divestment struggle's
movement culture. Ostensibly constructed to raise awareness about the
evils of apartheid and expose universities' financial connections to South
Africa by symbolically opposing their investment policies, the shanties

and the controversy they provoked came to represent much more. The struggles over the shanties developed into clashes over expression, student autonomy, and the kinds of places college and university campuses were supposed to be.

The building of the shanties contested public space. Although many noteworthy clashes over the shanties took place at private institutions—and elite eastern private institutions at that[1]—the construction of the shanties represented a battle for public space in the sense that student activists claimed a critical, centrally located spot within a campus and transformed it into the divestment movement's headquarters, a focal point for meetings, organizing, educating, and disseminating information under student-run, rather than official, auspices. In doing so, these activists transformed campus space in ways that left it more inclusive and accessible for wide-ranging ideas and debate.[2] This story of the shanties and their transformation into public space suggests that the boundaries between "public" and "private" space are not fixed and absolute, but permeable and socially constructed.[3] For instance, at several of the private institutions, such as Yale and Dartmouth, activists positioned the shanties so that at least one side bordered public streets or areas of the municipality in which the institution was located, consciously blurring strict notions of public and private and inviting the participation of the larger community. These examples demonstrated that there was more to campus space than its mere legal status as public or private. The divestment activists claimed an outdoor area of the campus that represented both a symbolic and actual center of campus life common to all members of the college or university and transformed it into a more public place than it was before, one more open for political speech and activity.

Though typically many campuses, even private ones, have public elements allowing outsiders to traverse portions of their spaces unfettered, shanty culture facilitated the participation of activists and sympathizers from outside the university community in new ways. At Yale University, colorful local figures such as a former Black Panther and a "free-spirited, flute-playing, chess-playing, potsmoker" lived in the shanties, sharing the movement culture with student activists. For one Yale student activist the shanties led to heightened interaction with the community that he parlayed into a postgraduate career, first as an alderman, then as associate vice president of Yale's Office of New Haven and State Affairs, overseeing the mobilization of university resources to strengthen the local community.[4] At Cornell, opinions diverged over whether the shanties made the campus more public. One professor recalled that the most interested "outsiders" were alumni and prospective students, which heightened the administration's desire to remove the shanties. Yet a student activist remembered, "A lot of the people who participated in the demonstrations had been active in the 1960s, especially community people from Ithaca, a pretty Left community that had a direct impact."[5] The divestment movement, though led by its student majority, was typically open to sympathizers whether or not they were enrolled.

At Dartmouth, movement activists and conservative students alike noted that the shanties tended to blur the boundaries between the college and the surrounding community. The DCD activist Rajiv Menon noted that the movement shrank when the shanties came down, a testimony to their efficacy at enlisting the support of locals outside the college.[6] At the University of Illinois the shanties attracted considerable attention from the Chicago-based news media, which in turn attracted many "townie" high school and community college students to hang out at the shanties and become involved with the movement.[7] The coverage motivated several local trade unionists to take an interest in divestment. This level of outsider involvement places the University of Illinois at one pole within the movement. Interaction with the community varied greatly, with some institutions exhibiting little evidence that the shanties expanded the movement's appeal beyond campus. That some institutions demonstrated low levels of outsider involvement is unsurprising given that the specific issue at hand involved college and university investments in South Africa. This makes the outsider involvement that arose all the more impressive—that the shanties, through creating a dramatic, visible link to oppression in South Africa, frequently broadened the issue beyond campus and encouraged the participation of outsiders.[8]

Conflicts over the shanties followed discernible patterns. College and university administrators sought to preserve "free and ordered spaces"[9] of learning, scholarship, and higher education that remained aesthetically pleasing to alumni and prospective students. Student activists attempted to disrupt precisely the same spaces by introducing an unavoidable structure into their midst, symbolically located in the heart of campus or close to the main administration building. The cultural geographer Don Mitchell has argued that what transforms a location into truly public space is when a group acts out of a compelling need and "takes" a space, making it public, though this rarely occurs under conditions of the takers' choosing. Constructing the shanties transformed campus areas into more public spaces and enhanced students' influence in shaping college investment policies. The shanties' locations in highly symbolic central areas of campus underscored how the divestment movement encompassed not just college investment policy or South African apartheid, but also "the right to a particular space" on campus. Within the divestment movement, what Mitchell calls the "where of protest"—the shanties' specific location within campus spaces—loomed large.[10]

By contesting particular spaces, student activists transformed American college campuses in ways that ruptured the image of the 1980s as a placid, conservative era. By reputation, the decade's youth embraced the credo of the filmmaker Oliver Stone's protagonist in *Wall Street* that "greed is good," with *Time* magazine running a cover story about their purportedly apolitical outlook. Yet the divestment movement provides a window into an influential minority of young people who dissented from the individualistic, militaristic, materialistic ethos for which the Reagan administration set the tone. Divestment activists harked back, consciously and unconsciously, to those of a generation before. The shanties in particular, while a legitimately innovative tactic,[11] paralleled one iconic 1960s episode, the Berkeley Free Speech Movement, in that each protest concerned both political expression on campus and the right to a particular space. Sometimes connections with the 1960s were less direct. Divestment activists confessed to knowing about 1960s-era activism "around the edges" and spoke of "a sense of connectedness," at the same time affirming that "people were reading books about those times, but they were not our main model."[12] Although divestment activists recognized varying levels of connection to 1960s oppositional politics, on one point the connection was unequivocal. Activists of the 1960s had raised the issue of social responsibility in college and university investments and criticized the ethics of South African investments specifically.

Divestment's Prehistory

Opposition to South African apartheid on campuses echoed earlier criticisms from the civil rights movement and the New Left. Civil rights activists frequently compared the segregated South to South Africa's apartheid regime. Martin Luther King, Jr., drew such parallels in his testimony on behalf of the Mississippi Freedom Democratic Party at the 1964 Democratic National Convention. Later that year, accepting the Nobel Peace Prize, King called for international economic sanctions against South Africa. In 1965 Students for a Democratic Society sat in at the headquarters of Chase Manhattan Bank to protest loans that helped stabilize the Pretoria government's international credit following the 1960 Sharpeville massacre, where South African police killed sixty-nine protesters and after which the African National Congress was banned. By the 1970s, students concerned with social responsibility in university investments—representing Princeton, Cornell, Union Theological Seminary, and Wesleyan—initiated calls for divestment. At Cornell the faculty joined the action, issuing a resolution for the university to avoid investments that supported South African apartheid.[13]

In the late 1970s, illustrating the transatlantic synergy that characterized the divestment struggle, movement activities stepped up as events in South Africa intensified. In 1976 the Soweto riots erupted as South African troops killed students protesting the compulsory teaching of the Afrikaans language. In 1977 the torture and murder of the Black Consciousness leader Stephen Biko while he was in police custody again focused international attention on South Africa and sparked a wave of antiapartheid activism on American campuses. That year, 700 American students were arrested in antiapartheid protests, including 295 at a single protest at Stanford University. As a result, three institutions divested and many more began reviewing their investment policies. The major corporations in which these institutions invested also felt the ripple effect of this movement, and many scurried to review their policies regarding employment practices in South Africa. The most notable result of the new corporate attention to South Africa was the Sullivan Principles, a set of fair employment guidelines devised by Leon Sullivan, a Philadelphia minister and General Motors board member. By 1979, most major U.S. corporations with large operations in South Africa had signed on to the Sullivan Principles, and American colleges and universities embraced them as a tool to influence corporations to avoid the negative stigma associated with investment in companies that exploited or ignored the injustices of the apartheid system.[14]

By developing a scale for judging the extent to which American corporations maintained a progressive stance in their South African business practices, the Sullivan Principles offered colleges and universities flexibility between total divestment from all corporations operating in South Africa and appearing insensitive to the plight of black South Africans under apartheid. Institutions practiced selective and partial divestment from firms that failed to comply with the principles, but retained their investments in companies that they could plausibly claim constituted a positive force in the country by providing black South Africans with jobs at a fair wage. As a result of the pressure generated between the newly established Sullivan Principles and the wave of anti-apartheid and divestment protests in the late 1970s, approximately three dozen additional colleges and universities initiated divestment policies by the decade's end.[15] Following this success, divestment activity once again subsided as focus shifted to other issues, most notably opposing Reagan administration Central American policies.

In 1984 events in South Africa once again catalyzed a wave of divestment. Uprisings of black South Africans in response to the country's new constitution—which gave political representation to "coloreds" and "Asians" (mostly Indian), but not blacks—caused the government to declare a state of emergency. This, coupled with the Anglican bishop Desmond Tutu's winning the Nobel Prize, again turned the international media spotlight on South Africa and increased pressure on the Reagan administration to adopt economic sanctions against the apartheid regime. Students in the United States responded, as they had in the 1960s and 1970s, by examining their institutions' ties to South Africa, and they found that American college and university endowments were invested to the tune of $400 million. This state of affairs hastened renewed calls for divestment.

The 1980s Divestment Movement: Racial Empathy for a New Generation

Perhaps not surprisingly, given its pedigree of 1960s activism, Columbia University led the new wave of divestment protest. The Columbia Coalition for a Free South Africa formed in 1982 to pressure the university to review its investment policies and divest accordingly. Ultimately, however, Columbia's pro-divestment forces became frustrated at the university's slow pace. Seeking more expedient progress, they blockaded the administration building, Hamilton Hall, for three weeks before desisting under a threatened court order. The protests at Columbia started on April 4, 1985, the anniversary of King's assassination, and three weeks later a National Anti-Apartheid Day organized by a coalition of student groups sparked pro-divestment activity on approximately sixty campuses across the United States. The Columbia protest—like protests at institutions as diverse as Cornell, Harvard, Tufts, the University of Massachusetts, Vassar, the State University of New York, Rutgers University, the University of Louisville, Oberlin College, the University of Iowa, the University of Wisconsin, UCLA, Berkeley, and UC–Santa Cruz—involved appropriations of campus space, mainly in building blockades and sit-ins. At Columbia, approximately 250 students wrapped a silver-link chain around Hamilton Hall's main entrance, sat down on the steps, and refused to leave until the university divested its South African holdings. The creation of a physical obstacle to university business as usual resembled 1960s-era student movement tactics, a fact the New York and national media seized on quickly. *The New York Times* commented that the Columbia students were "conducting the first real sit-in anyone can remember on the campus since the Vietnam War" and noted that the demonstrators were prepared to be arrested "in the same peaceful fashion" as their 1960s counterparts. Todd Gitlin, Students for a Democratic Society veteran turned Berkeley professor, rushed to note the 1960s influence, claiming that the era's "entire repertory of tactics" was available to 1980s activists and amply on display in the protests.[16]

This seemingly sudden reemergence of campus activism around the divestment movement overlapped and connected with other streams of campus activism, on issues such as opposition to CIA recruitment visits, Central America solidarity, and racial and identity politics. At Yale, for instance, the divestment movement was organized in the spring of 1985 by many of the same students who had played key roles in solidarity with a strike of unionized clerical and technical workers the previous fall. Yet among these issues, divestment galvanized student activists more than any other. A Dartmouth activist remembered a protest in the wake of the 1983 U.S. invasion of Grenada but recalled that only "five people and a dog" participated. By contrast, the spring

1985 demonstrations at UCLA, Berkeley, Columbia, and Cornell alone each mobilized more than a thousand participants at single demonstrations, not to mention hundreds more at events at Yale and Harvard as the divestment issue exploded. Mark Lurie, a white South African pro-divestment activist at Boston University, called divestment a "spark plug for getting young people in the United States motivated."[17]

When explaining what drew them to the fight, divestment activists typically cited the moral clarity of their opposition to apartheid. "The sense of evil was so dramatic," remembered Yale's Nancy Fishman, explaining why students embraced the movement. Matthew Lyons, a Cornell activist, concurred, describing apartheid as a "clear case of brutal injustice being done that only the most craven racists could deny." When articulating what drew them to the movement several activists professed admiration for the self-sacrifice of the oppressed black South Africans fighting against apartheid.[18] Similar to the way middle-class student activists identified with rural black southerners suffering under Jim Crow in the civil rights era, this empathy sharply contrasted with the image of 1980s youth as preoccupied with self-interested material pursuits.

What fueled the movement was students' realization of U.S. economic ties to the apartheid regime. Rajiv Menon, a leader in the Dartmouth movement who grew up in Holland, argued that if the focus had been only antiapartheid, "it wouldn't have taken off." "It was a way for American students in particular," he continued, "to feel proximity to what American money was doing to prop up the evil system." But if the students were motivated by opposition to U.S. economic support of South Africa, they were animated to an even greater extent by the financial links between South Africa and their own institutions. For Fishman, this was a revelation. She asserted that the movement derived its power and appeal by engendering an "understanding of the implications of one's money being involved . . . there was something directly compelling about that."[19]

Though the racial composition and leadership of pro-divestment groups varied from campus to campus—the movement at Columbia, for instance, featured significant black leadership—because of overall student demographics, especially at the elite schools, a majority of divestment activists were white. The Africa activist Prexy Nesbitt, who toured the country speaking on apartheid and divestment, observed that these issues offered a "way for white students to fight against racism" and to try to "seize control over governance questions" on their campuses. Sometimes this caused problems. Matthew Lyons remembered "important differences between white and black students . . . Initially, some white students were oblivious and insensitive at times. Black students had been addressing this issue for some time . . . Unintended oppressive patterns played themselves out—White students' assumptions about taking up space and being able to be in charge were sometimes alienating and divisive to black students."

Though the alienation and division Lyons described undoubtedly permeated campus divestment activism across the country, the movement also broadened discussion and awareness of racial struggles closer to home. Lyons added, "Many realized that it was important to deal with racism here and now . . . not just far away, and we did."

The Dartmouth student activist Scott Nova pointed out that "ultimately the movement dovetailed with issues of race on campus" and led to a greater institutional commitment to diversity. For their part, black students in the divestment movement often hailed from more modest socioeconomic circumstances. Many were the first in their families to go to college and unable or unwilling to risk arrest in divestment protests. As Nesbitt put it, "It was a class issue. I don't think black students were less concerned, but they had to consider the costs differently." This applied equally to white activists from less-advantaged backgrounds, sometimes discouraging them from at least the most drastic or risky forms of direct action.[20] Yet despite the movement's racial and economic diversity, activists unified around pressuring their institutions to divest. During the spring of 1985 they discovered their tactic of choice.

Cornell: Shanties, Free Speech, and the "Where of Protest"

In April 1985 Catherine Johnston of Cornell Community for Divestment applied for—and was granted by university authorities—permission to build a "symbolic permanent encampment" behind Day Hall, the main administration building, as part of her group's protest. The encampment included several different structures, including an "Inhumanities

Library," a Karl Marx/Nelson Mandela hut, and several smaller shanties. The largest of these, called the Hilton, housed fifteen people. The request to construct a shantytown less than a week into divestment protests suggests its importance to movement strategy. The shanties served as a physical and visual reminder for the university's tacit support of the apartheid regime, designed to pressure the university to change its policy on South African investments. When Johnston filled out the permit, she listed an initial end date that would have fallen before university commencement and alumni reunions; however, she quickly crossed out that first date and wrote "until Cornell divests."[21] This quick revision left the shanties' presence open-ended, necessitating a response from the administration that acknowledged—if not capitulated to—movement goals.

One veteran of the Cornell divestment movement underscored the significance of the shanties' location "right at the heart of things." He recounted, "The administration could not avoid it. It was a radical transformation of public space." The student activist Anne Evens bluntly stated, "We wanted to embarrass the administration," which wanted the shanties removed before alumni weekend. Student activists regarded this symbol of South African atrocities as a means of leveraging the university to divest itself of South African holdings. The activists' choice of building materials enhanced the embarrassment: the cardboard, wood, and tar paper shantytown juxtaposed with more refined architectural styles jarred campus aesthetics.[22] Given the shanties' spatial and stylistic assault on familiar campus visuals, the structures quickly developed into a flash point for conflict between student activists and the administration. But such an outcome was not inevitable. Indeed, Cornell might have followed an emerging pattern in the 1980s whereby college and university administrators, drawing on the perceived lessons of the 1960s, proved increasingly savvy about co-opting dissent by appointing advisory committees, fostering dialogue with student groups, and adopting other such methods to deflect campus unrest and skillfully preserve institutional interests. Cornell's decision not to mobilize such techniques was rooted in the university's own unique activist history.

In May 1969, against a backdrop of highly confrontational protests on American college campuses, some eighty members of the Cornell Afro-American Society occupied the student union, Willard Straight

Hall, as a protest against disciplinary reprimands. When the Cornell administration brokered an agreement for the demonstrators to leave, they famously exited brandishing shotguns and raising their fists in black power salutes, signifying a commitment to continued militancy. President James Perkins attempted to defuse the situation by urging faculty to appease the demonstrators by dropping the reprimands. Faculty initially rejected this as a capitulation to force that invited further upheaval, but they eventually reversed themselves under extreme pressure from both campus demonstrators and the administration. Many professors and students, not to mention alumni, chafed at this turn of events, believing that Perkins had coddled the demonstrators and failed to maintain order on campus. Although, at the very least, Perkins managed to avoid bloodshed in Ithaca, he paid for his handling of the situation with his resignation by the end of the year. After a transitional interval during which the university was run by insider holdovers from the Perkins administration, trustees selected as president Frank Rhodes, who listed breaking a University of Michigan teaching assistants' union among his major accomplishments.

Maintaining order and curbing campus turbulence were part of Rhodes's mandate as he assumed Cornell's presidency, and it was in this context that his administration faced the 1985 divestment protests. Yet there were some sympathetic individual administrators, which may account for the university's granting of the initial shantytown permit in what one faculty member referred to as a "historical accident."[23] Vice President William Gurowitz, who signed the permit, may have done so because he viewed the space behind Day Hall as preferable to the highly disruptive sit-ins earlier that week *inside* Day Hall. That is, granting a permit may have represented an attempt to control the "where of protest" rather than a display of tolerating dissent by allowing the shanties as a symbolic protest. Undoubtedly, though, the perceived impotence of the Cornell administration in the 1960s encouraged the Rhodes administration of the 1980s to avoid the appearance of indulging student activists. From the outset, the university sought to limit the scope of the protest by imposing conditions on the continued existence of the shanties.

An opportunity came when a fire broke out at the shanties. Though no one was hurt, university officials moved decisively to eradicate the two-and-a-half-week-old shantytown. Later that day, after a hastily conducted investigation, the Ithaca fire chief ruled that all "combustible waste and refuse" must be removed from the vicinity of Day Hall, but he pointed out that if those materials were dwellings, they would come under the jurisdiction of the city's buildings department. A memo later that day from David Drinkwater, Cornell dean of students, to the shantytown residents admitted to no such nuance, citing orders from the fire department that "all materials will be removed" and declaring the original permit's revocation. Hoping to salvage the shanties by addressing public safety concerns, student residents devised a detailed set of "Shantytown Fire Regulations," complete with provisions for trash collection, fire extinguishers, outside storage of gas canisters for cooking stoves, and maintaining a water supply. University officials, however, remained unimpressed. At seven o'clock the next morning the dean arrived with public safety officers and heavy machinery to remove the shanties. Anticipating this action, students had tied themselves to the shanties with wires, but the officers used bolt cutters to free the residents and remove them, apparently clearing the way to raze the structures. In a classic maneuver of nonviolent civil disobedience, students intervened by forming a human chain to block the machinery's path. Ultimately, the residents forced the university to relent—at least for that particular day.[24]

Pro-divestment forces seized on the university's action as another opportunity to connect campus struggles with those in South Africa. An "Emergency Memo from Shantytown" alleged, "They entered with bolt cutters drawn and cut and dragged the residents out of their homes, JUST LIKE SOUTH AFRICA." As a rule, confrontation with university officials over the shantytowns transformed the movement at institutions where conflict occurred. Movement participants recalled how the shanties on their campuses, initially intended to symbolize solidarity with black South Africans' oppression, rapidly took on a life of their own that was more closely connected to local concerns. Nesbitt, who toured shanties across the United States, observed that "constructing and protecting the shanties became more the issue on some campuses—it became about freedom of speech." At Cornell the shantytown promptly added to its global symbolism a central role in local movement culture. One leader claimed that the shanties "served a purpose as a center for movement activities, postering, flyers, information, etc." Another concurred, remembering that "people would hang banners, staff literature tables, people would congregate and exert a cultural presence." From the outset, residents of the Cornell shanties cited the encampment's dual purposes—its symbolic value and its status as "a vital information center." As the Cornell struggle took on a new legal dimension when the university obtained a restraining order barring the shantytown residents from interfering with the dismantling of the structures, the residents sent a memo to faculty and staff contending that "the issue has now become one of freedom of speech."[25]

In *Cornell University v. Loreelynn Adamson, et al.* the pro-divestment defendants claimed that the structures constituted a form of speech and that the university's intervention abridged that freedom. Though the New York Supreme Court ruled against the demonstrators, both sides were preoccupied with the "where of protest." Laying out a rationale for the shanties' removal after the residents' successful initial resistance, Senior Vice President William Herbster referred to them as "a dangerous and sprawling collection of scrap and waste in the center of campus." While ostensibly opposing the shanties on public safety grounds, Herbster tellingly hinted that their central location lay at the core of the university's concerns and that this particular form of free speech may have been freer if exercised in some less visible part of campus. He declared the university's intent to "restore the natural condition of the area," positing the carefully manicured, maintained, and organized appearance of this Ivy League campus—with its design-conscious collection of buildings oriented toward academic purposes—as "natural," while implying that the crudely constructed shanties represented a more "unnatural" use of Cornell's space.[26]

Though administrators fretted over the shanties' location, they also bemoaned the structures' aesthetics. Negotiations ensued with the residents for an "alternative means of expression" that would preserve free speech "without perpetuating a dangerous and unsightly collection of scrap and waste in the center of campus." The word "unsightly" and others like it glossed on the presumably deficient aesthetics of the shanties and resonated through the criticisms of administrators, faculty, and students who opposed the shanties in institutions across the country. An administrator asserted that though pro-divestment students saw the shantytown as symbolic protest, "there were many other students and faculty who did not see it that way and were offended by its presence."[27]

Those offended objected not necessarily to activists' political expression, but invariably to their "unsightly" aesthetics. Cornell's legal complaint noted that the shantytown was constructed of "cardboard, sticks, twigs, wood products, pressed wood, pine boards, wood shingles, canvas and other fabrics, plastic, and other scraps including wooden doors and posts, concrete blocks and metal products." These materials created jarring visual dissonance with standard Ivy League architecture. To the dismay of university officials and many students outside the movement, pro-divestment students claimed that the shanties' aesthetics of poverty linked them to South Africa. Erecting these structures prominently to assault campus aesthetics, pro-divestment students anticipated criticism and prepared responses to refocus attention on divestment's moral dimensions. "We realize that some members of the community may be offended by what they see, and we are sorry if that is so," wrote Cornell shantytown residents, "but, as one of our signs points out, 'Apartheid Isn't Pretty Either.'"[28] At Cornell's fellow Ivy, Dartmouth, the shanties' visual elements took center stage in an emotional campus debate.

"Unsightly Huts" and a "Real Big Eyesore"

By the time Dartmouth students constructed shanties, in November 1985, the structures had solidified themselves as the movement's iconic symbol and most potent strategy. A sociologist accounting for the shanties' wide dispersion cited the concept of modularity, whereby "activists in scattered locations, despite minimal organization, and without direct contact, somehow manage to unite in national social movements." Shared collective identity played a role in the shanties' proliferation. Higher rates of shantytown events occurred at prestigious northeastern liberal arts institutions as students mimicked movement tactics on similar campuses.[29] Pro-divestment students across the country also maintained more direct ties, relaying news of movement developments through formal and informal networks. A network of approximately thirty-five New England institutions disseminated information among students active in antiapartheid work. This informational network mobilized periodically for direct action, as when Boston University awarded an honorary degree to the Zulu chief Mangosuthu Buthelezi, who opposed both economic sanctions and the ANC. Students from several Boston institutions, along with others from New Hampshire and Vermont schools, joined BU students in protest.[30] Antiapartheid and pro-divestment speakers like Nesbitt, the South African "poet in exile" Dennis Brutus, and Mpahl Tutu, daughter of the Nobel laureate, crisscrossed the campus lecture circuit, educating and urging solidarity.

This intercollegiate exchange helped launch the Dartmouth shanties. A Dartmouth movement leader recalled that a Berkeley student activist brought a video illustrating the shanties' role in the protests there. The campus daily newspaper, *The Dartmouth*, heralded news of the Cornell shanties within a week of their creation. That October the newspaper reported on shanty construction on the green at the nearby University of Vermont. Two days before Dartmouth pro-divestment forces hammered the first nail, *The Dartmouth* ran a feature on their plans for the shanties, alerting the Dartmouth community to their impending construction. The DCD's Joshua Stein articulated its rationale, citing the Dartmouth trustees' inaction on South African investments and explaining the strategy of presenting the college with the uncomfortable choice of either divesting or enduring "unfavorable press." Stein noted that the high visibility of the structures on the Dartmouth Green—the geographic center and the heart of campus life—was uniquely suited for "alarming" the Dartmouth community and raising awareness. Of the assault on campus space, the DCD's Menon remarked, "It was an eyesore on an idyllic campus. You had to grapple with it. Within two days every student on campus would have walked by it."[31]

At Dartmouth, pro-divestment students who constructed shanties faced the stiffest challenge not from administrators—who, fearful of campus unrest and damaging media attention, actually took steps to accommodate the shanties—but from other adversaries within the Dartmouth community: alumni, parents, and, especially, conservative students. When two shanties first appeared on the Dartmouth Green, administrators initially stated that they could remain standing for three days. After this grace period, administrators stressed that the shanties needed to be taken down or they would be dismantled. But on the third day, pro-divestment students found that the board of trustees had ignored their initial set of demands, which included the college's total divestment from companies that conducted business with South Africa and the creation of an ethical investment committee with direct control over the college's investment policies. Echoing 1960s patterns of campus confrontation, DCD activists escalated the protest, building a third shanty adjacent to the others. With this move, the administration, perhaps wanting to avoid radicalizing more students through forcefully suppressing the protest, changed course. Not only did the administration allow the shanties to stand, it also provided assurances that campus police would protect the demonstrators. One administrator remarked, "Our primary concern right now is for the safety of the students who are expressing their right to protest. We are trying to be sensitive to the issue, but it is a difficult position for the College." The college's actions over the next several months reflected this difficulty as the administration vacillated between trying to appear to facilitate free expression and its underlying preference that the shanties would disappear.[32]

Other Dartmouth students, however, proved more vocal in opposing the shanties, with the criticism ranging from banal to satirical to menacing. For these students, the structures' high-profile location on the Dartmouth Green, which one called the "physical and emotional center of campus life," touched a nerve. *The Dartmouth* polled 211 students on the question "Do you think the shanty-town is an effective means of protest?" While opinion was split fairly evenly (46 percent answered "yes," 42 percent "no," and 13 percent "don't know"), more telling still were the additional comments that students who opposed the shanties scribbled. One freshman claimed, "They [DCD] have erected an illegal structure on everybody's Green, I'd like to play football there, and others should have a right to do that too." This criticism epitomized a growing attitude of privilege among 1980s youth, invoking entitlement to unmolested leisure time while avoiding the questions of social and moral obligation that the shanties sought to dramatize. Shantytown dwellers also embodied this privilege, since residing outside in the cold risked health and productive study habits—"it was a hard place to get a good night's sleep," as one remembered—potentially jeopardizing the academic benefits of an education that, at elite institutions like Cornell and Dartmouth, came with a substantial price tag.[33]

More common still was the complaint that the shanties were an eyesore and needed to be removed. Another freshman, who was uncommitted in his opinion on divestment, concurred: "It's great to make a point, but it makes the College unattractive to do it with this shantytown." For this student, campus aesthetics occupied a place of greater value than political expression or moral statement, a position well represented in debates surrounding the Dartmouth shanties. Numerous satires in the campus newspaper illustrated this response. One article announced that the Mandela Hall shanty had been awarded the "Frank Lloyd Wright architecture and design award for 1985," praising its "subtle, yet powerful juxtaposition of cardboard, tin, and plywood into a less than Baroque but more than post-modernist Bauhaus school shanty." This spoof revealed how the shanties' appearance had provoked pervasive campus discussion and debate, since such parodies rely on widespread familiarity. An editorial page column poked fun at the Biko Hall shanty in much the same vein, sketching a mock review of an artwork called *Shanty*. "How the artists were able to create such an aesthetically pleasing exterior synthesis of plywood, metal and spray paint I will never know," the author quipped, comparing the structure's use of color to the work of Willem de Kooning and Frank Stella. A tongue-in-cheek letter to the editor speculated that the administration was allowing the structures to stand because they offered a solution to the college's "housing woes."[34] While such satire represented both a humorous diversion and hinted at deeper anxieties about the shanties, the conservative students of *The Dartmouth Review* expressed their discontent with far less subtlety.

The Dartmouth Review denounced the structures as "putrid little outhouses" and criticized the administration's policy that the shanties could remain standing as long as they fulfilled an educational purpose. The column concluded, "The time has come to end this farce," and, in a foreshadowing, added, "and demolish the shanties." The *Review*'s Jerry Hughes highlighted shanty opponents' objection to their location on the Green: "anywhere else on campus, I don't think it would have been an issue." Both pro-divestment and anti-divestment letters to *The Dartmouth*, sprinkled with phrases such as "our beloved Green" and "our once beautiful Green," indicated the Green's emotional centrality to campus life. Several letters also contended that the shanties' incongruous appearance and visual dissonance alienated potential support for divestment from moderate students who could not embrace direct action protest tactics. Yet DCD activists responded to the often asked question, "Why put up the shanties which are ugly and ruin the beauty of the Green?" by countering:

[F]or us the shanties are beautiful. They symbolize a unity with people we will never meet, but whose oppression is as real as the shanties themselves, and infinitely more ugly. The shanties have served a purpose; it is only since their construction that a dialogue had opened between the trustees and the DCD and that divestment has become a daily debated issue. For us the issue of apartheid is much more important than the issue of the beauty of the green. The issue of the shanties is trivial compared to apartheid itself.[35]

Parts of this comment strike a disingenuous note, since the shanties aimed precisely to be ugly and to symbolize the real poverty and oppression of places like Soweto. Further, the DCD activists' claim that the shanties were beautiful sprang from their sense of identification and solidarity with black South Africans, which, in most cases, stopped short of the desire to live under the conditions the shanties represented. Yet this defense of the shanties reveals that aesthetic sensibilities are subjective, suggesting that not only is beauty in the eye of the beholder, it is also shaped by one's cultural and political outlook. The DCD students made the case for the shanties' value and "beauty" in educating and fostering dialogue, arguing that apartheid as a global moral issue trumps campus aesthetics as a local concern, a judgment the DCD and shanty supporters did not blush at making on behalf of the rest of the community. Strikingly, with the exact opposite reasoning—that local aesthetics trumps global moral concerns—twelve students affiliated with the *Review* did not hesitate to take upon themselves the task of ridding the Dartmouth community of the "unsightly huts."

Describing what motivated himself and his colleagues in the ad hoc Dartmouth Committee to Beautify the Green Before Winter Carnival, Jerry Hughes explained that the shanties were a "violation of our sense of the place, and it went too far and created a burden on the entire community without their consent." Calling the shanties "unsightly" and "an eyesore," a brief letter from the DCBGBWC to President David McLaughlin explained the rationale for removing the shanties. Though underscoring its commitment to free speech, the DCBGBWC affirmed its notion of the Green as a unique place whose pleasing appearance was not to be marred by protest: "We are merely picking up trash off the Green, and restoring pride and sparkle to the College we love so much." The letter laid out another justification for the shanties' demolition, reflecting deeper concerns. The shanties "exacerbate the bad national press Dartmouth is already receiving," the DCBGBWC wrote. "They confuse the student body, they create skepticism among devoted alumni, and they discourage prospectives when they visit the College."[36] These comments hint that what was really on the minds of the DCBGBWC was institutional prestige, alumni donations, and the future caliber of the student body. These items ultimately impacted the college's economic well-being through its endowment, which is precisely what pro-divestment students hoped might motivate their institutions to divest. Thus the aesthetic and spatial objections to the shanties often functioned as a surrogate for a deeper, more fundamentally political opposition to divestment activism.

This insight was not lost on the major television and print media outlets that covered the events at Dartmouth and in the divestment movement nationally. *The Nation* compared South Africa activism in the 1980s to that in Mississippi in the 1960s and wondered aloud whether it was asking too much to link the divestment movement to domestic racial issues, while *Newsweek* observed that at Dartmouth the shanties had accomplished precisely that. *Fortune* mocked both the shanties and administrators' attempts to have them removed on technicalities such as fire code violations, arguing instead for constructive engagement and warning of the dangers of a potential turnover of South Africa to "the Communist-dominated" African National Congress. The *National Review* objected to the relatively stern disciplinary suspensions meted out to the Dartmouth shanty dismantlers as compared with the pro-divestment activists, concluding that the moral was "you could do anything you damn well pleased as long as you validated it with a leftist cause." The *Review* also demonstrated insight into the movement's political significance: "It has to do with power within academic institutions, that is, just who runs them . . . it concerns imperialism, racism, sexism, you name it."[37] By acknowledging the power of the shanties rather than dismissing them, mocking them, or trivializing them, the *National Review*'s analysis testifies to the extent to which the shanties had become a focal point of campus political activity and symbolized a connection to a larger oppositional politics.

The shanties were not confined to elite institutions such as Cornell and Dartmouth. They also appeared in divestment protests at nonelite and public colleges and universities such as the University of Hawaii and the University of Utah, where the shanties were attacked by vandals and where pro-divestment forces ultimately prevailed upon a federal judge to maintain the shanties on free speech grounds against the administration's efforts to remove them. In the spring of 1986 the University of Illinois was the site of an intense divestment struggle. University authorities, after threatening students with arrest and disciplinary action, either pressured students to dismantle or dismantled themselves two different shantytowns built without authorization in the middle of the main quad. Student activists, led by the Divest Now Coalition, ultimately prevailed upon the university to negotiate acceptable conditions for rebuilding the shanties, which included an agreement to move the structures to a less central location. The demonstrators promptly erected six more shanties. As Tom Burke, one of the main figures involved in the construction, put it, "We decided to make it a *real big* eyesore." Burke touted the shanties' role in transforming the culture of the U. of I. campus, claiming that they "solidified and promoted that there was a left-wing student culture" and recalling "people hanging out around the shanties playing music, reciting rap poetry, and it was a safe space for gays and lesbians." This description of the shanties' inclusivity evokes the ideal of democratic public spaces where groups of people can come together on roughly equal footing to create a vibrant venue for a variety of activities, political and otherwise. The shanties became a campus focal point for divestment activities at the U. of I., where demonstrators ultimately gathered support from members of the football team—a major coup at a Big Ten institution—and by January 1987 the board of trustees voted to divest the university's holdings in businesses with operations in South Africa.[38] This decision occurred only after the trustees followed the widely used tactic of allowing a reasonable period of time to elapse before divesting, so as to avoid the impression that the decision was linked to protest or to the shanties.

Assessing Divestment and the Shanties

By the most obvious measure of the movement's accomplishments—namely, whether activists achieved their goal of forcing American colleges and universities to divest—the record indicates substantial success. Despite a minority of instances where university officials dragged their feet or stubbornly refused the appearance of caving in to movement pressure, by 1989 more than 80 percent of colleges and universities instituted divestment policies. Ultimately, more than 150 institutions pursued some form of divestment. At campuses where protest occurred, 60 percent of those institutions divested at least partially, as compared with less than 3 percent at the schools where no protest occurred. In turn, these policy changes were linked to a larger stream of antiapartheid momentum nationally that included the divestment of $18.5 billion from state and local government pension and investment funds, Congress's 1986 override of President Reagan's veto of an economic sanctions package, and the decisions of several major corporations, led by General Motors and IBM, to pull out of South Africa. Finally, antiapartheid actions in the United States synergized with international pressure that ultimately witnessed the end of South African apartheid and the election of Nelson Mandela as South Africa's president.[39]

Considered by these standards, the divestment movement emerges as an impressive success story. But the shanties also allowed student activists to transform college and university campuses, if only temporarily in many cases, into more democratic, more truly public spaces, open to a wider range of political, social, and cultural expression. That these transformations were often short-lived and always contested does not, however, mean that they were without lasting effect. First, the lives of student activists were transformed in the process, with many remaining engaged in activism oriented toward social justice. The Yale divestment alumnus Nancy Fishman, senior law and policy analyst at the New Jersey Institute for Social Justice, maintained that the "lessons learned" from the movement were applied to subsequent struggles. Cornell's Matthew Lyons, an archivist and historian of social movements and systems of oppression, concurred, adding, "The issue of racial oppression is central to my outlook on the world, and that's certainly an outgrowth of that time." The 1986 *Fortune* article that compared the shanties to panty raids, finding the latter a superior force for potential social good, lacked this long-term view of the movement's legacy.[40] The divestment movement and the shanties, through their transnational concern with achieving social justice abroad in the historic liberation of South Africa from apartheid, and through changing the political culture on campus, resounded with domestic struggles to democratize American society.

Moreover, they were part of a larger "war of position" between 1980s progressives and the decade's increasingly confident conservative voices, which prevented the Right from ever fully dominating American life during these years. But participants in traditional activist movements like the nuclear freeze, Central America solidarity, and divestment were not the only combatants battling against the decade's political conservatism, economic stratification, and corporate rapaciousness. Diverse actors from the decade's cultural life arose to oppose the tide of Reagan-era America, re-enchant social conscience, and, sometimes haltingly, engage politics.

4

POPULAR CULTURE AND THE CULTURE WARS

Schoolchildren in the 1980s, faced with the time-honored assignment of creating time capsules filled with ephemera for future generations to unearth, doubtless stuffed them with quaint artifacts that swiftly reached obsolescence. Cassette tapes and videocassette recorders, for instance, were doubtless included in such projects. But what kind of content might these children's descendants discover from the capsules, and would it reflect the decade's conservative tenor? Certainly there would be no shortage of examples, such as the film *Risky Business* (1983), which venerates the desperate entrepreneurial drive and status-driven ambition that lead a young man to open a brothel in his parents' house. Or *Fatal Attraction* (1987), a film so saturated with AIDS-driven anxiety and misogyny that its climactic sequence morphs into a horror movie, with the temptress career woman-as-monster gunned down by the betrayed wife. Perhaps these schoolkids deemed Madonna's "Material Girl" the defining statement of 1980s sensibility—with its iconic refrain and its assertion that "the boy with the cold hard cash is always Mister Right"—loading a copy of the song's memorable video into the capsule. Of course, in doing so, they would have ignored the heavy dose of irony "Material Girl" used to critique the very same acquisitive tendencies it putatively celebrated, but then the schoolchildren would have been far from alone in not probing beyond the title in assessing the song's significance.

For those delving deeper into popular culture in the 1980s, a more complex picture emerges. On one hand, media and entertainment mergers on a grand scale created huge conglomerates that placed a new emphasis on quarterly profits and the necessity of moving "units"— often considering the content of those units as an afterthought. On the other hand, the sheer scale of money and finance, combined with the residue of 1960s idealism and social engagement, opened up new possibilities. The emergence of "mega-events"—led by the 1985 Live Aid concerts—that featured big-name recording industry stars were a case in point. Drawing on a host of 1970s predecessor musical benefits— from the Concert for Bangladesh to Britain's Rock Against Racism movement to the No Nukes! concerts that harnessed the power and energy of rock music to raise money and awareness for social and environmental causes—the event ushered in a new wave of social consciousness in popular music.

"There's a Choice We're Makin'"

Live Aid, a seventeen-hour musical extravaganza organized by the Irish rock musician Bob Geldof with concerts in London and Philadelphia, televised to an estimated 1.5 billion people in 150 countries, mobilized an array of head-spinning celebrity power—Mick Jagger, the Who, Phil Collins, Elton John, Tina Turner, U2, Madonna, Sting, Paul McCartney, and Bob Dylan—to raise charitable aid for Ethiopian famine victims. Despite this seemingly benign and even beneficent purpose, Live Aid managed to engender a surprising amount of criticism. The points of contention were numerous. Echoing the language of "compassion fatigue" that surfaced during the Reagan years, one group of critics questioned the motives of the star performers who donated their services, citing the event's publicity-boosting and image-shaping capacities as factors that made participating a solid career move. The rock critic Greil Marcus went further, calling it "an enormous orgy of self-satisfaction, self-congratulation."[1] Though such invective was directed toward allegedly self-centered performers rather than toward the cause of international famine relief itself, it coincided with callousness toward the less fortunate on the domestic front, as the decade's diatribes against "welfare queens" attest.

Suspicion of musicians' social conscience represented only one of the indictments hurled at Live Aid. Others wondered if the money would actually reach those who needed it most. Reports surfaced about hundreds of thousands of tons of grain rotting in ports, held hostage by Ethopia's inferior transportation infrastructure and "obstinate Marxist regime" that prioritized hauling Soviet-donated military equipment. Still, organizers anticipated these difficulties and took steps to prevent them, such as earmarking the first $2.7 million for purchasing trucks and trailers to transport the food and partnering with established relief agencies like the Red Cross, Oxfam, and CARE to assess how the cash might most readily be converted into life-sustaining food and supplies, while eliminating delays. The reports of rotting food proved exaggerated extrapolations of conditions on the ground, with the food merely sitting in storage while the trucks were retooled to distribute the provisions.[2] That such inflamed anxiety emanated from diverse points on the political spectrum—not only the Right—testified to the era's skepticism about socially conscious action.

Detractors also bemoaned Live Aid's lack of incisive political perspective. Some charged that black artists were underrepresented among Live Aid performers. Though "We Are the World," the hit single recorded by a star-studded ensemble to raise African relief funds, was co-written by two of the recording industry's biggest stars, Lionel Richie and Michael Jackson, both African American, the lineup at Wembley and JFK stadiums featured only a sprinkling of black performers. Run-DMC, at the time rap's most popular group, suffered the double indignation of being initially rejected, only to be added to the lineup at the eleventh hour and then having their MTV appearance preempted mid-performance in favor of Sting. Given that the recipients of the concerts' proceeds were Ethiopian people of color, the relative absence of racial diversity provoked probing questions from the media. Organizers defended the criticism, maintaining that top black performers like Jackson, Diana Ross, and the Pointer Sisters were invited but declined. Geldof's response to media questioning illuminated the dynamics of organizing mega-events: "I asked the biggest because the biggest will draw the most money. It's pragmatics." According to the 1980s music industry's market logic, the biggest were overwhelmingly white performers or black performers with wide crossover appeal to white audiences, which explained the paucity of rap acts. Geldof elaborated: "Would a racist go to all the trouble to keep these people alive? People who just happen to be black? And by the way," he continued, "the fact that they are black is incidental. They could be luminous orange for all I care." Geldof rebutted criticism, maintaining that the specifics of the event were less relevant than raising "a lot of money to feed a lot of people." The African American vocalist Eddie Kendricks of Temptations fame, who sang harmonies for Hall and Oates at Live Aid, concurred, observing, "Hunger knows no color."[3]

Those inclined to a jaundiced view of Live Aid raised comparisons to 1960s rock festivals epitomized by Woodstock. No less an icon of 1960s social conscience than the singer Joan Baez encouraged such associations, opening Live Aid with her famous benediction to the "children of the eighties" that "this is your Woodstock and it's long overdue." Baez spoke to the generation's longing for community, of which older generations had told them they had missed out. For many observers the comparison fell flat. They pointed out that Live Aid's crowd were no social rebels opposing the Vietnam War, but solidly mainstream citizens with short hair who "waved the Stars and Stripes." Another living link to the 1960s, the legendary promoter Bill Graham, pointed out that Live Aid's star-studded lineup motivated fans more than political commitment, claiming, "If there was no famine, we'd have sold as many tickets." A *Los Angeles Times* reporter surveying fans at the London performance agreed, noting that when asked why they came to Wembley Stadium, fans much more frequently cited rock musicians from U2 to Elton John and Paul McCartney than "the cause."[4]

Commentators on the left lamented the centrality of corporate sponsorship to the event's success. Indeed, Live Aid relied on a roster that could have been culled directly from the Fortune 500, including corporate giants Pepsi, AT&T, Eastman Kodak, and Chevrolet. One critic focused particular suspicion on Pepsi, noting the happy confluence of "We Are the World"'s oft-repeated phrase "There's a choice we're making"—written by Richie and Jackson, both well-compensated endorsers of the popular soft drink—and the Pepsi advertising slogan "the choice of a new generation." Geldof defended Live Aid as "morally justified," arguing that the greater goal was keeping people alive: "If I can get Pepsi to sponsor an event, and make us money, it's fine by me—regardless of what they get out of it." Though this ends-justifying-the-means approach led to a flattening of Live Aid's political content and a missed opportunity for consciousness-raising about the African famine's structural roots in the global political economy, a big-picture perspective vindicates Geldof's position.[5]

Most obviously, Live Aid generated $67 million for African famine victims. Add to this more than $50 million from album and merchandise sales of USA for Africa's "We Are the World" and $11 million from Band Aid's "Do They Know It's Christmas?" and revelations of popular music's unique fund-raising capacities started to dawn on those in the industry. By fusing popular culture and politics, however domesticated those politics appeared, Live Aid paved the way for new constituencies, exposing young music fans to political issues. This in turn opened up space for cultural events to broach politics. Bob Dylan's offhand remark at Live Aid, that he wished some of the proceeds could benefit struggling American farmers, led directly to the Farm Aid concert later that year, which raised $10 million and launched what remains an annual event. In a less direct way, Live Aid fostered a mixing of popular music and social conscience that enhanced the popular appeal of more politically potent cultural expressions such as Sun City.[6]

The multifaceted Sun City project was convened by Steven Van Zandt, of Bruce Springsteen's E Street Band, under the aegis of Artists United Against Apartheid. The group recorded a Billboard Top 40 single, a critically acclaimed album, and a heavily rotated music video that took direct aim not only at apartheid—which might have been opposed with relatively easy moral clarity—but also against the Reagan administration South Africa policy. The multicultural and polymusical ensemble that Van Zandt assembled to record the title song and video unambiguously assailed the damaging effect of Ronald Reagan's policy of constructive engagement and the hopelessness it caused among oppressed South Africans. An all-star cast representing styles as diverse as rap (Run-DMC), rock (Bruce Springsteen, Lou Reed, Pat Benatar), punk (Joey Ramone, Stiv Bators), long-standing politically progressive singer-songwriters (Jackson Browne, Bonnie Raitt), reggae (Jimmy Cliff), funk (George Clinton), and jazz (Miles Davis), to name just a few, zeroed in on American complicity in apartheid, lamenting the lack of solidarity with 23 million black South Africans and demanding to know why "we're always on the wrong side." To hammer home the issue's moral immediacy, the "Sun City" video interspersed shots of the eclectic performers, footage of Martin Luther King marching and civil rights demonstrators beset by police dogs and fire hoses, and contemporary scenes of South African oppression and unrest. Sun City also featured an educational component; the album included bonus materials detailing facts and figures about apartheid, and for educators, the artists provided a package describing how to integrate the album and video into the classroom. Most significant, though, Sun City's politics targeted the world closest to home, the world of music and entertainment. Sun City itself was a popular South African resort, a "playground for moneyed whites"—in the midst of one of the segregated black homelands, Bophuthatswana—that was a favorite venue for entertainers from the United States and other Western countries.[7] The hit record's memorable refrain "I ain't gonna play Sun City" trumpeted a clarion call to political conscience for musicians and entertainers at a pivotal moment on the road to the liberation of black South Africans from apartheid.

Where Live Aid's transatlantic spectacle used a bully pulpit made possible by state-of-the-art satellite technology, Sun City's salvo at the role of entertainers in legitimizing the apartheid state mobilized music industry money, talent, and media coverage to up the ante for politicizing popular culture. Both projects underscored the considerable potential of such collaborations for raising public consciousness. These events illuminated issues that transcended national boundaries—Live Aid's focus on African famine and Sun City's spotlight on the ethics of musicians' South African performances—and showed westerners how their lives intertwined with those in less-privileged corners of the world. This transnational focus was particularly evident in Amnesty International's Conspiracy of Hope concerts and its Human Rights Now! tour. In 1986 the Amnesty International USA executive director Jack Healey partnered with U2 to stage a series of six U.S. concerts to celebrate the organization's twenty-fifth birthday and to publicize its international efforts to free political prisoners. Conspiracy of Hope specifically targeted the release of six prisoners, including a "disappeared" Guatemalan schoolteacher, a South African union leader, and a Soviet computer specialist who documented the Communist state's human rights abuses. The concerts aspired to raise "not just money"—although the $2.4 million total was nothing to sneeze at—"but consciousness," aiming especially to educate young Americans about their relatively privileged access to human rights. To this end, event organizers engaged rock fans as "freedom writers," inserting kits in concert programs with pre-addressed postcards to facilitate the goal of distributing twenty-five thousand letters to each nation housing one of the "prisoners of conscience." Within two years, three of the six prisoners were freed, making good on the prophecy of the show's finale, an ensemble rendition of Bob Dylan's "I Shall Be Released."[8]

Conspiracy of Hope and Human Rights Now! showcased an eclectic, multicultural array of musical styles to convey their internationalist humanitarian agenda. Conspiracy of Hope performers at the eleven-hour Giants Stadium finale ranged from the headliners, U2 and Sting, to Peter Gabriel, Lou Reed, Bryan Adams, Joan Armatrading, and the Neville Brothers; from the 1960s holdovers Joan Baez and Peter, Paul and Mary to the jazz guitarist Stanley Jordan, the salsa star Rubén Blades, and the Nigerian musician Fela, himself a dissident recently freed from prison with help from Amnesty International. For the 1988 Human Rights Now! tour, which commemorated the fortieth anniversary of the United Nations Universal Declaration of Human Rights, Bruce Springsteen joined Sting and Peter Gabriel, the African American pop folksinger Tracy Chapman, the Senegalese sensation Youssou N'Dour, and assorted musical performers from each of the fifteen host countries on five continents that the tour visited. The two tours dramatically raised the profile of Amnesty International, an organization theretofore known better in Europe and the Third World than in the United States. In the early 1980s Amnesty International's membership languished under the 100,000 mark, with a typical member in his or her forties. After Conspiracy of Hope, this number ballooned to 200,000, and after Human Rights Now! the figure escalated to 420,000, with an average age of twenty. The concerts made Amnesty International hip for young Americans. One journalist hailed its "Third World orientation" and its role in calling Americans' attention to human rights in previously unconsidered corners of the world.[9]

U2's Bono summarized the value of the mega-events: "There are those who wished the doors that have opened with Live Aid and Band Aid would close. Some people have suggested that we get this charity business over with" and return to rock-end-roll hedonism. "But there are those of us anxious to keep the doors open," the Irish rock star continued, predicting a new era of engagement. For all of the mega-events' star power, the potential for shameless celebrity exploitation of charitable causes for self-promotion, and the pitfalls of corporate sponsorship, their very "mega-ness" unleashed substantial power to address real problems and make ameliorative change. Indeed, by increasing the sense of global vigilance, Conspiracy of Hope's high-profile musicians made it harder for nations to abuse human rights. Moreover, the evolution of mega-events tended toward greater politicization. Whereas critics dismissed Live Aid as lamentably apolitical, Conspiracy of Hope and Sun City spotlighted specific objectionable policies and regimes. Ultimately, Live Aid ushered in an era in which progressive forces in the music industry opted to join mass culture's political, ideological battle lest their voices be crowded out. This decision rested on a growing recognition of the potency of culture as politics that even political journalists conceded was more edifying than electoral politics. Though the mega-events were no substitute for full-fledged political movements, they created cultural space for influential musicians to reach legions of fans with political and humanitarian messages. Bruce Springsteen, the emergent archetype of the politically committed rock musician, summarized music's sheer reach: "I like to believe that music can change people's minds and feelings about humanity, and in doing so may change the way they look at the next guy."[10]

The Gipper and the Boss

At a 1984 New Jersey rally, looking to cement his lead over the Democratic presidential candidate, Walter Mondale, and enhance his legitimacy in a traditionally Democratic industrial state, Ronald Reagan grasped at the star power of a favorite son. "America's future rests in a thousand dreams inside your hearts," the president exhorted. "It rests in the message of hope in songs of a man so many young Americans admire— New Jersey's own, Bruce Springsteen." In a warm gesture of ingratiation, Reagan summarized, "And helping you make those dreams come true is what this job of mine is all about," then segued to a call-and-response lovefest with the audience. As Reagan ticked off a list of his administration's achievements, supporters were prompted to reply, "U.S.A." To untrained eyes and ears this spectacle resembled Springsteen's own legendary live performances with their impassioned rituals of audience participation.[11] More savvy onlookers recognized the irony in the president's attempt to cloak himself in the populist rocker's reputation. Why should a Republican Cold Warrior and conservative family values advocate try to ride the coattails of a working-class-hero rock star, a sympathetic chronicler of serial murderers, laid-off autoworkers turned armed criminals, downtrodden Vietnam veterans, and nostalgic losers?

A smidgen of the responsibility for Reagan's easy appropriation lay with Springsteen himself. After all, Springsteen consented to Columbia Records' marketing strategy for the *Born in the U.S.A.* album, designed to tie in with election-year fervor. The iconic jacket design featured a cover shot by photographer-to-the-stars Annie Leibovitz of the man fans called "the Boss" against an American flag backdrop. That the photo was of Springsteen's backside was of little consequence, no sly subversion of the patriotic tones the flag imagery evoked. As Springsteen explained, "We took a lot of pictures, and in the end, the picture of my ass looked better than the picture of my face, so that's what went on the cover." Still, even Springsteen acknowledged the power of nationalistic symbols in an age when the president's expanding popularity was hitched to his grand project of restoring American self-esteem. "The flag is a powerful image," Springsteen conceded, "and when you set that stuff loose, you don't know what's gonna be done with it."[12] If Springsteen bore complicity in the album's opportunistic packaging, it was difficult to hold him accountable for the widespread misinterpretation of its content.

The misunderstanding centered on the album's title track. The song's verses told an unemployed Vietnam veteran's hapless tale, from meager beginnings to bleak future, in starkly unambiguous terms. Punctuated by a refrain that repeated the words "born in the U.S.A." four times over a pounding bass drum, the song both sketched the dismal prospects of working-class America and illustrated the stubborn patriotism that persisted anyway. That the song could be co-opted by the political Right reflected what one journalist called the "Springsteen phenomenon"—the confluence of a national resurgence of self-confidence, a serendipitously patriotic title, and rock superstardom powerful enough to induce Chrysler's CEO, Lee Iacocca, to offer $12 million for the rights to the tune. The writer contrasted this phenomenon with Springsteen's music, a rich body of work spanning more than a decade, mixing rock and roll and folk idioms, sympathetically giving voice to a gallery of social outsiders, and echoing the sixties ethos of personal liberation and flight from authority. For a public increasingly content to skim the surface of mediated images, the Springsteen phenomenon overpowered this musical legacy. This allowed the conservative columnist George Will the opening to try to claim Springsteen as a model for hardworking American self-reliance. "He is no whiner," Will extolled, distinguishing Springsteen from what conservatives viewed as flotsam who turned toward the federal government during economic hard times. "The recitation of closed factories and other problems," Will continued, "always seems punctuated by a grand, cheerful affirmation: 'Born in the U.S.A.'" In his haste to claim Springsteen as a "national asset," Will overlooked or willfully ignored Springsteen's irony-laden indictment of the American dream unfulfilled.[13]

Springsteen realized that Will and Reagan were not alone and that many of his newer fans shared such a potent desire to "feel good about the country that they live in" that they took *Born in the U.S.A.*, album and song, as a patriotic affirmation rather than dwelling on the searchingly desperate narratives of his songs. After a few days of befuddlement about how he should handle the president's remarks, Springsteen told a Pittsburgh audience, "The President was mentioning my name the other day, and I kinda got to wondering what his favorite album musta been." Referencing his 1982 masterwork that one reviewer called an "acid-etched portrait of a wounded America that fuels its machinery by consuming people's dreams," Springsteen quipped, "I don't think it was the *Nebraska* album." He then launched into "Johnny 99," the tale of a laid-off autoworker turned stickup murderer. The rock critic and Springsteen insider Dave Marsh observed how the Reagan incident played a pivotal role in Springsteen's politicization. Throughout the remainder of the *Born in the U.S.A.* tour, his onstage remarks grew more pointed and charged with the language of economic stratification, poverty, homelessness, the plight of workers in deindustrializing America, and the corresponding loss of dignity. "What's happening now is people want to forget," Springsteen told *Rolling Stone*, "and you see the Reagan reelection ads on TV—you know: 'It's morning in America.' And you say, well it's not morning in Pittsburgh. It's not morning above 125th Street in New York."

Not limiting his critique to bread-and-butter domestic issues, Springsteen took on Reagan-era foreign policy, integrating Edwin Starr's 1970 antiwar hit "War" into the tour's final shows in Los Angeles. Where Starr had scored a number one hit with the song's funky, guttural refrain during the Vietnam War's most anguished days,

Springsteen used "War" to impart the lessons of the 1960s to 1980s youth. Against the rising specter of American interventionism in far-flung locales from Grenada to Central America and the Middle East, Springsteen told the crowd, "I'd like to do this song for you 'cause if you're seventeen or you're eighteen out there, the next time they're gonna be lookin' at you." In a thinly veiled reference to presidential popularity, he warned, "In 1985, blind faith in anything—your leaders—will get you killed."[14] Springsteen not only increasingly talked politics in his performances, he made connections with local audiences at the grass roots. His management team helped him research local groups helping ordinary working and out-of-work people, from union locals representing laid-off steelworkers to homeless advocacy groups to food banks. Springsteen helped these organizations raise money, including personal contributions ranging from $10,000 to $25,000 a show, and raised their profiles in the community by talking up their good works nightly.

From Springsteen's political and community engagement on the *Born in the U.S.A.* tour and onward, his politics and art grew increasingly unitary. This was evident from his participation in the Sun City project and the Human Rights Now! tour; his 1995 collection of acoustic ballads *The Ghost of Tom Joad*, which updated the Depression-era social commentary of John Steinbeck and Woody Guthrie for the 1990s; his Oscar-winning original song for the film *Philadelphia* (1993), which did much to humanize the plight of AIDS victims; and his throwing his hat in the ring in mainstream politics with endorsements and benefits for the Democratic presidential candidates John Kerry in 2004 and Barack Obama in 2008. Springsteen had butted up against a moment of truth in the Reagan "Born in the U.S.A." episode, faced down the thunder on the right in his own voice, and in the process the beloved entertainer and gifted songwriter added the mantle of committed artist for social justice.

Resisting, Hollywood Style: Left Politics in the 1980s Film Industry

It is difficult to imagine a more obvious symbol for the 1980s reaffirmation of national strength than Sylvester Stallone's John Rambo character, his biceps bulging through multiplex screens. The macho warrior simultaneously reflected and shaped a new paradigm of masculinity, repudiating the 1970s sensitive male epitomized by Alan Alda's character in television's *M*A*S*H* and replacing it with a "hardbody"—an invulnerable, rippling specimen of manhood. At the same time, the image harked back to cinematic and national traditions of rugged individualism and vigilante heroism. *Rambo: First Blood Part II* (1985) revolved around finding American POWs in Vietnam and murdering their captors in a baptism of vengeful bloodshed. This symbolically revised the outcome of America's longest and most disastrous war, affirmatively answering the question Rambo poses to his superior: "Sir, do we get to win this time?" Rambo, the 1980s archetype, paralleled President Reagan's own attempt to cultivate what one political scientist called a "macho presidential style," a robust, decisive antidote to the waffling passivity of the Carter years. The record shows that Reagan, the movie star president and lifelong film aficionado, was paying attention. Testing his microphone before a speech applauding the release of American hostages in Lebanon, the president quipped, "Boy, I'm glad I saw *Rambo* last night. Now I know what to do the next time this happens." Stallone's film warrior and Reagan's aggressive Cold War posturing so meshed in the public consciousness that novelty "Ronbo" posters cropped up, sporting the president's head on Rambo's rippling, machine-gun-laden torso, unifying cultural and political expressions of the decade's newly aggressive attitude.[15]

Complementing the tenor of Reagan-era presidential style and foreign policy, *Rambo* represented the quintessential 1980s Hollywood action blockbuster. Beginning in the late 1960s, massive conglomerates, emboldened by weakening motion picture revenues and industry restructuring, commenced to absorb venerable film companies from Paramount to United Artists and Metro-Goldwyn-Mayer. In the 1980s, corporate consolidation intensified with a new synergistic frenzy, maximizing film revenues through videocassette rentals, video game tie-ins, licensing opportunities at fast-food chains, and the mergers of Warner Communications (parent of Warner Bros.) with Time, Inc., and Rupert Murdoch's News Corp's acquisition of Twentieth Century Fox. With the new era of consolidation came new pressures for Hollywood, namely, heightened accountability for meeting corporate executives' targets of quarterly financial performance. The media outlets enshrined opening weekend box office gross as the prime marker of a film's cachet. In this climate, Hollywood adopted a strategy based on a logic that exploited the enhanced earnings potential of pushing forward a smaller number of carefully crafted blockbuster, "high concept" movies, often laden with cross-marketing opportunities. *E.T.* and *Raiders of the Lost Ark*; *Ghost Busters* and *Top Gun*; action films *Rambo: First Blood Part II*, *Die Hard*, and *The Terminator*; and the raft of sequels that eventually saw five *Rocky* and *Star Trek* films each, not to mention four *Supermans*—all partook of this logic. Film savants who aspired to something more elevated—and relished film's potential as expressive art—fretted about the quality issue: a growing sense that the Hollywood product was being cheapened and playing to the lowest common denominator, that Tinseltown, as the proverb ran, "just wasn't making them like they used to."[16]

Still, 1980s Hollywood, amid financial and political constraints, managed to produce a number of films that contested the era's dominant sensibilities. Against the fantasy of rewriting the Vietnam War in Stallone's *Rambo*, Chuck Norris's *Missing in Action*, and *Uncommon Valor*, the Vietnam vet and director Oliver Stone posited a darker, more realistic view in *Platoon* (1986). The film combined arresting depictions of combat, which drew widespread praise for their authenticity, with a compelling coming-of-age narrative to pull off a rare 1980s double: critical and box office success. Garnering Academy Awards for Best Picture and Best Director and ranking as the year's third-top-grossing film, *Platoon*, unlike *Rambo*, did not shirk Vietnam's moral complexities. Rather, it portrayed cultural and social divisions within the military, suffering inflicted on Vietnamese civilians, and even crucial plot elements that turned on American soldiers assassinating their own. Stone commented that he wanted to offer a picture of war not from the point of view of the ideologues who make the decisions to go to war, but of the young men who actually experience it. If enough people took the film's lessons to heart, Stone postulated, it could alter thinking about the country's future involvement around the globe. Critics overwhelmingly concluded that Stone achieved these aims. *The Washington Post*'s verdict was typical: "This is not the Vietnam of op-ed writers, rabble-rousers or esthetic visionaries, not"—alluding to Vietnam films like *Apocalyspe Now* and *The Deer Hunter* that quested for the mantle of high art—"Vietnam-as-metaphor" or, referencing *Rambo* and its ilk, "Vietnam-the-way-it-should-have-been." "It is," the reviewer decreed, "a movie about Vietnam as it was, alive with authenticity, seen through the eyes of a master filmmaker who lost his innocence there." But it was the film's audiences that truly testified to *Platoon*'s authenticity and achievement. The film connoisseur Vincent Canby recounted an anecdote about a rowdy band of gung ho filmgoers who tried to behave as if *Platoon*'s grim battle scenes were another *Rambo* but found the exercise difficult and unsatisfying. Though a few Vietnam veterans objected that *Platoon*'s pot-smoking, alienated grunts obscured the reality that many of the soldiers were stolidly upstanding middle Americans, most praised the film's authenticity and its refutation of the *Rambo* myth. Reports of veterans weeping and calling out "that's the way it happened" in response to the film were not uncommon. A father writing to *The New York Times* expressed gratitude for the film's tempering his thirteen-year-old son's enthusuaism for *Rambo* and the desire for glory that it catalyzed. *Platoon* worked a "dramatic cure," the father wrote. "Now he's having second thoughts about a military career"—after viewing scenes of young soldiers "enduring sleepless nights and days in a place of dust, filth, and blood" where "it was not so easy to dodge enemy bullets, and death wasn't clean."[17] Repudiating the Reagan-Bush era's attempts to erase the specter of Vietnam, *Platoon* reminded audiences of the human costs of American interventions abroad from the not-too-distant past.

Of course, the immediate context of *Platoon*'s deglamorization of Vietnam was U.S. aggression in Central America, a topic that a cluster of 1980s films addressed more directly. The first of these took aim allegorically, reaching farther south and further back chronologically than the immediate U.S. presence in Central America. *Missing* (1982) probed the Nixon administration's involvement in the 1973 military coup that overthrew the democratically elected leftist leader Salvador Allende, replacing him with the brutally repressive General Augusto Pinochet. Tellingly, it was an outsider, the Greek-born French filmmaker Constantin Costa-Gavras, who launched the minor cycle of 1980s films criticizing American interventionism. Based on a true story, *Missing* documents the kidnap and murder of its protagonist, the American journalist Charles Horman. Costa-Gavras's deft choice of subject matter complements historical accounts that contend that American citizens' opposition to the Chilean coup was pivotal, building on the Vietnam antiwar movement's momentum to establish "a well-grounded foreign policy opposition" that persisted to challenge 1980s interventions in Central America. Though critically acclaimed, *Missing* provoked a libel suit against Costa-Gavras and its distributor, Universal Studios, in which the former U.S. ambassador to Chile and other plaintiffs alleged that the film misled audiences to believe that U.S. officials "ordered or approved" Horman's murder. Though the suit was later dismissed, it foreshadowed the resistance that films critical of American interventionism might occasion.[18] With that in mind, it is all the more remarkable that even a modest output of Hollywood product dwelling on Central America came to fruition.

Debuting amid clamorous debate over contra aid, the British director Roger Spottiswoode's *Under Fire* (1983) profiled an American photojournalist's crisis of conscience while covering the 1979 Sandinista Revolution in Nicaragua. Deluged with evidence of right-wing Somoza regime atrocities, the film's protagonist, played by Nick Nolte, ultimately concludes that taking a moral stand outweighs professional standards and abets the leftist guerrillas. Though several critics dismissed *Under Fire* as "underdone," "overblown," and well-meaning but "fatally confused," the film nevertheless provoked debate about its efficacy as cinema, its politics, and its stance toward journalistic ethics. One observer noted the film's striking audacity in a Hollywood landscape not famous for risk taking, calling it "the only American movie in recent decades to side with a foreign government against which the United States has aligned itself." In a 1980s Hollywood—where the erstwhile hawkish Reagan secretary of state Alexander Haig sat on the board of directors of United Artists and right-leaning producers surfaced, seeking to counteract "films with an anti-Establishment message"—*Under Fire's* mere existence was remarkable. Courting public controversy through political subject matter risked profitability, studio executives' ultimate test for green-lighting projects.

Despite lukewarm box office performance, *Under Fire's* political sentiments engendered passionate reactions. Enthusiasts such as the Massachusetts congressman Edward Markey, who sponsored a bill prohibiting sending troops to Central America without explicit congressional authorization, praised the film, claiming it would give the American public "insight into the way Central American politics work" and clarify the "social and economic conditions that spawned the revolution in Nicaragua." A veteran foreign correspondent was less sanguine, taking exception to its sanitized depiction of the Sandinistas, which omitted mention of their suppression of trade unions and the press and the forced evictions of thousands of Miskito Indians.[19] Like *Under Fire*, *Romero* (1989), which starred Raul Julia as the saintly Salvadoran bishop and proponent of liberation theology who was assassinated while giving Mass in 1980, featured anti-interventionist sentiments, noble intentions, and questionable cinematic execution. With both *Missing* and *Under Fire*, *Romero*, directed by the Australian filmmaker John Duigan, viewed Latin American conflict from a perspective outside the Western Hemisphere, aligned with neither the United States nor its backyard neighbors.

Of the major films focusing on Central America in the 1980s, only with Oliver Stone's *Salvador* did an American filmmaker take direct aim at U.S. foreign policy. *Salvador* pulled no punches, depicting the worst terror and violence perpetrated by the tiny Central American nation's right-wing government and its notorious death squads, including the Romero assassination and the rape and murder of four American churchwomen. The film directly implicated the United States for its complicity in the atrocities. It underscored the idea that the Salvadoran military regime saw in Reagan's Cold War rhetoric acknowledgment that its reign of terror would be not only tolerated but subsidized in the name of anticommunism. The twisted tale of *Salvador*'s production and financial backing highlighted the political schizophrenia of 1980s Hollywood. When the film's raw violence and political slant caused Orion Pictures to get cold feet and withdraw from the project, Stone drew on Hollywood's left-liberal community to raise enough cash to secure a deal with the independent British producer Hemdale, which also distributed the film. A Washington lobbyist for the Salvadoran opposition FMLN recalled that sympathetic Hollywood studio executives wrote out checks freely, "feeling they were part of something bigger than themselves." Yet such sympathy did not translate to directly producing films critical of U.S. foreign policy for the corporate entities that underwrote their livelihoods. In the end, Hemdale could not give *Salvador* the full-scale marketing blitz a major studio release would have received, and its audiences suffered accordingly.[20]

Meddlesome foreign interventions were not the only quarry in filmmakers' crosshairs; directors also found much to question about the nation's domestic life. Oliver Stone's *Wall Street* (1987) and Michael

Moore's *Roger and Me* (1989) underscored a range of social, economic, and cultural discontents from opposite ends of the socioeconomic spectrum. *Wall Street* probed the suspect moral scruples of the nation's financial capital amid the bull market of the mid-1980s. A morality tale that pulled back the curtains on the evolving relationship between the ruthless corporate raider Gordon Gekko (Michael Douglas) and his young protégé, Bud Fox (Charlie Sheen), Stone's film displayed uncanny timing. In the film's most famous scene, Douglas, awarded the Best Actor Oscar for his performance, delivered a rousing address to shareholders in a paper company targeted for acquisition, climaxing with the revelation "Greed is good." Gekko touted not just free market ideology but downright avarice as salutary, and not only in business endeavors, but as a tonic for national malaise. By the time of *Wall Street*'s release, the national news media had detonated a real-life insider trading scandal starring an eerily Gekko-like Ivan Boesky and the stock market bubble had burst, unleashing the 1987 crash. This cinematic exposé of the moral pitfalls of high stakes finance also illustrated the decade's veneration of corporate culture. Stone captured this in *Wall Street*, hiring the investment banker Kenneth Lipper as a technical adviser to enhance the film's authenticity, consulting him on matters ranging from how rapacious to make the traders to what brand of computers to use on the trading floor. Reviewers noted the film's "manic, electrifying pace," its "endless computer terminals and telephones bursting like rockets everywhere," and its "tantalizing, Sidney Sheldon–like peek into the boardrooms and the bedrooms of the rich and powerful." The film titillatingly celebrated Wall Street's moneyed aura even as it lambasted its moral degeneracy. In the end, though, *Wall Street* indicted the decade's pin-striped culture heroes scathingly. Stone pointed out that the film dealt with the "relativity of wealth," citing Gekko's encouragement to Fox to transcend the $400,000-a-year plateau of a "working Wall Street stiff" and go for "really, really rich— $100 to $300 million," highlighting the greed and dishonesty that underlay the age of hostile takeovers and leveraged buyouts.[21] *Wall Street* skewered the integrity of the decade's financial world elites and the acquisitive mentality of the broader culture.

Roger and Me offered an illuminating counterpoint to *Wall Street*, exposing the consequences of corporate decision making for those at the bottom of the socioeconomic ladder. The filmmaker Michael Moore's premise involved a quixotic quest to track down General Motors' CEO, Roger Smith, and persuade him to spend a day in Flint, Michigan, "the unemployment capital of the world," to view the deleterious effects of company policy. The film alternates tragic and comic vignettes to profile Flint's corporate largesse and working-class precariousness. A deputy dutifully dispatches his daily round of evictions, a woman sells rabbits for "pets or meat," high society types fete themselves in a lavish Great Gatsby–themed party, and a quartet of pastel-clad women golfers at a country club moralize about the deficient work ethic of laid-off autoworkers. As his first filmmaking effort after working as a journalist, Moore financed *Roger and Me* in a classic shoestring effort involving yard sales and bingo games and adopted a self-consciously amateurish aesthetic for wryly comedic effect. But for the targets of the film's withering satire—such as the city fathers seeking to revitalize Flint's economy by creating the Disneyesque theme park Autoworld in a tribute to the industry that had downsized and deflated its citizenry—this was no laughing matter. As for Smith, the man with the bull's-eye on his back, Moore explained, "the homeless didn't just drop out of the sky, and we wanted to find who was responsible. We wanted to name names."

Critical reactions to Moore's quest for accountability varied widely, and observers vigorously debated whether the film even qualified as a "documentary." Harlan Jacobson of the journal *Film Comment* rebuked Moore for playing fast and loose with the chronology of Flint's demise in order to make a "tidy Hollywood narrative" implying that the thirty thousand layoffs that bespoke a decades-long tale of American deindustrialization actually transpired in a concentrated burst just prior to the film's starting point. Not surprisingly, GM's public relations director dusted off his Webster's dictionary to remind *New York Times* editorial page readers that *Roger and Me* did not fit the parameters of "documentary," a title reserved for "products that are factual and objective." In an acrid *New Yorker* review, Pauline Kael took exception to Moore's ironic tone, asserting that his voice-over commentary on encounters with Flint's regular folk—from the rabbit lady to an Amway color consultant—ridiculed innocent targets and made her "feel cheap for laughing." To Kael, Moore positioned his "leftism as a superior attitude," inviting audiences to feel culturally superior to "insufficiently hip" unfortunates. Moore characteristically defended himself, arguing that what his "mockumentary" was really lampooning were the pro-foundly unequal circumstances of wealthy and poor Flintonians. Certainly *Roger and Me* sought to entertain; its wry humor and subversive sensibilities assumed a sophisticated audience and resembled the absurdist irony of *Saturday Night Live*. But the film also aimed to shock and disrupt its audience's middle-class comfort—in scenes like the rabbit lady's on-camera skinning of a once-furry creature while calmly monologuing about how she was raised with a creed of self-sufficiency. Amid the dire conditions in which the film's protagonists found themselves, *Roger and Me* showed how Flint's working class was taking action, albeit at times pathetic, rather than copping out as victims. Other reviewers recognized the larger truths the film exposed. *The Washington Post* asserted, "The party Moore's crashing here, though, is the Reagan '80s." The film critic Roger Ebert most deftly articulated the film's value, rejecting the idea that *Roger and Me* should stand as a paragon of realistic analysis. Rather, it offered "something more important and rare than facts," Ebert contended. "It supplies poetry, a viewpoint, indignation, opinion, anger and humor." In Eastern Europe, audiences in a crumbling Soviet bloc viewed the film as a sobering warning about the potential danger of a too hasty embrace of capitalism as they cast off Communism.[22] With *Roger and Me*, the waning 1980s unleashed a provocative filmmaking voice with a left sensibility that has persisted as a Hollywood gadfly into the twenty-first century.

That a film detailing the human costs of corporate America's greed and ineptitude could receive distribution from one of the world's largest corporations, Time Warner, suggests the contradictions and implicit limitations of broaching political material in popular entertainment. But it also demonstrates that by the late 1980s the possibilities had expanded from what they were earlier in the decade. The curious, cautionary tale of *Red Dawn* (1984) suggests some reasons why. Peter Bart, longtime editor of *Variety* and a senior studio executive of MGM/United Artists in the mid-1980s, recounted how what was originally a story of teenage resistance fighters and the "brutalization of the innocent," à la *Lord of the Flies*, was transformed by the company's zealous CEO into a "flag-waving, jingoistic," anti-Soviet spectacle. Key to the movie's transformation was the close consultation of Reagan's former secretary of state, the MGM board member Alexander Haig. The movie that ultimately emerged, with its vision of a United States besieged by invading Russians and Cubans, offered cinematic support for Reagan's foreign policy goal of fighting Communists in Nicaragua to avoid fighting them in Texas. Bart recalled how "the people who made the movie cynically distorted its original anti-war theme." Starved for hits, MGM's CEO had eschewed remaking *Lord of the Flies*, seeking instead to cash in on the market for zealous anticommunist militarism and "try for *Rambo*." "There was something nasty about it," Bart reflected, "a movie deliberately engineered to induce paranoia rather than honest emotion."[23] The ideological disfiguring of *Red Dawn* hints at some of the obstacles faced by filmmakers with progressive tendencies in the 1980s and explains why much of the most arduous political work in Hollywood took place off camera.

Against the stereotype of 1980s apathy, Hollywood notables lent their celebrity to activism that stood up to the prevailing Reaganite wind. Ed Anser, costar of the iconic 1970s sitcom *The Mary Tyler Moore Show* and its spin-off *Lou Grant*, remarked, "Reagan obsessed us." Joined by the former *M*A*S*H* star Mike Farrell, Michael Douglas, and other Hollywood luminaries, Asner formed the Committee of Concern for Central America, which organized to oppose the administration's Central America policy. Asner also cofounded Medical Aid for El Salvador and staged an episode of political theater on the State Department steps, presenting a $25,000 check for clinics in areas controlled by leftist guerrillas fighting the U.S.-backed Salvadoran military. This blend of publicity stunt and principled stand provoked a firestorm within the Screen Actors Guild (SAG), of which Asner was president. He was roundly criticized by two former SAG presidents—the conservative National Rifle Association activist Charlton Heston, and President Reagan himself. Unsympathetic SAG members charged that Asner was not sufficiently clear that he was speaking as an individual rather than on behalf of the union. Emboldened by supporters within SAG, though he acknowledged a "slight goof" in failing to identify himself as a private citizen, he defended the prerogative and the necessity of Tinseltown's stars to speak out: "We are all American citizens and our visibility gives us a special responsibility." Asner paid the price for his stand. Within three months, the tissue baron Kimberly-Clark withdrew its sponsorship of *Lou Grant* and CBS killed the show. Though executives conceded the difficulty of canceling a show so widely praised for its high quality—it was "the Jewel in our craft," admitted CBS's president, Bud Grant—they ultimately put the kibosh on it, citing declining ratings. Anser took exception, arguing that the show deserved greater support from the network, citing instances of other quality programs with loyal followings that network television managed to carry despite less-than-stellar ratings. "Politics most definitely did have something to do with it," Asner asserted, concluding that pressure from advertisers was the "thumb on the scale" that ultimately ousted the show.[24]

If Asner represented one pole of exemplary activism, more typical of entertainment industry political activity were the efforts of the Hollywood Women's Political Committee, which helped finance a range of liberal causes. The HWPC was founded in 1984 by Jane Fonda, the producer Paula Weinstein, and some two hundred other prominent Hollywood women to raise cash and consciousness for left-oriented initiatives, from the environment and education to peace and pro-choice, that faced neglect or hostility during the Reagan years. The committee attracted celebrities, including Barbra Streisand, Goldie Hawn, and Morgan Fairchild, harnessing their star power to galvanize liberal politics in the industry. "We gave them a narrative, a cause, a more progressive place to be than just the Democratic Party," recalled Lara Bergthold, who served as the HWPC's last executive director. The HWPC's activities included weekend seminars to bone up on issues to support direct action advocacy, facilitating U.S. Central America policy protests, and partnering with the National Organization for Women to mobilize for the landmark 1989 abortion rights rally in Washington, D.C. But the HWPC's forte lay in getting Hollywood notables to pony up for candidates whose views passed muster—some $6 million over its thirteen-year career. The HWPC's attention to issues rather than individual politicians prompted *The Economist*'s comment that Democratic candidates could no longer get away with "using Hollywood as a glitzy but silent teller-machine."

This fidelity to issues rather than individuals played a large role in the committee's dismantling. In the mid-1990s the HWPC developed a reputation as the only political action committee ever to publicly call for abolishing PACs. The organization disbanded, joining the call for campaign finance reform and citing a distaste for what one member called money's ascendancy as the "driving force" of American politics. Still, even as these protestations over capital-intensive politics rang out, the HWPC postmortem revealed another culprit in its disintegration:

Clintonism. With the end of the Reagan-Bush tenure, the drift of the Democratic Party rightward toward the center muddied the impulse to mobilize as an opposition force. It was no accident that the HWPC's demise coincided with the achievement of raising $4 million for Clinton's 1996 reelection at a Los Angeles presidential gala that the organization cohosted. Shortly before the event, their ostensible friend repaid this courtesy by signing a welfare reform bill into law that the Left viewed as capitulation to Republican breast-beating about welfare cheats. To the HWPC, Clinton's cooperation with welfare reform represented a decisive betrayal, and the committee disbanded shortly thereafter. Though the money that the HWPC tapped still remained for progressive causes to access, the growing difficulty of distinguishing friends from enemies—what the leftist journal *Dissent* called the "inability to identify minimally progressive candidates"—caused the committee to fold its tent in disgust.[25]

The Culture Wars: Visigoths in Tweed, Fairies in the Garden

In 1987, the fifty-six-year-old college professor Allan Bloom's unlikely bestseller, *The Closing of the American Mind,* asked readers to imagine a thirteen-year-old boy doing his homework while wearing his Walkman headphones or watching MTV. Bloom recounted how the hypothetical boy "enjoys the liberties hard won over centuries" by "philosophic genius and political heroism, consecrated by the blood of martyrs" and revels in "comfort and leisure" buttressed by the unprecedented productivity of the post–World War II American economic boom. From this quick sketch of privileged contentment and technological abundance Bloom swiftly proceeded to his narrative of decline, diagnosing the teenager as a "pubescent child whose body throbs with orgasmic rhythms; whose feelings are made articulate in hymns to the joys of onanism." Revealing a bit of sex and gender anxiety—he laments the teen's imitation of "the drag-queen who makes the music"—Bloom's concluding judgment on his imaginary scenario torpedoes one of the United States's signature cultural contributions to the world, rock and roll, as "a nonstop, commercially prepackaged masturbational fantasy." With choice language and obvious generational dissonance, Bloom discharged an early salvo in the culture wars that raged from mid-decade into the next century.

This vignette illuminates many of the familiar targets of the culture wars: postmodern society's corrosive effect on youth, liberalized sexuality, and homophobia. The larger work in which it was enmeshed, *The Closing of the American Mind*, encompassed many more of these targets, including cultural relativism, the erosion of the canon of Western civilization's great literary works at the hands of a nascent multiculturalism, and the demands for representation by historically oppressed groups. Much of the discontent from the Right swirled around American college campuses, where 1960s intellectual movements from feminism to black power had survived and thrived to transform the curriculum. In place of Bloom's beloved Plato and *Paradise Lost*, late 1980s college students were as likely to find forgotten proto-feminist classics like Kate Chopin's *The Awakening* on their reading lists and to take whole courses exploring "Black Women and Their Fictions." Needless to say, cultural purists and conservatives inside and outside the academy were horrified by the "Visigoths in Tweed" transforming the terrain of liberal arts education, with black (later African American) studies and women's studies movements leading the way. Declension narratives like Bloom's soon yielded to outright attacks in the closely intertwined controversy over political correctness. The concept, once proudly adhered to by Marxists-Leninists seeking to toe the party line, reemerged in the early 1990s simply as "P.C.," a pejorative invoked by the Right. The label aimed to tar a generation of professors who came of age in the 1960s—and sympathized with postmodern intellectual revelations, Third World self-determination, and redress of racial and sex discrimination—with the charge of institutionalizing rigid codes of language and behavior in a left-wing version of McCarthy-like repression. The conservative columnist George Will objected to professors' insertion of radical perspectives on sexism and racism into such general education curricular standards as freshman composition, citing a slippery slope of "political indoctrination supplanting education."[26]

The hue and cry of conservatives over political correctness viewed alternately suggests the tremendous level of cultural influence the Left had consolidated by the early 1990s. Historians have increasingly recognized that the spawn of 1960s social and political movements, from black power to feminism, from gay liberation to opposition to foreign interventions, not only survived in the era of Reagan and Bush, but in many cases were institutionalized.[27] The very ubiquity of the "tenured radicals" decried by the neoconservative Roger Kimball, and the enhanced representation of previously marginalized groups in the curricula they taught, provided powerful testimony to the influence of once-radical visions of the 1960s on mainstream culture. After all, the largest source of private support for women's and African American studies programs was the Ford Foundation, a venerable philanthropic institution with a long-standing interest in social justice and equity, but certainly no bastion of radicalism.[28]

Moreover, many on the Right feared the spillover of what Kimball called "ideologically motivated assaults on the intellectual and moral substance of our culture" beyond the grassy quadrangles of elite colleges into other sectors of society. The rarified world of the fine arts and its financial underwriting through the National Endowment for the Arts represented an area of immediate concern. The photographers Robert Mapplethorpe, whose work featured homoerotic and sadomasochistic images, and Andres Serrano—whose infamous photograph of a plastic crucifix immersed in his own urine, a creation upon which he bestowed the appellation *Piss Christ*—emerged as causes célèbres snared in a public controversy over federal arts funding that arrayed powerful conservative voices against the art world's presumed moral laxity. These voices were led by the legendary Republican senator from North Carolina, Jesse Helms, who introduced a notorious amendment forbidding public funding for "obscene" or "indecent" works. A diverse range of left-of-center perspectives, from radical journalists to Rhode Island's establishment liberal senator Claiborne Pell, bemoaned congressional Republicans' trip, led by their constituents on the religious right, down the primrose path toward censorship. Helms balked at the charges, asserting that his amendment intended simply to end the use of taxpayer money to "support outrageous 'art' that is clearly designed to poison our culture." Through 1989 and into the early 1990s the debate over the federal funding of controversial artwork raged, unearthing a number of salient ironies. First, the spark that ignited the NEA controversy, the Serrano and Mapplethorpe cases, represented a statistically insignificant two out of some eighty-five thousand grants in the agency's twenty-five-year history to that point. The art critic Robert

Hughes, trying to stake out a sensible middle ground, argued that although Helms's amendment technically stopped short of censorship, "one would have needed to be remarkably naïve to think that censorship was *not* the root of the controversy." Hughes perceived efforts to stanch the flow of government dollars to "offensive" art as "only the tip of a general effort growing on the right to repress *all* 'offensive' art, subsidized or not."[29]

The historical record of government incursion into the cultural realm—most notably demonstrated by the timidity of Hollywood films in the wake of the House Un-American Activities Committee's anticommunist probes of the 1940s and 1950s—suggested that the real danger lay not so much in overt censorship of a couple of bad apples like Mapplethorpe and Serrano, but in adopting a defensive posture that avoided controversial material as a survival strategy. Amid the flak, which included President George Bush's directive that "not a dime" of taxpayer money should go into "'art' that is clearly and visibly filth," the NEA implemented this approach. It abandoned a rigorous peer-reviewed granting process in favor of internal preemption of potentially troublesome proposals. Holly Hughes, one of four performance artists, along with Karen Finley, John Fleck, and Tim Miller, whose grants the agency revoked in one infamous episode of political cold feet, quipped that the NEA Four, as they became known, were transformed "from political artists to political footballs." The four sued the NEA on the basis that the grants were denied for "purely political reasons." When documents revealed that the NEA chair John Frohnmayer had instituted a flagging procedure designed to quash grants that right-wing politicians might seize upon to raise public outcry, the NEA settled out of court and restored the grants. A part of the case lived on as *NEA v. Finley*, wending its way all the way to the Supreme Court, which in 1998 reversed two lower court decisions, upholding the NEA's prerogative to consider "general standards of decency" when deciding which art to fund. More significant, the art controversy's targets suggest that what was at stake was the public acknowledgment of hot-button lifestyle and cultural realities. The NEA Four's work dripped with themes of gay sexuality and radical feminism, providing opportunistic politicians a chance to hurl slabs of "red meat" at conservative constituencies whose anxieties were aroused. Robert Hughes interpreted the Right's antigay attacks as an attempt to capitalize on the demonization vacuum left by the demise of Soviet bloc Communism. "Now that their original crusade against the Red Menace had been rendered null and void," Hughes observed, "having lost the barbarian at the gates, they went for the fairy at the bottom of the garden." The results for the American arts scene were swift and severe. Already subsidized at only a fractional proportion of their Western European counterparts, American artists faced the further shrinkage of federal dollars. In 1995 conservative legislators savaged the NEA's approximately $150 million budget, which worked out to less than a can of soda for the average American taxpayer, leaving arts councils and individual artists to scrabble over a relatively paltry $98 million.[30]

Artists did not simply wilt in the hostile environment. They fought back with direct action rallies and demonstrations, mounting forums on freedom of expression in the arts, and a redoubled commitment to politicized art. Faced with a new pledge, initiated by Helms, in which artists accepting federal dollars promised to conform to standards of decency, many arts organizations, having submitted to the byzantine NEA grant-making process, turned down their awards in distaste. But beyond the initial spate of invective against the pledge and artists' contempt for bureaucrats determining what qualified as offensive and what constituted legitimate art, the NEA backlash ushered in a wave of new work with an oppositional attitude. In the early 1990s a plethora of performance artists responded to the new taboos against sexual and homosexual content by taking off their clothes. The movement was so pervasive that one critic dubbed 1992 "The Year of the Nude." Transgressive titles and subject matter abounded. The performer Penny Arcade urged not capitulating to "censorship" with "self-censorship," mounting a one-woman show entitled *Bitch! Dyke! Faghag! Whore!* In *My Queer Body*, the NEA Four performance artist Tim Miller responded to detractors inside and outside the federal government by imagining himself as the "performance artist laureate" at the 2001 inauguration of the first black lesbian president and incorporating images of anonymous gay sex over Ravel's *Bolero*. But beyond this in-your-face backlash reaction to the conservative crusade against "obscene art," many committed artists raised serious questions about the government's role in artistic creation. When Alexander Gray, a staffer for a New York arts foundation, argued that the "cutting edge" in the "next generation of artists doesn't need the NEA," many artists concurred. In the now infamous performance piece "We Keep Our Victims Ready," Finley smeared her naked body with chocolate frosting to symbolize the degradation of women and joked about the artistic liberation she felt, since, as she remarked, "I don't have to worry about being funded anymore." Nor did the spirit of resistance confine itself to ultra-hip New York–based performance art. Like-minded multimedia spectacles cropped up in the provinces, from the "Evening of Objectionable Art" in Buffalo to "Cabaret Gorilla: An Evening of Censorship Awareness" in Kansas City. Considering that the most explosive tinder in the arts controversies centered on feminism and gay culture, a look at the 1990s cultural landscape suggests, in the vibrant careers of the Guerrilla Girls and Gran Fury, that the provocative use of art and the political mobilization of the arts community—from pro-choice politics to AIDS activism—far from withered under the Right's attack. One journalist remarked, "What Jesse Helms has done has backfired," observing, "I now know more about lesbian sexuality than I had hoped to know, quite honestly, because I have seen artist upon artist find the authentic voice that has been told it cannot speak out."[31] To find these voices, artists ventured outside traditional channels of patronage, a lesson that many creative forces even more removed from potential funding sources had already discovered.

That avant-garde and political artists were arriving at the conclusion to reject public subsidies as the 1990s revved up was ironic, considering that mainstream artists and entertainers had enjoyed more than a modicum of success at infusing popular culture expressions with political content in the previous decade—more than most observers might have expected. Transcending the much-trumpeted 1980s bent toward conservatism and materialism, pop stars rediscovered, through mega-events like Live Aid, their industry's economic capacity and public relations power for charity and political work. An ever more vertically integrated and corporately synergistic Hollywood nevertheless managed to create incisive celluloid expressions deglamorizing militarism, critiquing interventionist foreign policy, and exposing the era's venerated corporate culture's proneness to moral bankruptcy. Behind the scenes, in their lives as private citizens, a raft of film industry personnel proved willing to escalate their public commitment to a variety of progressive causes in opposition to the official policies of the Reagan-Bush era. To a large extent, their own personal and professional success, a healthy sense of security, and a stake in its continuation enabled such engagement. For those outside the relative comfort of the pop and motion picture establishment—those alienated from mainstream goals, mores, and sensibilities—opposition to the era's prevailing authorities took on a different shape.

5

NOISE FROM UNDERGROUND
Post-Punk Music, Culture, and Politics

The music of Nirvana, Alice in Chains, Soundgarden, Sonic Youth, Stone Temple Pilots, the Red Hot Chili Peppers, Pearl Jam, Green Day, and their ilk have enjoyed a remarkably long half-life, and indeed, in one form or another, many of these bands are still active. Too diverse to encapsulate under any banner other than "post-punk," with roots in the 1980s and early 1990s, their musical expressions are now enshrined in classic rock radio formats and iPod playlists across the country and internationally. Their creations continue to exert gravitational pull on legions of aspiring young bands and band wannabes. Indeed, post-punk—which catapulted to widespread public attention with the 1991 release of Nirvana's *Nevermind*—transformed and continues to influence mainstream music. Not all of these developments have led to improved music. A veteran of the Boston underground music scene of the 1980s and 1990s satirized contemporary punk pop's slickly produced and formulaic sound—epitomized by Blink-182 and its imitators—quipping, "It just sounds like you put the money in the gumball machine, turn the crank, and out comes punk." But on the whole, post-punk has wrought a greater concern with the authenticity of musical expression and diversified approaches to songwriting, and has emerged as a culturally venerated music that is fundamentally about something.

Of course, the post-punk label means to evoke punk proper—the thrashing, stripped-down, in-your-face brand of rock and roll that exploded in Margaret Thatcher's Britain in 1977 with the Sex Pistols and the Clash and, with less fanfare but a few years earlier in the United States, with the CBGB's scene led by the Ramones and Television. From the beginning, punk music was oppositional and contrarian. On both sides of the Atlantic it opposed the seemingly discredited countercultural idealism of the 1960s and what punk musicians regarded as bloated, pretentious, inauthentic, mainstream rock and roll music. In the United States during the 1980s, the Reagan administration's conservative social policies and ardent militarism were common targets for the rage of hardcore punk particularly and post-punk generally. Unlike the decade's mainstream pop, which invoked themes of personal pleasure, sexual novelty, and transcendent escapism, post-punk more often examined public life, however caustically. Musicians and fans infused their frustrations, including those over the nation's conservative direction, with political, or at least proto-political, salvos at that rightward trend.

During the 1980s, post-punk music in the United States germinated underground, enjoying limited commercial success. While a handful of college radio stations disseminated the music, mainstream commercial radio ignored it. Post-punk bands were not seen in MTV music videos, the decade's signature popular culture medium. Yet post-punk persisted through the 1980s, coming to public light as "alternative" music and forging its way into the mainstream in the 1990s. Significantly, post-punk was not a top-down phenomenon, in which powerful record companies, units of still more powerful corporate conglomerates, through advertising and marketing hype foisted their musical acts on the public to ensure their popularity. Post-punk fans and musicians alike developed an identity as a community, one of whose salient attributes was opposition to the era's dominant musical, social, and political institutions.

Many cultural scholars, examining this music's relationship to the recording industry, have focused on the paradox of whether commercially produced music can truly challenge the institutions of capitalist society.[1] Indeed, before the age of musical downloads and file sharing, vertically integrated media conglomerates wielded massive, even prohibitive influence over what music was available to consumers. But for post-punk, at least, the meanings fans and performers ascribed to their own experience of enjoying and making music were less commercially mediated than the decade's major-label-disseminated popular music backed by generous advertising budgets and—the mother of all pro-motional bonanzas—heavy rotation on MTV. Interaction at live per-formances, discussions in "fanzines," musical innovation, underground subculture, and grassroots enthusiasm loomed significantly more im-portant to post-punk.

Post-punk musicians and fans forged a shared identity in opposition to mainstream culture and politics. People in this community did not dress the same way or share the same values as their peers who em-braced the era's dominant social values. Post-punk fans often pursued jobs designed merely to pay the rent rather than career-oriented em-ployment. They tended to oppose authority of all varieties—from the federal government to the local police. Though it would be an over-statement to portray a post-punk community unified in a set of ortho-dox political beliefs, most performers and fans deplored, for example, the Reagan administration's intervention in Nicaragua. But what ac-tions did they take to voice their outrage? Were the most engaged a minority of literate and politically sophisticated middle-class fans, or did post-punk fans of various social backgrounds share the same out-look?[2] Many post-punk fans behaved apolitically, whereas people who never attended a Black Flag or Sonic Youth show opposed militarism in more activist ways, such as demonstrations and tax resistance. To be sure, diverse political attitudes existed among fans, exposing the gulf between culture and politics and suggesting limits to the extent to which a musical genre can unify its fans. Eighties post-punkers in the United States were not anywhere near as unified either musically or stylistically as the spiky-haired British punkers of the 1970s.[3] Post-punk did not foster the kind of organized critique that mobilized public opin-ion to oust Reagan or the first George Bush electorally or through street rioting. Prior to 1991 it did not achieve sufficient sales figures to confer significant social or economic power upon even its most successful per-formers. Yet post-punk and its fans persisted throughout the 1980s de-spite this marginality, creatively challenging the conservative consensus. Understanding the meteoric rise of this music to popular acclaim after 1991 necessitates delving into post-punk's protracted period of under-ground ferment.

From 1980 to 1991 post-punk enabled communities of fans to ex-plore identities in opposition to mainstream social and political mores. "Community" often conjures up utopian imagery of an egalitarian cooperative ethos, but in fact, communities are just as often defined relationally, by contrasting members with "others" on the outside looking in. The 1980s post-punk scene was not equally permeable to everyone; it sometimes demonstrated exclusionary impulses. Different subsets of post-punk—hardcore being the most obvious—periodically displayed hostility to those who didn't live up to rigid strictures of punk authenticity. Yet on the whole, post-punk tended toward progressive political impulses, from inclusionary stances on race, class, and gender issues to rejecting yuppie materialism and interventionist American foreign policy. This worldview echoed through post-punk fanzines, bands' music and lyrics, the causes with which post-punkers aligned themselves, and live performances.

Manifestly, post-punk fans and performers shared a distaste for the conservative social policies and militarist foreign policies of the 1980s, and tellingly, the community did not foster any splinter group that called itself Post-Punkers for Reagan. Opposition to mainstream culture, values, and politics was central to the identities of post-punk fans. And while an oppositional identity did not necessarily translate into oppositional activism, post-punk helped its fans maintain attitudes of resistance in their everyday lives that added up to an important critique of the mainstream. As the rock critic Greil Marcus wrote, "while revolution made by music is a joke, rebellion sustained by music might not be."[4] Post-punk musicians and fans sustained a subcultural rebellion whose reverberations echoed throughout the larger culture after 1991.

Defining Post-Punk

Musically, post-punk refers to a wide variety of guitar-based musics, ranging from the stylistic minimalism of early hardcore bands like Black Flag, the Dead Kennedys, and Minor Threat to the complex aural arrangements of Sonic Youth. Demographically, post-punk was overwhelmingly a phenomenon of white youth culture. Hardcore, a discrete subset of post-punk, emerged to unleash its straight-ahead no-frills sound as, more often than not, the voice of working-class rage. Inspired by the music and attitude of 1970s punk, post-punk had sufficiently established itself as a discrete musical genre by the early

1980s. A sampling of bands sketches the genre's boundaries. The Dead Kennedys, Black Flag, and Minor Threat comprise a trio of influential, stylistically minimalistic bands that struggled to make the music more accessible to fans, from the Dead Kennedys' Jello Biafra's infamous court battle with the Parents Music Resource Center to Minor Threat's policy of exclusively playing in all-ages venues.[5] Sonic Youth and the Minutemen culled from punk's raw materials and added various musical experiments and innovations to expand the genre. Members of Sonic Youth were associated with the No Wave musical movement and the New York avant-garde composer Glenn Branca before starting the band, while the Minutemen, who incorporated jazz and funk riffs, were once called "America's Most Conceptual Bar Band."[6] The Minneapolis-based Hüsker Dü began in 1981 as a hardcore band with a reputation for playing fast, then recorded the 1984 concept album *Zen Arcade*, about a day in the life of a skinhead, ultimately signing with Warner Bros. in 1986 for its final two albums, which interspersed acoustic ballads with distorted electric guitar songs.

The Replacements and R.E.M. shed light on post-punk's elasticity. Both came from the small club, independent label roots that epitomize post-punk, yet both achieved popular acclaim well before the genre's commercial breakthrough in 1991. The Red Hot Chili Peppers shared similar underground roots but relied heavily on African American–inflected musical forms such as funk, rap, and hip-hop.[7] What tied these disparate bands together was less a shared musical aesthetic than a set of influences from 1970s punk, including a do-it-yourself production ethos emphasizing authenticity rather than technological perfection; aural dissonance that consciously challenged mainstream popular music; transgressive subject matter in lyrics and associated visual imagery; and live performances that attempted to bridge the distance between the performers and the audience.[8]

Post-punk prized what the Minutemen termed going "econo," cutting production costs through often unpolished independent production and even establishing fledgling alternative distribution systems. This aesthetic echoed the British rock critic Simon Frith's observation that 1970s punk embodied "a people's version of consumerism, the idea that record buyers had a right to maximum market choice, that record buying should involve customer expression rather than producer manipulation." Since the late 1960s, independent record labels largely served a research-and-development function for the majors, who scooped up acts as soon as they reached a bankable level of popularity. But this practice reflected the vision of the corporate owners of the major record labels more than that of the music's performers or its fans. Many fans, such as one who wrote a letter to the seminal fanzine *Flipside*, recognized a trend that the "independence" punk bands "once cherished is increasingly being lost as bands get popular and sign record deals." "The independent record distribution scene," the letter continued, "has just become a smaller model of the larger 'mainstream' record market."[9] While this fan's testimony indicated awareness of corporate domination of making and distributing music, his regret signified fans' substantial emotional investment in the indies.

Post-punk fans believed they were making important consumer choices by buying independently produced records, and musicians believed they were challenging major label hegemony by making their music available through the independents. A review of 1980s fanzines shows that the independent labels played to this ethos of ethical consumerism in their advertisements. When Catch Trout Records, a Charlottesville, Virginia, independent ran ads with the slogan "CATCH TROUT . . . making music worthless again," reclaiming "worthless" as a positive attribute, the appeal courted a fan sensibility that resisted the commodification of its favorite music. Likewise, the distributor Rough Trade's ads proclaimed "Specializing in **INDEPENDENT** import and domestic Hardcore, Experimental, Industrial, Dance and the Undefinable," emphasizing the most important word this way to underscore that independently produced music was a quality fans valued. The California mail-order outfit Mamma Jamma's gimmick to sell its stock involved the promise of "ALL YOUR FAVORITE *INDEPENDENT LABEL RECORDS & TAPES*C.D.S.," again suggesting through prominent size and capitalization that fans prized independence. In invoking independence to promote musical and purchasing loyalty, one ad stands out. The Las Vegas record store the Underground sought to sell the business with the following appeal: "Since 1980, The Underground has been Las Vegas' only alternative music store supporting the independent industry."[10] Presumably, what the Underground was selling as a business opportunity was its loyal customer base, whose coherence was defined by fans' loyalty to the "independent industry."

Though major labels largely controlled independent producers by

The nuclear freeze movement mobilized 750,000 for this mass demonstration in New York City's Central Park, June 12, 1982. (Jenny Warburg)

CISPES rally in Los Angeles, 1981. The Central America Solidarity Movement's actions provided opportunities to educate the public about the effects of U.S. foreign policy on our neighbors to the south. (CISPES National Office Photo Archives)

CISPES demonstrators applaud a Jesse Jackson speech at the U.S. Capitol, 1985. Nineteen eighties opposition from diverse origins targeted a common foe. (Rick Reinhard)

Cornell shantytown, 1985. The shanties were constructed to occupy a centrally located campus space and disrupt business as usual. As one activist remarked, "The administration could not avoid it. It was a radical transformation of public space." (David Lyons)

The shanties at Dartmouth, 1986: "an eyesore on an idyllic campus." This assault on campus aesthetics provoked the wrath of campus conservatives. (Stuart Bratesman/Dartmouth College)

The Live Aid finale, 1985. Widely hailed as a reawakening of social conscience amid the materialistic 1980s, aided by satellite technology, Live Aid also served as a model of the transnational "mega-event" in which the performers' star power leveraged mammoth financial returns for a worthy cause. (Ebet Roberts)

Sonic Youth at CBGB, 1989. Rooted as much in the avant-garde as in punk, it took Sonic Youth a decade to achieve a fraction of the acclaim Nirvana reaped almost overnight. After aiding Nirvana's rise, Sonic Youth bucked a stereotypical trend, becoming increasingly politicized *after* signing a major-label deal. (Ebet Roberts)

Harold Washington at the West Lawn Branch Library, 1986. First elected in a racially polarizing campaign, as his mayoralty wore on, Washington was making strides toward effectively reaching out to groups of white Chicagoans (like this one) before his untimely death. (Chicago Public Library, Special Collections and Preservation Division)

On the campaign trail in 1984, Geraldine Ferraro proved more compelling to many than her partner at the top of the ticket, Walter Mondale: "Ferraro is one hell of a lady," a Cleveland policeman gushed. "I just wish we could have Reagan with her." (Minnesota Historical Society)

ACT UP was notable for its militancy and direct action tactics, epitomized by its signature chant, "ACT UP! Fight Back! Fight AIDS!" (Clay Walker)

KISSING DOESN'T KILL: GREED AND INDIFFERENCE DO

Gran Fury, a collective of artists associated with ACT UP, designed arresting graphics to combat misinformation about the AIDS crisis and agitate for a more urgent response. "Kissing Doesn't Kill" appropriated the visual style of a popular ad campaign to debunk mythology about how the disease is transmitted. (1989 Aldo Hernandez, courtesy of Creative Time) dominating distribution channels, there were exceptions. Alternative distributors such as Mordam Records, Dutch East India, and Rough Trade persevered through the 1980s and beyond.[11] The story of Mordam Records illustrates the incomplete nature of the majors' hegemony over distribution. Ruth Schwartz founded Mordam in 1983, aided by a collaboration of the Dead Kennedys' Alternative Tentacles label and Tim Yohannan's influential fanzine, *Maximumrocknroll*. Schwartz hoped that independent labels and magazine publishers would band together under Mordam's distributorship for financial viability. Along with this economic strategy, Schwartz articulated opposition to the majors: "What independent music is about, is anger against major labels and the music business on all levels." She favorably contrasted the mind-set of personnel involved in independent music at Mordam—"we're a bunch of fans!"—with "big major multimedia corporations," of which she claimed, "They're not there for the artists. They're not there for the artist's fans."[12] While it is easy to romanticize independent music personnel as heroic holdouts against corporate co-optation, their populist language bespoke real commitment. Despite the fact that majors exercised the majority of control over what music was available to consumers throughout the eighties, the marginal but persistent presence of independent distribution remained an important expression of autonomy and opposition for post-punk and its fans.

Another salient legacy of punk in post-punk centers on noise. Seventies punk deployed a new brand of harsh guitar noise, from the jagged chords of the Sex Pistols to the Ramones "primitive buzzsaw sound." Post-punk likewise mobilized noise to its advantage. In the 1980s, musicians as diverse as the Dead Kennedys and Sonic Youth self-consciously enshrined noise—"a jangling, aural buzzing, cacophony"—as a signal convention of the genre. To post-punk audiences, noise acted as a kind of rite of passage. Membership in the musical community depended not only on passing a toleration threshold for amplified sonic dissonance, but on reveling in its inaccessibility to patrons of mainstream pop.

Post-punk also borrowed from punk's penchant for transgressive subject matter, crafting lyrics and visual images calculated to shock middle-class sensibilities and invert what was prestigious in mainstream culture.[13] Band naming strategies illustrated this tendency, resulting in the Circle Jerks, Crucifucks, Social Distortion, the Dead Kennedys, and the Butthole Surfers, for starters. Visual images associated with post-punk ranged from the Butthole Surfers' films, showed at live performances and depicting penis reconstruction surgery, to the all-women band L7's T-shirts picturing a dominating female forcing cunnilingus on a submissive male. Even the arty Sonic Youth explored a fascination with the Manson Family in "Death Valley '69" and "Expressway to Your Skull," which was narrated from the point of view of a cult member who crooned, "We're gonna kill the California girls." Using transgressive subject matter sometimes proved problematic, since the musicians had little control over how their work was interpreted, but in the conservative 1980s, lyrics could be transgressive simply by opposing popular sentiment, such as Reagan-era militarism. In "Themselves," the Minutemen sang, "All these men who work the land / Should evaluate themselves / And make a stand / Can't they see beyond the rhetoric? / The lies and promises that don't mean shit."[14] "Themselves" fit into the Minutemen's repertoire of antimilitarist songs, its lyrics challenging mainstream rural Americans who celebrated Reagan's program of restoring military strength and voted for him in large numbers.

Post-Punk and Its Fans

Punk bequeathed to post-punk a tradition of performers who tried to reduce the distance between themselves and their fans both literally and figuratively. This approach rejected the arena rock of the 1970s and beyond, which paired rock demigods backed by elaborate stage sets and flanked by giant columns of stack amplifiers with mass audiences who were forced to pony up escalating sums of hard-earned cash for the privilege of attendance. *Flipside's* editors bemoaned the closing of one punk venue, Al's Bar, and applauded the opening of another, Godzilla's, proclaiming, "Bring punk back to the CLUBS where it belongs, fuck the arenas!!!" Post-punk venues offered a cheaper alternative to the high ticket prices found at arena concerts. Fans experienced shows from a standing position, with no assigned seating, allowing them to roam around the club freely. This in turn allowed more fans to attend shows because the legal capacity of clubs expanded when there were no seats. Hardcore bands like Washington, D.C.'s Minor Threat agitated for minors to be allowed into clubs that served alcohol. D.C. clubs secured a compromise, allowing minors into the clubs if their hands were marked with an X, signifying that they could not drink. The X mark came to symbolize fan solidarity in D.C.'s hardcore community.[15]

Like punk, post-punk brandished a do-it-yourself ethos that lessened the gap between audience and performer by eliminating technical virtuosity as a prerequisite for making music. These democratized attitudes surrounding music making encouraged fans to start a band and make their own music. Fans came to feel that they were not so different from the musicians they admired. The fans also resisted the labeling and categorization of their musical passions. When asked in a survey "What are your three favorite bands?" several respondents who were self-identified post-punk fans refused to be pinned down, with responses such as "keeps changing regularly," "too many to mention," "don't play favorites with innovative music," and "no favorites all faves." Unlike the decade's heavy metal fans, who relished the opportunity to nominate bands they believed epitomized the genre, post-punk fans, out of respect for the music's diversity, routinely declined to identify individual groups as representative of the genre. Instead, they took pains to demonstrate their openness to musical innovation, listing blues, country-western, jazz, folk, classical, rockabilly, Brazilian, Cajun, and even Hawaiian mambo as musical styles that inspired them.[16]

Post-punk fans contrasted their musical tastes with the pop mainstream. They preferred recorded music to radio, eschewing the music that received popular airplay. Despite the meteoric rise of MTV, post-punk fans resoundingly rejected music videos and the commercially popular artists they showcased. Their rejection of radio and music videos in favor of independent-label-recorded music showed resistance to the role of the majors, and the corporate power that buttressed them, in shaping musical taste. Post-punkers insisted on the individuality of their musical preferences. Asked what elements of his favorite local bands' music were most important, one fan, a musician himself, cited "interesting & original arrangements." Another fan who played guitar listed her reasons for liking the Boston bands Letters to Cleo and O-Positive as "originality, different from the mainstream, fun." When identifying the most important elements of a good band, fans included responses such as "originality and chutzpah," "weirdness and originality," "distinct band sound," and "fuckedupness." Though one fan thought "beer" vital to a good band and another admitted a fondness for "cute" bands, musical originality was clearly prized.[17]

Fans valued sincerity and honesty in live performances, citing these qualities, along with "a sincere sense of abandon," as reasons to embrace their favorite bands. Local live performance scenes emphasized independence from the mainstream music industry. Post-punk's lore is crammed with tales of local live music overcoming traditional commercial and social authorities, such as the December 1981 Social Distortion show that was broken up by police and continued ad hoc from the band's warehouse rehearsal space.[18]

Though a group of post-punk fans and performers explicitly repudiated any engagement with politics, another contingent considered themselves activist-musicians or viewed their fandom itself as a political statement. Still others rejected any overt connection between music and politics but believed post-punk could support political activity through events such as benefit shows. Despite ambivalent voices, post-punk musicians and fans tended toward rebellion against the Reagan-Bush era's dominant social and political trends. Often this rebellion proved inchoate or did not take the form of activist politics, but reflected the kind of everyday resistance that ultimately exerted subtle effects on the decade's cultural balance of power.[19]

Post-Punk and Antimilitarism

Post-punk's politics appeared most explicitly in its rejection of militarism. As military spending rose and interventions from Lebanon to Grenada and throughout Central America became commonplace, post-punk musicians opposed military aggression. Antimilitarism ranked among hardcore's most popular and salient themes. In part, this reflected a self-interested desire to avoid military service. The reinstatement of the draft was a growing fear among the nation's young under Reagan, especially among hardcore's working-class constituency. Throughout post-punk as a whole, the pervasive theme of antimilitarism amounted to more than a dollop of skepticism toward the dominant culture's bellicose rhetoric. The decade's cult of militarism extended beyond official foreign policy, gaining a foothold in popular culture. Screen heroes, led by Sylvester Stallone's Rambo character, glorified nationalism, vigilantism, and violence. Tom Clancy's novels of international intrigue, such as *The Hunt for Red October* and *Red*

Storm Rising, epitomized a wave of bestseller fiction that buttressed American patriotism against a Soviet menace that in hindsight proved near to its ultimate demise. Popular culture's embrace of militarism and nationalism attracted post-punk's derision and opposition.[20]

In 1981 the Dead Kennedys rewrote their song "California Über Alles" and retitled it "We've Got a Bigger Problem Now." This song mentioned Reagan by name and explicitly deplored the implications of his rise to power, raising the specter of American youth serving as cannon fodder in a "Third World War." That same year, in a visual indictment of the consequences of militarism, the cover of Hüsker Dü's *Land Speed Record* pictured three officers overlooking rows of military coffins with American flags draped over them. "Stars and Stripes" by the Circle Jerks highlighted the consequences of nuclear proliferation, chiding Reagan's supporters: "Ha, ha, ha you're all gonna die / and you voted for that guy." The lyrics of these songs focused sarcastic criticism and a sprinkling of mischievous humor on the Reagan administration's martial tone. Their use of irony, a hallmark of post-punk attitude and aesthetics, reflected the legacy of seventies punk's critique of sentimentalism. Post-punk aesthetics allowed for disagreement with institutional authority but resisted easy identification with any specific political position. Even a band as overtly political as the Minutemen prefaced a live version of "Little Man with a Gun in His Hand" with the jibe "This one's for the Gorbachevs and the Reagans . . . May they sleep well tonight."[21]

In addition to the lyrical assault on militarism, post-punkers expressed opposition more directly. The 1982–83 Rock Against Reagan hardcore tour culminated with a Fourth of July concert on the Mall in Washington, D.C. Left-wing groups routinely erected information tables at hardcore shows. At Minutemen shows the band's guitarist and songwriter D. Boon distributed U.S. OUT OF CENTRAL AMERICA bumper stickers and encouraged fans to boo Ronald Reagan. Fanzines brimmed with fan letters opposing the conservative national political culture. "Somebetty," a Bloomington, Indiana, fan, listed such progressive organizations as Women Strike for Peace and Women's Institute for Freedom of the Press for fans to join. Writing in *Flipside*, a fan named Jim deplored a disturbing trend he perceived in American life—abridgments of civil liberties, such as drug testing and the use of police roadblocks to arrest drunk drivers, and military escalation he compared to Nazi Germany. Signing off, he quipped, "Remember a vote for a Republican is a vote for War in '88. Ed Norton for President."[22] Jim's letter evoked antagonism toward the main currents of national politics more clearly than any vision of where that opposition might lead. His suggestion that Norton—the simpleton character on the iconic 1950s television sitcom *The Honeymooners*—would be a preferable presidential candidate mined popular culture for an alternative to Reagan. This rebellious refusal of the mainstream political possibilities emblematized post-punk's fascination with pop culture kitsch, a frequent surrogate for more direct political engagement.

Post-punk kitsch, iconoclasm, and ironic irreverence complicate attempts to analyze fans' politics. Asked "Who is your favorite recent public figure?" fans most frequently produced ironic responses drawn from popular culture and crafted for shock value. Poking fun at the question, they mocked the notion of reverence for public figures, repudiating politics proper. Paradoxically, however, many post-punk fans did not hesitate to identify which political causes and issues they considered most important. Support for a pro-choice position on abortion rights emerged at the forefront of their concerns, followed by "funding AIDS research," "environmental issues," "better education," and "cutting military spending." At the same time, fans rejected the conservative causes that marked the Reagan-Bush years, such as the "war on drugs," "fighting crime," and "cutting welfare spending." Ultimately, post-punk fans demonstrated ambiguous attitudes toward politics. On one hand they displayed a knee-jerk impulse to reject any interest in politics—suggesting that post-punk culture might more accurately be regarded as alternative rather than oppositional. Yet upon self-reflection, fans acknowledged specific political issues that they cared about, sometimes enough to merit active engagement. Not surprisingly, the issues that elicited the most fervent responses were those that most directly affected young people. This ambiguity illuminates a more complex picture of 1980s youth than the media portrait typified by *Time*'s 1990 cover story that used broad strokes to paint the "twentysomething" generation as politically apathetic.[23]

Though many fans viewed the presence of politics in the music warily, some professed admiration for bands associated with particular issues. An Austin, Texas, fan identified Fugazi with pro-choice, poverty, and anti-police-brutality issues, and one from Boston remarked that her favorite bands were involved with women's issues. The majority revealed a discomfort with music that was intentionally political, at the same time maintaining an openness to and acknowledgment of a relationship between music and progressive politics. A Providence record store buyer typified this attitude, preferring music "free of statements." "Bands playing benefits or quietly making donations to pet projects/causes is fine," he contended, but he cautioned, "Singing about social/political issues that everyone already agrees on as if it were a bold or daring statement is silly. Singing a song against child abuse for instance." Though underscoring his belief in the futility of bands playing overtly political songs, this fan affirmed music's legitimacy as an element surrounding and supporting political activity, and he sought to move beyond "preaching to the converted" in favor of a strategy that reached a broader audience. Tellingly, the fan described his own politics as "Democratic Far Left," a spirit that applied to numerous post-punks even if many would have shunned the label. Though post-punk lacked a unified "Democratic Far Leftist" vision, there was a symbolic fit between its values, lifestyles, musical expressions, and political leanings, which all aligned to resist mainstream society and, frequently, electoral politics.[24] Post-punkers rejected the conservative Republican aesthetic of the Reagan-Bush era more than fashioning themselves as political insurgents.

Race, Gender, and Proletarian Play: Identity Politics in Post-Punk

Though post-punk represented an overwhelmingly white form of youth culture, racial matters generated wide-ranging commentary. Letters to the editor in *Flipside* and *Maximumrocknroll* (*MRR*) consistently brought discussions of race to the fore. Often the letter writers responded to letters from previous issues, allowing for whole dialogues about race to unfold in the fanzines. The editorial staffs printed letters from fans who criticized their counterparts for displaying unenlightened racial attitudes. The editors' replies sought to elevate and refine the racial discussions appearing in their publications.[25]

A 1985 issue of *MRR* featured several letters responding to the right-leaning political views of the New York City hardcore band Agnostic Front. Though never espousing any particular political program, the band members were, for instance, critics of the welfare state and champions of militaristic foreign policy. Some of the letters defended

Agnostic Front, claiming that they could not be held responsible for the right-wing politics of certain skinhead groups connected to violence at some New York shows. Tim Yohannan's editorial reply, however, repudiated this defense and further impugned the band's politics by reprinting a section of an interview in which band members defended U.S. military intervention in Nicaragua as an appropriate response to "Communist aggression." This exchange typified the ideological dynamics of the fanzines. Though the 'zines printed letters expressing conservative points of view, the editors consistently used their editorial power to refute the positions of these fans. The concluding letter criticized Agnostic Front for defending the racism of Great Britain's right-wing National Front. The letter quoted a passage from an Agnostic Front interview that amounted to a damning apologia for the National Front's racism.[26] Placing this letter last in the series of letters about the controversial band, *MRR*'s editors deftly positioned it as the authoritative voice.

Fanzines generally characterized racial prejudice as unique to a specific subgroup of hardcore skinheads. In 1987 Skinheads Against Racial Prejudice (SHARP) formed to counter what they viewed as the mainstream media's unfair characterization of skinheads as racist. Referring to the growing power of television talk shows in the 1980s, a female skinhead from Richmond, Virginia, wrote, "I'm sick and tired of being called a nazi and a white supremist by people who watched Oprah Winfrey and Morten Downey, Jr.!!"[27] A cadre of post-punkers proactively sought to change the music's image as a prohibitively white brand of youth culture. The all-white Red Hot Chili Peppers fused elements of punk, funk, heavy metal, and rap, expanding the music's parameters beyond its roots in 1970s punk, which often bleached out black musical influences. The Minutemen incorporated jazz and funk riffs to widen the already capacious genre's boundaries. Members of Sonic Youth and Firehose collaborated as Ciccone Youth for a single album that combined punk and rap styles and covered hits by such acts as Madonna and Robert Palmer, spoofing the artifice of mainstream pop.[28] Organizers of the Rock Against Reagan concerts encouraged black rap and Latino bands to perform alongside white hardcore bands. Fans who witnessed Rock Against Reagan's racially mixed musical lineups tried to influence their counterparts in other cities to organize similar events and to get bands to perform at benefits for causes such as antiapartheid groups and Chicano Mexican community centers.[29] Though in one sense fan activism for events to promote racial unity acknowledged that racial discord existed within the community, it also adopted the forward-looking stance that post-punk's progressive impulses would be better served by musical hybridity and multiculturalism, as well as by social intermingling with black and Latino communities and cultures.

Though hardcore's subculture was palpably working class, the larger alternative rock scene represented a diversity of socioeconomic backgrounds. Post-punk thrived in what one might call the interstices of the class structure. Writing of British punk in the 1970s, Simon Frith argued that punk did not represent the authentic "voice of unemployed youth" so much as a strident expression of "the bohemian challenge to orderly consumption."[30] In other words, Frith was suggesting that punk anger was less rooted in class anger and orthodox political challenges to the established social order than it was enmeshed in a creative, and even fun, cultural project of shaking up the moral complacency of modern consumer capitalism. Frith's model applied equally well to post-punk, which also featured vigorous explorations of "proletarian play"—that is, rough-and-tumble behaviors and styles not normally associated with middle-class respectability and comfort. During the Reagan-Bush era this meant that post-punk relished flouting a set of mainstream material aspirations stoked by media images that venerated affluence and conspicuous consumption.

Fanzines spoofed and scorned middle-class consumer mentalities and searched for bohemian alternatives. A letter to the editor in *MRR* from Doug, a fan recently enrolled at the University of Idaho, described his exposure to punk subculture in San Francisco. Doug praised the tolerant nature of the Bay Area and its alternative music community. He then admitted to a period of disillusionment with the scene, when he considered becoming "a contributing member of twisted society." Ultimately, however, provoked by northern Idaho's conservative political climate, he decided to reaffirm his nonconformity despite the physical and verbal harassment he often encountered. He explained how, upon arriving in Idaho, he observed "the intense brain-washing and propagandization of the government-controlled media." In the same overstated mode Doug alluded to "the shocking, hideous truth of those in power (pro war, sexism, racism, corporate-control, mind control, rich supremacy)." His choice of villains reveals that his disaffection involved not only the conservative agenda of the Reagan era but also the media's complicity in institutionalizing that worldview. Doug's language, despite obvious dramatic embellishment, bore more than a passing resemblance to what First Lady Hillary Clinton, a decade later, famously called a "vast right-wing conspiracy" between conservative politicians and the media. His remark about "rich supremacy" expressed distaste for the decade's abandonment of the social contract and its corresponding emphasis on personal gain, which he contrasted with his own personal sacrifice in "resisting the fruits of Reagan's reign."[31] Doug shared with like-minded post-punk fans a politics that featured an aversion to consume or participate in anything that might reek of class privilege, a sentiment that existed regardless of whether their parents were doctors, capitalists, or hailed from legitimately working-class backgrounds.

Post-punk attitudes toward consumerism reflected a critique of corporate rapaciousness and a spunky economic populism. In 1986 an *MRR* reader sought to mobilize others to join a boycott of Coors products to protest the Rockies' leading beer producer's support for a raft of conservative causes. He informed readers of the *National Boycott Newsletter*, a publication that covered activist causes "from the destruction of the rainforests to which corporations fund the contras." Another fan protested inflated ticket prices at shows, urging his counterparts not to attend and bands not to play high-priced shows. Several bands sympathized and took steps to provide access to their shows for the widest range of fans. The bands Fugazi and Minor Threat maintained a policy of playing only all-ages shows and shunning venues that charged more than $6 per ticket. Similarly, Pearl Jam battled mightily, infamously, and litigiously with Ticketmaster's exorbitant ticket surcharges, arguing that the practice inflated already high prices, excluding regular fans who could not afford such purchases.[32] Although the courts ultimately upheld the surcharges, Pearl Jam's stand against Ticketmaster demonstrated resistance in an era when mainstream musical acts remained content to perform arena shows at steep ticket prices without questioning such policies.

Post-punks who explored "proletarian play" experienced an exhilaration that helps explain their participation in this distinctive subcultural "scene." An anonymous female fan remarked of her initial attraction to hardcore:

The first show I went to was great. I felt I had finally found a place where I belonged. Slamming was a trip. It was dangerous, it was senseless; to me it was a perfect manifestation of the chaos inside of me. In those days I was very optimistic. I was sure I was becoming part of a group that was unified and supportive. I thought we were going to change something and make a difference in the world . . . when I was knocked down someone picked me up; when my lip bled, someone wiped it off. When I was hit I felt the pain, but pain was not new to me and the feeling of camaraderie in the crowd of dancers was well worth any bruises I accumulated.[33]

This fan's excitement with slam dancing and the sense of community it engendered permeated not only hardcore but post-punk generally, entering the mainstream in the early 1990s as "moshing." The rock journalist Rachel Felder observed, "Moshing releases aggressions," putting "parameters around physical violence" but also allowing young fans to express anger.[34] In other words, it represented a way of playing at violence or roughness that allowed participants to mark their difference from the banal niceties of middle-class culture.

For female fans the rough play sometimes proved less cathartic than frustrating. Some expressed disillusionment with the escalating roughnesss of slam pits, and they blamed skinheads for the violence. One considered her options for coping with the problem: "I suppose I could become a skinhead girl and if I acted tough enough, maybe I would be accepted that way. It is funny that I have to speak of looking a certain way in order to be accepted in a scene that is supposed to condemn conformity."[35] The exclusivity this fan described contradicted the professed politics of the subculture, which supposedly represented a haven for youth opting out of the mainstream. Accounts like hers opened the door to questions about how oppositional hardcore really was, given its male dominance and its aversion to challenging traditional gender roles.[36]

A female Iowa City fan picked up on this and penned a letter to the editor of a leading fanzine recommending classic feminist texts by Simone de Beauvoir and Susan Brownmiller to enlighten fans on gender issues and expressing frustration with hardcore's reconstitution of traditional gender roles.[37] Though female hardcore fans may have faced limitations because of gender, in post-punk outside of hardcore many women enjoyed expanding musical possibilities. Women flourished in 1980s post-punk, asserting themselves as instrumentalists and song-writers and escaping the stereotypical girl vocalist role. By the late 1980s and early 1990s, all-women bands flourished, led by L7, Babes in Toyland, and Bikini Kill. Their music, lyrics, attitudes, and styles used post-punk as a forum for wide-ranging expression challenging gender stereotypes. Women post-punkers juxtaposed traditionally feminine clothing, such as undersized "baby-doll dresses," with tough-looking boots. Kim Gordon, Sonic Youth's bassist, proved particularly influential to the decade's wave of all-women bands.[38] Gordon's songwriting consis-tently addressed issues that affect women specifically, such as sexual harassment and anorexia. The battle over women's public sexual per-sona persisted as a primary concern of post-punk women. Members of L7 tried not to wear clothing that was too revealing, fearing that their music would not be taken seriously. They condemned the female heavy metal artist Lita Ford, who exploited her sexuality to increase her popu-larity, wearing garter belts and pantomiming sexual intercourse with the microphone in music videos. Suzi Gardner, L7's lead vocalist and guitar player, implied that she felt adopting a version of female sexuality such as Ford's would encourage fans to trivialize the band's music.[39] Post-punk women's thoughtfulness about how to represent themselves underscored the difference between these women and many main-stream women musicians at the time, even those as controversial and intermittently subversive as Madonna, who nevertheless routinely sexu-alized their personae to heighten their commercial appeal. In an era when mainstream popular culture aggressively buttressed patriarchy, post-punk's subversion of traditional feminine style amounted to the kind of everyday rebellion that frequently erupts in groups outside offi-cial channels of power or prestige.[40]

1991: Nirvana's *Nevermind*, Lollapalooza, and the Politics of Co-optation

During the 1980s, post-punk remained marginal in the marketplace as bands enjoyed little commercial success. After 1991, however, post-punk exploded into the cultural mainstream, as betokened by the documentary film *1991: The Year Punk Broke*. The title was a telling double entendre, highlighting the music's remarkable ascent to popular acclaim while also connoting the fear of compromised authenticity and co-optation that accompanied mainstream success. In 1991 guitar-based rock-and-roll music in the "post-punk" tradition made a quantum leap commercially, led by Nirvana's *Nevermind*, which sold 3.5 million copies in the last four months of that year alone. The popular press lauded "Smells Like Teen Spirit," the album's hit single, as a generational anthem. Grunge rock, a post-punk subgenre associated with a group of Seattle bands including Nirvana, spawned its own fashion trend, with pricy designer lumberjack shirts reaching high-fashion runways, and with kids who were previously devotees of Top 40 radio, chic jeans, and Vuarnet sunglasses "flying the flannel," in the lexicon coined by the Firehose bassist, Mike Watt, to describe mainstream youth's beeline for the post-punk bandwagon. Major record labels rushed to sign bands previously regarded as lacking commercial potential, capitalizing on the genre's newfound popularity. Commercial success changed the discussion surrounding the music, prompting the mainstream press to ask whether it could maintain its oppositional posture. Articles titled "Alternative to What?" and "Is Lollapalooza Losing Its Outsider Status?" examined the mainstreaming of post-punk, raising more questions than they answered about whether music with commercial aspirations, however alternative, could retain its critical edge. But why did post-punk become popular at that particular moment? Uncanny parallels abounded between 1991 in the United States and British punk circa 1977. The musical innovation of both cultural epochs displaced a rock and pop culture dominated by superstars who remained distant from their fans. British punk and American post-punk both surfaced when their countries of origin were mired in economic recessions. British punk, epitomized by the Sex Pistols, and American post-punk led by Nirvana emerged to fill a national void in moments where youth were ripe for a resurgence of music with a rebellious spirit.[41]

To the untrained eye (or ear), Nirvana and its ilk shot to prominence overnight, emerging with a sonic vengeance from the Seattle drizzle. But, as with many overnight successes, this picture belies the deeper roots and protracted struggle that led to post-punk's flowering. One enthusiast argued that though music in the 1980s was often derided for its lack of innovation, post-punk cognoscenti regarded it as rock's "most fertile decade," as the era's lesser-known independently produced music bubbled with creative ferment. While many of post-punk's most influential bands started out on independent labels like SST, Touch and Go, and Sub Pop, by the late 1980s the major labels caught on to the music's commercial potential. In 1986 Hüsker Dü left SST and signed with Warner Bros. for its *Candy Apple Grey* album. In the wake of the signing, some of the original fan base felt alienated and charged the band with "selling out" and abandoning its politics. Hüsker Dü's Bob Mould defended the move to a major label as a bid to reach a wider audience, arguing that the band remained true to its ideals and that its conception of politics was broadening beyond the formula of topical songs each addressing individual issues. Debates such as this one, carried out ritually in the fanzines' pages, closely foreshadowed popular press debates in the wake of Nirvana's success.[42] By decade's end, a growing legion of seminal post-punk bands—including Firehose (two-thirds of whose members were from the Minutemen), the Replacements, Dinosaur Jr., and, perhaps most important, Sonic Youth—questing for expanded audiences and a greater opportunity to earn a living through their craft, made the break and signed with major labels.

Bands like Sonic Youth, which took almost a decade to garner a fraction of the popularity that Nirvana achieved virtually overnight, faithfully toiled "underground" throughout the 1980s, opening cultural space for Nirvana's popular success. Though prior to signing with Geffen in 1990, Sonic Youth was affiliated with a number of independent labels such as Homestead, Blast First, and SST, the band's career path challenged typical arguments about "selling out" and cultural co-optation. Their early work was characterized by aural experimentation—such as tuning the band's two guitars one quarter note apart to produce a dissonant wall of sound—and impressionistic lyrics often delivered with an ironic distance and frequently defying interpretation. Beginning with *Goo*, Sonic Youth's 1990 major label debut, the band's politics actually became more overt. Songs like "Swimsuit Issue," "Tunic (Song for Karen)," and "Youth Against Fascism" supplied eminently hip music with savvy commentary on topics ranging from sexual objectification and the male gaze to eating disorders and combating hate speech.[43] The band's increasing politicization after signing to a major label gave the lie to the old saw that bands signing to majors were sellouts incapable of delivering any meaningful message. Sonic Youth personally aided Nirvana's rise by providing a liaison with a Geffen Artist and Repertoire representative in 1990 and selecting Nirvana as the opening act for their 1991 European tour.

Along with increasing major label interest in "underground" music, another factor enabled Nirvana's commercial breakthrough—an increasingly cohesive sense of identity among post-punk fans, honed over a decade of shared experiences in the clubs, in the pages of fanzines and underground newspapers, and in the aisles of retail outlets devoted to making independent music available to its discerning followers. A set of recurring political sensibilities pervaded these locales, helping this community to cohere. Patrick, a Colorado Springs native, typified the community's outlook. When defending the place of politics in post-punk, he remarked, "People think that enough has been said about Ronald Reagan, war, nuclear holocaust, cops and governments. Well, I don't." "A lot has been said and a lot of people have been working really hard," he continued, "but the things that we hate have not gone away. So why should I not sing about what sucks and what should be done about it just because others feel the same way and have voiced their opinions before me?" Patrick proceeded to defend the Dead Kennedys against charges of "selling out," praising the band for broadening the reach of its message and urging fans to pool their "collective power together against the system" as a strategy for survival.[44] Though he left his choice of targets unspecific, with "the system" evoking a dose of generalized paranoia, those in the post-punk community would have been able to pinpoint the system's chief elements: militarism, social conservatism, rampant materialism, and Reagan himself. At the very least, Patrick's comments conveyed post-punkers' sense of engagement with politics adversarial to the decade's main currents.

Other fans called for a move to "other directions of political work," advocating moving beyond political lyrics that simply preached to the converted. A fan named Dave cautioned fans not to fall into the "subculture trap"—maintaining a cool and unique style and attitude at the expense of limited influence on those outside the community. Arguing that post-punk was vulnerable to charges of exclusivity, he pleaded for a more inclusive community, offering to compile a contact list of fans' addresses so that "serious political punks" could "get together and start talking." Besides the opposition to the dominant political culture evident in Rock Against Reagan concerts and "I hate Ronnie" contests, post-punks also defined their politics in contrast to previous generations. Letters from fans cite examples of 1960s radicals who have renounced their politics and "traded in their lovebeads for three-piece suits."[45] Young post-punk fans consistently differentiated themselves from 1960s youth, rejecting the earlier era's wide-eyed idealism for a more skeptical and even cynical outlook. This sensibility coincided with a more pragmatic engagement with politics that rejected utopian solutions in favor of an issue-by-issue approach tempered with realism about what could be achieved amid the more conservative landscape. In the summer of 1991 the first Lollapalooza tour helped solidify the post-punk community's self-image.

The Lollapalooza festival was the brainchild of Perry Farrell, the lead singer of Jane's Addiction. Farrell and his associates in music management organized a lineup of seven bands representing a range of musical styles, from Jane's Addiction to the Henry Rollins Band and Ice T and Body Count, and announced a tour to seventeen U.S. locations. The initial Lollapalooza proved successful, drawing large crowds for a ten-hour show of varied musical fare, with leading post-punk bands represented prominently. The festival featured information display tables sponsored by various political and social action groups. Many of the tables emphasized non-radical initiatives—from voter registration to abortion rights to condom distribution—suggesting that by the early 1990s the post-punk community grasped the utility of participating in electoral politics to pursue modest reforms and the necessity of battling the tide of socially conservative activism moving in the opposite direction. Still, with Greenpeace, Refuse and Resist, NARAL, and gun control advocates setting up shop, the festival's atmosphere was decidedly left leaning. Farrell had invited representatives from the center and right of the political spectrum, notably the National Rifle Association and the armed forces, but—despite his protestations that it would have been too easy to have "this hip, left-wing event" and his claim "I don't want to make out I have the answers, all I want to do is pose the questions"—tellingly, they declined to show. "Why should I bother getting into a pissing match with a bunch of left-wing rock & roll punks?" the army's spokesman mused. If Lollapalooza's politics weren't exactly a call to storm the barricades, the festival's success promoted generational cohesion and political common ground. Even the mainstream press appreciated this heightened sense of community, epitomized by *Newsweek*'s dubbing Lollapalooza "A Woodstock for Post-Punks."[46]

The breakthrough of Nirvana and post-punk in 1991 represented the serendipitous convergence of increasing major label attention, the cohesion of post-punk fans through festivals such as Lollapalooza and the International Pop Underground Convention, and a shared oppositional identity forged over a decade-long period of ferment underground, in bars, clubs, and dives far from the cultural spotlight. Politics, though only one of several ingredients in this identity, were nevertheless vital. The rock writer Jon Garelick compared Nirvana's *Nevermind* to Jon Landau's memorable comments on Bob Dylan's *John Wesley Harding* album in a 1967 review. Landau argued that although Dylan didn't mention the Vietnam War explicitly, a "profound awareness" of the war and its consequences for American life could be felt throughout the album. Garelick contended that *Nevermind* exhibited a similar consciousness about the 1991 Persian Gulf War, during which Nirvana recorded the album. Garelick suggested that Nirvana's rage on *Nevermind,* which helped it tap into powerful and inchoate generational emotions, registered an implicit rebellion in the national dialogue. One Nirvana enthusiast wrote, "When I heard that *Nevermind,* an album whose first line is 'Load up on drugs and bring your friends,' had gone to number one the first week of 1992, my first thought was, 'Bush will not be reelected.'"[47] Though the fan got the lyric wrong—it was "guns" rather than "drugs" that Cobain had mumbled—her premonition proved correct, as the greatest number of young people to turn out for a presidential election since 1972 voted George Bush out of office.

The success of post-punk, or "alternative" music, as the recording industry came to call it, combined with Bill Clinton's election shifted the cultural context in which the music operated. Articles with titles like "Alternative to What?" pointed out that this supposedly rebellious music was easily retrofitted to sell Subarus and Miller beer. Writers in the mainstream music press questioned the authenticity of some of the most popular alternative acts, such as the Stone Temple Pilots and Blind Melon, suggesting that they were second-rate examples of the industry's rush to capitalize on the popular musical style du jour. The industry's mobilization of a musical movement that it regarded only a few years earlier as lacking commercial potential illustrated consumer capitalism's capacity for overcoming barriers to commerce—even ones as laden with dissonant noise as post-punk. Yet its staying power, as demonstrated by the long-standing recording careers it launched and its ubiquitous airplay on classic rock radio formats, testifies to post-punk's substance and enduring appeal to those longing for music that expresses an authentic spirit of resistance.

6

FIGHTING THE POWER
The Response of African American Politics and Culture

In his 1982 State of the Union address, contemplating an unprecedented $100 billion deficit and looking to stave off the recession that plagued his early administration, Ronald Reagan focused the nation's attention on entitlement programs. He depicted a welfare system rife with waste and fraud, remarking, "Virtually every American who shops in a local supermarket is aware of the daily abuses that take place in the food stamp program." Even members of his own party bemoaned the president's approach. The GOP senator Bob Packwood griped, "We've got a $120 billion deficit coming and the President says, '. . . a young man went into a grocery store and he had an orange in one hand and a bottle of vodka in the other, he paid for the orange with food stamps and he took the change and paid for the vodka. That's what's wrong.'" Reagan's own aide deflated the anecdote's veracity, noting to a House subcommittee that change from food stamp transactions was limited to 99 cents and thus, "it is not possible to buy a bottle of vodka with 99 cents." Yet the story reveals the lack of empathy and factual accuracy that typified public discussion of welfare and poverty in the 1980s, from the highest ranks of government to the general public.[1]

The tale also demonstrates the increasingly confident moralism with which Americans judged between the truly needy, whose interests the president pledged to protect, and an undeserving underclass whose existence was "discovered" by journalists and social scientists throughout the decade. Popular media and academics alike argued that the underclass suffered from a "tangle of pathology," including poverty, joblessness, drug use, illegitimacy and single motherhood, homelessness, and violent crime. Though most of these afflictions were on the rise among all Americans during the 1980s, these observers routinely foregrounded African Americans. Buttressed by social science, the popular media installed race as a metaphor for poverty, leaving the face of the decade's "new poor" conspicuously black. This simple construction masked a world of irony and paradox. National anxiety about the underclass occurred at a time when unprecedented numbers of black Americans managed to emulate the much-loved Huxtables on television's *The Cosby Show* and secure a place in the middle-class professional world. This raised salient questions about how such mobility could coincide with the continued deterioration of living conditions for the majority of African Americans in cities.[2]

This was a persistent dilemma. The 1968 Kerner Commission Report, which looked into the causes of racially charged rioting in Newark and Detroit, famously concluded that "our nation is moving toward two societies—one black, one white—separate and unequal." Citing black frustration and feelings of powerlessness as the riots' root causes, the report recommended expansive federal initiatives to improve services, schools, and job opportunities in black communities. Unfortunately, these suggestions surfaced at the moment when the escalating bill for the Vietnam War emboldened Republican congressional leaders to exact cuts in President Lyndon Johnson's War on Poverty. By 1968 the national appetite for ambitious social agendas was evaporating. Almost a full generation later, the National Urban League's 1985 annual recommendations closely paralleled those of the Kerner Commission, calling for restored social spending amid the Reagan cutbacks, an array of job-training initiatives, equal employment measures, family support programs, and inner-city economic development.[3]

Amid unrelenting black poverty and urban crises in an era when many legal barriers to equality had been eradicated, many white Americans concluded that the fault must lie somewhere in black America itself. Conservatives, including a celebrated handful of prominent black conservatives, examined underclass "pathologies" and suggested that the complex of federal welfare programs itself contributed to rising poverty and should be dismantled. In a much-trumpeted, provocative analysis of welfare dysfunction, the political scientist Charles Murray argued that federal policy incentivized failure, dependency, and promiscuity, in part through lenient attitudes toward crime and punishment. Deftly eliding explicit mention of race, the *National Review* questioned the underclass's self-discipline, suggesting that the myriad social problems of a burgeoning "undeserving poor" could be addressed only through increased prison construction and tighter social controls.[4] By contrast, liberal observers placed the onus for the swelling underclass and welfare state maladies on racism and white backlash. In a more sophisticated vein, the renowned sociologist William Julius Wilson emphasized the role of ongoing structural changes, such as urban deindustrialization and the flight of the black middle class, that relegated the "truly disadvantaged" segment of the black population to the inner cities, where they were especially vulnerable to unemployment and poorly positioned to benefit from affirmative action programs.[5] Though attitudes about the underclass varied according to the onlooker's politics, black Americans understood that the legislative gains of the civil rights movement, with their promise of equal opportunity, had not translated into social and economic equality in fact. The promise of Reaganomics— that fueling the supply side would stoke the prosperity of ordinary Americans—stalled, leaving most still waiting for the trickle down.

The weeds that choked the urban underclass had deep roots. In the late 1940s and 1950s, amid widespread economic growth, a telltale loss of well-paying manufacturing jobs was already afoot, culminating in the full-blown deindustrialization of the 1960s, 1970s, and beyond. Beginning in the 1950s and 1960s, buoyed by federal mortgage policies that discriminated against African Americans, middle-class whites embarked on a mass exodus from American cities to the suburbs. Though the Supreme Court ruled the restrictive covenants that barred would-be black homeowners and renters from white neighborhoods unenforceable in the late 1940s, the standard operating practices of American Realtors worked to keep residential segregation in place, leaving the racial boundaries of northern cities even more sharply delineated than their southern counterparts. Indeed, one landmark sociological study concluded that residential segregation stood at the forefront of structural factors that perpetuated black poverty and inequality. The funk icon George Clinton aptly encapsulated the spatial and racial dynamics of the situation with his memorable declaration: "God bless Chocolate City and its vanilla suburbs."[6]

With "white flight," American cities faced depleted tax bases and corresponding declines in services. Though chronic disparities in wealth inhibited home ownership for the majority of black citizens to begin with, the disintegration of inner cities resulted in declining real estate values that further hampered black homeowners' ability to build personal wealth. Efforts to redress the educational inequalities caused by white disinvestment in America's cities—such as the 1970s contentious busing crisis—failed to level the playing field for the nation's urban public schools. Relentless deindustrialization moved manufacturing jobs to foreign shores with cheaper labor costs, leaving black workers lacking the training for employment in the service-based postindustrial economy. By 1987 the hemorrhaging of jobs resulted in a situation where black unemployment, far from receding in the "post-Civil Rights Era," remained more than double the white rate, with no relief in sight from a Supreme Court that through the years of Reagan-Bush appointments became increasingly hostile to affirmative action though limited gains continued.[7]

Facing great challenges, African Americans refused to adopt a position of supine surrender during the Reagan years. On the contrary, the black community tried to combat the hostility and neglect it confronted, engaging in a variety of efforts aimed at a broad spectrum of goals. Electoral efforts to promote black politicians harnessed the promise of black political power in the era following the Voting Rights Act. This produced a wave of new black mayors, who, despite impressive obstacles, forged changes in municipal affairs that changed the face of local politics and democratized city government, however incrementally. A national quest to unify a multiethnic, multiracial coalition of Americans left behind by the Reagan recovery produced a black presidential candidate of unprecedented legitimacy whose failures paved the way for the Obama breakthrough of the next generation. Urban grassroots community organizers opted to work outside the compromise-laden arena of electoral politics, freeing themselves to agitate more directly for changes in health care, housing, education, and job training to improve conditions for black city dwellers. The diffuse, fragmented nature and the mixed record of achievement of black activism discouraged thoughtful analysis from a media establishment that increasingly craved catchy sound bites to encapsulate complex issues. In a world where close to 95 percent of television executives and print journalists were white, and black ownership of commercial radio and television stations languished at 1.7 percent, the national media tended to ignore grassroots community organizing efforts in favor of "sexier" narratives of the danger and outlaw glamour of life in the 'hood.[8] Because of this, many of the most vibrant and effective African American political statements of the decade emanated from the cultural realm, from the pens of black women novelists to the rhymes of militant rappers. Despite a context of deindustrialization, cuts to social spending, and ascendant conservatism that put a ceiling on their achievements, African Americans continued to pursue the means to improve their lives, confounding stereotypes of underclass passivity and pathology.

A Tale of Two Mayors: Black Mayors and Urban Politics in the 1980s

Recalling the Cleveland black community's support for Carl Stokes in his 1967 bid to become the first African American mayor of a major American city, the campaign secretary Geraldine Williams explained, "We thought he would have the interests of the blacks more at heart." Stokes's subsequent election, along with that of Richard Hatcher in Gary, Indiana, catalyzed a wave of successful efforts to enhance black political power by electing black candidates to mayors' offices. The proliferation of black mayors represented a direct outgrowth of the civil rights movement and the 1965 Voting Rights Act, which galvanized black political participation, swelling the numbers of registered black voters from 1.5 million to 3.1 million within a decade. From Stokes's and Hatcher's victories, the number of black mayors escalated to 48 in 1973, and 316 in 1990. Like the white ethnic Americans who dominated big-city politics in the early twentieth century, urban blacks yearned to have one of their own in power to better address their needs and steer jobs and improved services their way. In practice, the calculus of black mayors achieving beneficial results for black communities proved trickier than many supporters anticipated. Only a handful of the nation's cities featured black majorities, so that even attaining the mayor's office necessitated multiracial support. Once elected, successful black candidates faced a standard of appearing fair and addressing the needs of all citizens rather than solely serving their black political bases. This political imperative exceeded what was expected of their white counterparts and often conflicted with the elevated hopes and expectations of black voters that black mayors would redress chronic urban ills that disproportionately plagued their communities. All of this was set against a larger structural landscape of continuing deindustrialization, white and black middle-class suburbanization resulting in shrinking tax bases, and a wave of Reagan conservatism that augured severe cuts to social spending from the federal government. In this climate, the cities' need for private sector economic revitalization typically forced black mayors to cooperate with local business leaders, often at the expense of improving services and the quality of life for black neighborhoods.[9]

Despite these constraints, the 1980s witnessed continued African American inroads into city halls, resulting in modest but real benefits to the lives of black citizens. Black mayors dramatically altered the face of municipal government, installing greater proportions of black and minority municipal employees. Mayor Tom Bradley of Los Angeles, often criticized for not standing up for black interests forcefully enough, significantly expanded the ranks of black Angelenos in higher-paying white-collar jobs. Atlanta's Andrew Young, using a top-down approach to economic revitalization that prioritized business interests, nevertheless increased the role of black decision making in the city's bureaucracy. Even moderate black mayors, often emerging from their cities' white-dominated political machines, pursued affirmative action in hiring and awarding municipal contracts. This held true across the country, from the Rust Belt cities of Chicago, Detroit, and Gary to urban areas of the formerly segregated South such as Atlanta and New Orleans, where remedying patterns of historical discrimination still loomed large. In Detroit, Mayor Coleman Young's administration typified black mayors' approach to reforming police-community relations, a mandate for black urban Americans since the mid-1960s. Young changed the profile of the police force, hiring greater numbers of African Americans and women. Yet the assumption that expanding the uniformed minority presence in black communities and in police leadership positions would heighten empathy and reduce violent conflict was not always enough. Two of the era's major racial conflagrations, the 1985 bombing of Philadelphia's MOVE house and the 1992 Los Angeles insurrections following the Rodney King verdict, occurred in cities with black mayors where the racial composition of the police force had undergone significant reform.

The careers of Washington, D.C.'s Marion Barry and Chicago's Harold Washington provide contrasting case studies of black mayoral leadership during the 1980s, but they nonetheless share some telling commonalities. Barry, known in popular memory as a poster boy for black urban misrule, embodies a welter of contradiction. Exemplifying the familiar, though often inaccurate, archetype of a black mayor who cut his political teeth in the 1960s civil rights movement, Barry rose to prominence as a member of the vanguard Student Nonviolent Coordinating Committee. Washingtonians first came to know him as an activist for home rule in the District, which for almost a century was governed by a presidentially appointed board of commissioners. Barry, harnessing the direct action tactics of the civil rights movement, spearheaded a Free D.C. movement that boycotted local businesses that refused to display messages of support for home rule. Though the Free D.C. movement halted under threatened legal action, Barry kept nurturing his public profile, serving on the school board in the early 1970s. When home rule finally prevailed, he was elected to the District's first city council. In 1978, rallying around a platform of greater inclusion for African Americans and other minorities, reforming city governance, economic empowerment, and better social services, the District elected Barry mayor.[10]

D.C. voters were energized by Barry the man as much as by his platform. *The Washington Post*'s endorsement cited his promises of decisive, dynamic, innovative leadership as qualifications that made his tepid Democratic primary opponents pale by comparison. Of course, it was another set of personal qualities—bespeaking a psychological complexity on a par with Shakespearean tragedy—that undermined Barry's administration and led to his undoing, though his career would feature a resurrection or two. This was a story of noble ambition thwarted by catastrophic character failings: corruption scandals too close for plausible denial, womanizing, and drug use. His dramatic fall reached a national audience with the 1990 release of a grainy FBI videotape showing the mayor smoking crack cocaine in a hotel to which a former extramarital interest had lured him. The accompanying audio proved even more damning, broadcasting the handcuffed Barry's infamous reaction to the sting: "Bitch set me up!" This episode received wide media dissemination, playing into the national narrative of underclass pathology—drugs, sexuality overspilling social constraints, and the disintegration of urban morality.[11]

Media focus on Barry's personal frailties masked a flawed but palpable record of accomplishment. Lost in the lurid articles and salacious TV news reports in the drug bust's wake were an array of less-publicized achievements, including reforms that benefited all Washingtonians across color lines. During his first two terms Barry revitalized an unresponsive city bureaucracy, initiated reforms that ultimately created a nationally recognized system of financial management, and recorded modest improvements in city services and crime prevention. In the early 1980s, prior to economic recovery, he nurtured a productive relationship with the D.C. business community that spared the city much of the high job loss that plagued urban areas across the country. He instituted several policies that particularly assisted D.C.'s black community. He created an enduring summer jobs program that has served hundreds of thousands of D.C. youths, improved the rate of minority-owned firms hired for city contracts, and restored ten thousand blighted housing units. This record goes a long way to explaining the durability of Barry's support in the black community, even in the face of scandal.[12]

The brief mayoral career of Chicago's Harold Washington, though less morally ambiguous, shares some commonalities with Barry's career that illuminate the decade's urban politics. Washington's journey to the mayor's office forced him to wrestle with the defining element of Chicago politics: the machine. With roots dating to the early twentieth century, symbolized most famously by the longtime mayor Richard J. Daley, the Chicago Democratic machine dominated the city's politics through a tight system of patronage and party loyalty. To an extent, black Chicagoans participated in the system. Since Franklin Roosevelt's New Deal of the 1930s, they had voted overwhelmingly Democratic. Black politicians intermittently reaped patronage positions for their support, and loyal black voters occasionally were rewarded with projects that addressed community needs. But on the whole, white, ethnic working-class Chicagoans were the big winners of this self-replicating system that ensured their control of decision making in city government, with black interests remaining "subordinate." To counter this, "self-determination" and "community control" represented two galvanizing principles of Washington's campaign and his administration.[13] Ironically, Washington's path to political prominence, unlike Barry's, started not through protest against the white power structure, but through diligent dues paying within the machine itself.

In the early part of his career, like most successful black politicians in Chicago, Washington dutifully helped the machine harvest votes and consolidate power. In return he was rewarded with a seat in the Illinois state legislature and was expected to reciprocate loyalty through his political behavior in Springfield. Washington soon departed from the script, demonstrating independence by supporting legislation that confronted police brutality in Mayor Daley's Chicago. Beginning in the late 1960s, heightened focus on racial consciousness and identity increasingly forced Washington to walk a fine line between his need for machine political support and racial solidarity. Though he introduced a bill that ultimately made Illinois the first state with a Martin Luther King Day holiday, he remained quiet about the brutal police raid that killed two leaders of the Chicago Black Panthers. Though playing both ends in casting himself as an "independent machine politician," Washington's unsuccessful 1977 run for mayor against the Daley organization Democratic candidate sealed a future outside the machine. In 1980 he was elected to Congress, where he quickly made his mark and garnered appointments to key committees.

Washington emerged as an outspoken critic of President Reagan's policies. He advocated a nuclear freeze, argued for diverting 20 percent of the defense budget to social and urban programs, and condemned interventionist policies in Central America. Moreover, he relished his new post in Congress, far from the insular world of Chicago city politics. Approached about a possible challenge to the former Daley protégée and Chicago's first female mayor, Jane Byrne, Washington replied that he would consider a run provided the black community could register fifty thousand new voters. Though some viewed this high bar as evidence of Washington's contentment in Congress, others, led by the black businessman Edward Gardner and a new group called POWER (People Organized for Welfare and Employment Rights), took up the challenge. POWER brought the voter registration campaign directly to unemployment lines and welfare offices to mobilize the city's most disenfranchised citizens. The result: a whopping hundred and thirty thousand predominantly black new registered voters, which led to Washington's eventual entry in the 1983 mayoral campaign.[14]

In a hotly contested three-way primary race against Byrne and the legendary mayor's son Richard M. Daley, Washington eked out victory with a 36 percent plurality. His win demonstrated the energy behind the expanded voter registration totals and catalyzed unprecedented excitement in politics for black Chicagoans. "Black people just thrilled" to watch a series of debates in which an informed, articulate, and experienced candidate of their own argued the merits of police reform with the embattled Byrne and the wooden Daley. One observer beamed, "It was like watching Michael Jordan with a basketball." Undoubtedly, racial pride had something to do with the high turnout that netted Washington 85 percent of the black vote in a town where many blacks maintained a decades-long allegiance to the machine that some derided as "plantation politics." Washington also benefited from a white vote split between Byrne and Daley. Though victory in Chicago's Democratic primary traditionally meant a free ticket to the mayor's office in this overwhelmingly Democratic city, many white Democrats—including key party leaders—did the unthinkable, moving their support behind the Republican candidate, Bernard Epton.[15]

Running unopposed in the Republican primary, Epton garnered a mere 11,000 votes, compared with Washington's 415,000 in the Democratic race. Yet in the general election the previously obscure Epton found himself the beneficiary of legions of "recent converts." Some of Chicago's newfound ambivalence to the Democratic candidate reflected anxiety over Washington's promise to combat the inequities of the machine. One Democratic alderman supporting the Republican remarked of Washington, "Why should I give him the guillotine with which to chop off my head?" Hesitancy about Washington's candidacy also may have stemmed from his well-documented, though relatively minor and decades old, tax troubles. Others more candidly acknowledged the central factor behind the exodus from the Democratic candidate. One committeeman explained, "The people in my area just don't want a black mayor—it's as simple as that." The heightened racial politics of Chicago's mayoral race boiled over for a national audience at a Sunday Mass at St. Pascal's Church attended by Washington and Walter Mondale, the early front-runner for the 1984 Democratic presidential nomination. When 150 pro-Epton demonstrators jeered and shouted epithets, Washington and Mondale beat a hasty retreat rather than let the protest disrupt the Palm Sunday service. Though Epton later criticized the demonstrators, the incident epitomized a campaign that exploited racial anxiety without explicitly mentioning race. One tagline accompanying the candidate's television commercials warned "EPTON—BEFORE IT'S TOO LATE."[16]

Though 80 percent of Chicago's citizens were Democrats, Washington squeaked out victory with only 52 percent of the vote, which broke down to 99 percent of the black vote and 12 percent of the white vote. Though these figures represented the fallout of a racially polarizing campaign, the white voters who supported Washington tended to be upscale "lakefront liberals" who, together with a sizable Latino contingent and overwhelming support within the black community, signified a fledgling multiracial, multiethnic coalition that played an even greater role in his 1987 reelection. The new mayor faced a major hurdle not usually confronted by white urban mayors: demonstrating his legitimacy as the leader of all Chicagoans across racial lines. This problem was exacerbated by tactical blunders from some of Washington's supporters, notably Jesse Jackson, who had pumped the primary victory rally crowds, shouting, "It's our turn." This stoked white fears that black political power would involve efforts to exact retribution on the city's white population and provoked an infamous backlash by white city council members. Another looming challenge Washington faced—along with black mayors across the nation—was how to leverage jobs and services to improve the lives of the poor and minority citizens in his constituency from the pro-growth business community that represented the cities' best hope for economic revitalization in an age of declining public investment. Before Washington could address this, however, he confronted the herculean attempts of machine loyalists to thwart his efforts to govern. Machine forces controlled the council committee positions from which power emanated and which had stood for decades as a bastion of white privilege. One of Washington's great challenges was to open up Chicago city government and provide a measure of control to its minority citizens.[17]

Washington spent his first three years as mayor in Chicago's infamous Council Wars, jockeying to achieve a working majority to allow him to govern. Upon realizing this goal in 1986, he quickly revamped governance along more egalitarian lines. This included "good government" measures that took direct aim at the patronage system's grip on the city. He signed a decree that prohibited politically motivated hirings or firings and limited campaign contributions by companies holding city contracts. He diversified key leadership positions, appointing a black police chief to head a department renowned for unscrupulous use of force against minority citizens. He worked to make conditions fairer for the poor and minorities, notably passing a Tenants' Bill of Rights. For some black radicals, Washington's fairness was itself an issue. Desiring greater redress after years of exclusion from Chicago's public life, many black Chicagoans believed that Washington should "put black people first"—just as Mayor Daley had funneled disproportionate shares of jobs and services to his supporters. They viewed Washington's resistance to doing this as "too fair." As the activist Lu Palmer argued, he "never became what I would consider the black mayor" for which much of the city's black population longed. This stubbornness about fairness was in keeping with Washington's program of giving Chicago a good government makeover. It was also good politics, helping him build trust and enhanced support among white Chicagoans, since his already overwhelming popularity in the black community allowed him to expand his outreach to white constituencies.[18]

Any evaluation of Washington's record encourages projection, since his career was cut off prematurely by a fatal heart attack only months after his 1987 reelection. In the early months of his second mayoral term, having wrested control from the machine and consolidated his political power, he started to implement a program of progressive reforms. In the past, Community Development Block Grants (CDBGs) and other federal resources were channeled through the machine-appointed bureaucracy and dispensed at its discretion to Chicago's neighborhoods. Often these funds were diverted to such pet projects as purchasing snow-removal equipment or padding teacher pensions, which had little to do with the neighborhoods' greatest needs. In a professionalized, within-the-system version of the New Left ideal of decentralization, Washington rerouted federal funds directly to the communities and enhanced the power of nongovernmental community organizations to participate in decision making. William Foster, a housing rehabilitation activist, noted, "Community groups now can come into the Department of Housing and sit down with commissioners and develop programs. That's a first for this city." A *Nation* columnist observed that these community groups included strong contingents of "activists and leftists" who were now "not only respected by the administration—many of them are in the administration." Though some observers viewed education—along with housing—as areas lacking "tangible improvement" for "Chicago's vast black underclass" during Washington's mayoralty, a closer look indicates that gradual education reforms involving decentralized, community-based strategies were under way at the time of his death.[19]

Through empowering communities, modifying the police department, pursuing affirmative action initiatives, and strenuously grappling to transform Chicago government, Washington democratized the city's political culture substantially enough to prevent his more conservative successors from restoring the old order. By the time of his death, through good governance and commitment to fairness, Washington had alleviated white anxieties about the meaning of a black mayor, significantly increasing his support among whites. A local columnist remarked, "Harold was winning over white Chicagoans. They were slowly beginning to lose their fear."[20] Moreover, the columnist pointed out, Washington's white following was not limited solely to affluent liberals: "even working class whites" evinced greater support for Washington in his reelection. Washington's rise to power raised eyebrows, with even the conservative *National Review* grudgingly acknowledging the power of "an informed and mobilized black constituency working with white liberals who have nowhere to go."[21] Washington's multiracial, multiethnic coalition in Chicago provided the inspiration for a viable political movement on a national stage.

Run, Jesse, Run

In the summer of 1983, when many black Chicagoans were still celebrating Harold Washington's victory, Chicago's other famous black leader, Jesse Jackson, headed home to the South. Leading a "Southern Crusade," he aimed to register thousands of black voters. This mission grew out of a recognition of the region's pivotal role in President Reagan's 1980 election. The Gipper had prevailed by a narrow margin in several states within a region where Democrats left the votes of some three million unregistered African Americans on the table. Enhanced black political power could sway the balance of the 1984 presidential race, underscore African Americans' importance to the Democrats, and move issues that mattered most to black people to greater prominence in the Democratic agenda. This logic inspired Jackson's swing through the South. In a development that he did little to discourage, the campaign generated a momentum of its own, with Jackson as the focal point. Delivering the message about harnessing the political energy of the voter registration drive, cries of "Run, Jesse, Run" greeted Jackson at rallies across the South.[22]

Though black leaders had discussed the idea of a black candidate to run for the 1984 Democratic nomination earlier in the year, Jesse Jackson was far from the inevitable choice. His detractors within the black community were numerous. Many established black politicians endorsed the traditional strategy of supporting whichever white Democratic candidate was perceived as most sympathetic to black interests. Some argued that a black candidate would dilute support for the eventual Democratic nominee, thereby enhancing the danger of Reagan's reelection. Yet a growing consensus among key black leaders emerged that in an increasingly conservative national political landscape, mainstream Democrats might abandon support for the social programs, educational initiatives, and job-training measures that were important to black Americans. Thus the push for a black candidate gained increasing urgency. The premise was that a black candidacy, even if victory was unattainable, would mobilize large numbers of black voters, forcing the Democrats to address African Americans' concerns rather than taking their votes for granted.

Still, no consensus existed for Jackson as a standard-bearer, and many viewed him as divisive. He encompassed a welter of contradictions within one individual, and his résumé could provoke profoundly different reactions depending on one's perspective. Competing interpretations of Jackson's legacy within the civil rights movement abounded. Some viewed him as Martin Luther King's heir apparent and moral successor; others contended that Jackson opportunistically bathed in the fallen hero's blood, literally, then courted the cameras to enhance his stature. In Chicago, where Jackson had spent most of his adult life, some praised his ability to build black community through his leadership of Operation PUSH (People United to Serve Humanity), while others detected calculating self-aggrandizement, noting that he frequently upstaged Harold Washington, as though vying to become the city's preeminent black leader. Supporters argued that Jackson's preternatural sense for grabbing media headlines represented a uniquely powerful tool among black leaders. For critics, it was obnoxious behavior that caused friction that divided African Americans and led white Democratic leaders to overlook worthy but quieter, less self-promoting black voices. A former Jackson aide summarized, "He repels and attracts in equal measure," adding, "If you feel like you want an argument, just go to any tavern and say the name Jesse Jackson."[23]

A combination of personal traits and serendipity enabled Jackson to emerge as the candidate. He possessed the requisite ability to command the media and raise money. His lack of political background and experience within Democratic Party inner workings actually worked in his favor, since he did not share the reluctance of other black leaders to step forward. "It was something, interestingly enough, that people were not knocking each other down wanting to do," explained Jackson's campaign chairman, Richard Hatcher. "They saw it as placing themselves at great risk, financially, politically with the party, lot of reservations." The reticence of black political leaders to alienate the Democratic Party, a traditional source of support, left a vacuum that Jackson seemed a natural to fill. A *Time* feature claimed that "he is the only black leader with the drive and audacity to mount such an extraordinary political campaign." The campaign's symbolic centerpiece was the Rainbow Coalition, which Jackson invoked liberally in public appearances on the trail. With an intellectual lineage dating from the quest by the seminal New Left organization Students for a Democratic Society to fashion an "interracial coalition of the poor" and Martin Luther King's Poor People's Campaign, the Rainbow Coalition envisioned "blacks, Hispanics, Indian and Native Americans, Asians, women, young people, poor people, old people, gay people, laborers, small farmers, small-business persons, peace activists and environmentalists" uniting to become a political majority to defeat Reagan, the Republicans, and the corporate largesse that supported them. Viewed as the "disenfranchised and ignored" by callous Republicans and Democratic "friends" alike, the groups of the Rainbow Coalition shared a common bond.[24]

As the campaign unfolded, Jackson enjoyed better-than-expected fortunes, and the Rainbow Coalition gained rhetorical force. Despite a prevalent view that his candidacy was symbolic, Jackson outlasted a handful of better-capitalized Democratic candidates, including the Ohio senator and former astronaut John Glenn. Ultimately Jackson placed a respectable third to Mondale and the Colorado senator Gary Hart, taking 21 percent of ballots cast in primaries, winning the South Carolina and Virginia primaries, and earning a total of 384 delegates, a number that many agreed would have inflated with fairer Democratic Party rules in a number of state primaries. Jackson himself undermined any further viability and unifying vision with his campaign's biggest blunder. In an off-the-record confidence to a black reporter, he referred to New York City as "Hymietown" and Jews as "Hymies." Though Jackson apologized for the remarks, the response came slowly and encouraged public scrutiny of his record for anti-Semitism. Particularly at issue was the Jackson supporter and Nation of Islam minister Louis Farrakhan's distressingly anti-Semitic tirade that referred to Judaism as a "gutter religion." This episode attracted saturating media attention and widespread criticism that Jackson's disavowal of Farrakhan was insufficient and tardy. Media accounts cited the Jackson-Farrakhan affair as evidence that the relationship between African Americans and Jews, close during the civil rights era, was increasingly strained. The dustup did not bode well for the Rainbow Coalition. Hatcher recalled the "Hymietown" controversy as a negative turning point that placed a ceiling on Jackson's appeal, contending that it was "like somebody dropped an atom bomb right in the middle of our campaign."[25]

Before and after the Democratic convention, observers across the political spectrum questioned the extent to which Jackson succeeded in forging his Rainbow Coalition in reality. His astounding black support, which surged to 85 percent of the overall black vote as the primary season wore on, occasioned characterizations of the coalition as "monochromatic." Leaders of other ethnic constituencies noted a disconnect between the candidate's vision of the Rainbow Coalition and a desire of key campaign staffers to keep it "a black thing." National media were quick to point out his tepid reception from Hispanic voters and his lack of substantial white support, which remained in the single digits throughout the primaries. Though affluent, educated whites could and did hop aboard the Rainbow Coalition bandwagon, the movement had trouble attracting working-class white voters, exposing the classic fault lines of contemporary liberalism.[26]

Still, for those who appraised the Rainbow Coalition in less purely statistical ways, signs of promise abounded. Jackson was the first African American presidential candidate the mainstream Democratic Party establishment took seriously. This earned him a spot at the bargaining table at the national convention, which he opened up to unprecedented minority participation. Managing only 5 percent of the white vote meant that Jackson clearly fell short of creating a legitimate interracial coalition of the "rejected and locked out," but he did make some inroads among white voters, who accounted for more than three-quarters of a million of his 3.4 million overall votes. Though his stronger showing among whites in New York, California, and Massachusetts than in Illinois and Ohio betokened better appeal with upper-class liberals than with blue-collar Democrats, Jackson's message of economic justice illuminated the possibility for a cross-racial alliance along economic lines. This was evident at a Pennsylvania campaign stop, where, eschewing the comforts of a hotel, Jackson and his wife, Jacqueline, spent the night with a white unemployed steelworker and his wife. "This campaign is focused on the concerns of the common people, people who are not visible on the American scene," Jackson told the press, drawing a contrast between the couple hosting the Jacksons and the more celebrated conspicuously consuming yuppies who were beneficiaries of the Reagan recovery. Jackson used the opportunity to redress misconceptions about the country's downtrodden: "Reagan has been able to put color on the face of poverty, but most poor are White women, infants, children and old people." With this comment Jackson took direct aim at Reagan-era America's increasingly potent and callous stereotypes of black welfare queens, arguing for turning the "racial battleground into economic common ground."[27] Though heir to the liberal legacy of Hubert Humphrey and the Great Society, it is impossible to imagine the lackluster Mondale pulling off this feat of empathy with the democratic masses, a forum in which Jackson sparkled. With flourishes such as this, Jackson staked a claim as the conscience of the 1984 Democratic campaign.

This moral vision derived from civil rights–era battles, often led by Jackson's mentor, Martin Luther King. Reflecting on Jackson's legendary ambition, the African American political leader Andrew Young speculated that Jesse felt a special responsibility to live up to King's "moral legacy," though King operated in an era when the liberalism of Presidents Kennedy and Johnson was the mainstream. By contrast, Young observed, "Jesse has had to deal with the likes of Reagan." The Republican president was not the only adversary. In a more conservative age, facing massive budget deficits, hostility to social spending, and renewed Cold War tensions, Jackson's main Democratic rivals, Mondale and Hart, battled to "occupy the dead political center." Though mainstream Democrats patronizingly dismissed Jackson as more adept at oratory than at articulating a tangible program, over the course of the campaign he asserted a consistent agenda. Jackson stood for domestic programs that empowered the various elements of the Rainbow Coalition: job creation and training, enhanced federal aid to education, greater taxes on the wealthy and corporations. These social and economic initiatives were to be financed in part by a 20 percent cut in defense expenditures. This reduced military spending swam against the tide of Reagan's aggressive foreign policy and, in an age when the Cold War was still extant, contradicted what was politically possible for Jackson's Democratic rivals. But this stance complemented Jackson's larger vision of America in the world, including sanctions against South Africa's apartheid regime, greater sensitivity to the aspirations of Third World nations, the cessation of U.S. military intervention in Central America, and equal recognition of the rights of Israelis and Palestinians to a secure homeland. At a time when mainstream Democrats scurried to claim the centrist mantle, one columnist lauded Jackson's efforts to "apply King's insight to the cutthroat electoral arena."[28]

The quest in 1984 paved the way for greater success four years later when Jackson again campaigned for the Democratic nomination. In 1988 a better-organized Jackson campaign amassed the second-highest delegate total, trailing only the eventual candidate, the Massachusetts governor Michael Dukakis. Moreover, Jackson strengthened the Rainbow Coalition's legitimacy with a redoubled effort at garnering white working-class and Hispanic support. Whether renegotiating loans for farmers in Iowa and Missouri, cavorting with the seven-foot-plus pro wrestler Silo Sam at a Teamsters' meeting, or empathizing with struggling Wisconsin autoworkers, Jackson hammered home a message of economic justice that traversed racial and ethnic barriers. This campaign strove to find the "common ground" he invoked more than a dozen times in his memorable address to the Democratic National Convention. Seeking to unify a multicultural and multiracial "quilt" composed of various "patches" of American groups left out by the "reverse Robin Hood" dynamics of Reaganomics, Jackson passionately championed the cause of the working poor with a message of economic populism.[29]

After a strong showing in the primary season's Super Tuesday and a dazzling win in Michigan, Jackson stood out for a brief shining moment as the front-runner for the Democratic nomination. With the possibility that a black candidate might have a legitimate shot, the first in U.S. history, for a major party presidential nomination, the national discourse on the battle for the Democratic nomination pivoted instantly to race. Articles with titles like "Taking Jesse Seriously" and "Why Can't Jesse Be Nominated?" circulated in the national media, reevaluating the "conventional wisdom" that assumed that Jackson could not win the nomination. This was accompanied by hand-wringing about whether the Democratic Party establishment would accept his nomination and by heightened scrutiny of past Jackson bugaboos: his actions in the aftermath of the King assassination, his embrace of the Palestinian Liberation Organization leader Yasser Arafat, his poor accounting of federal funds distributed to Operation PUSH, his relationship with Farrakhan, and the Hymietown controversy. From the Left, critics charged that his image as the self-appointed "national black leader" allowed other Democratic candidates to avoid addressing issues of concern to African Americans.

Jackson was far from the perfect candidate. Still, even in his ultimate defeat and mobilization behind Dukakis's candidacy, as in 1984, Jackson injected the moribund Democratic discussion with progressive moral convictions about economic justice and stopping militaristic, interventionist foreign policy. In doing so, he kept the fire alive for what Howard Dean, a generation later, called the "Democratic wing of the Democratic Party." Additionally, as several observers apprehended at the time, Jackson played an important trailblazing role for future minority candidates. One columnist elegized, "No one who has seen the white hands of farmers and the elderly straining to touch Jackson" could doubt that his campaign would leave the country "less racist than it found it," adding, though, that "Jackson may have to settle for being the one on whose shoulders others stand to climb through."[30]

Talking Back: Community Activism and Cultural Politics

The trajectories of Barry, Washington, and Jackson collectively amount to a moral about the efficacy and the limits of electoral politics. The three pursued their constituencies' needs in an age of dominant conservatism, declining taxpayer appetite for social service expenditures, and the demise of well-paying manufacturing jobs that ongoing deindustrialization wrought. Add to this an urban revitalization movement that gentrified poor and minority neighborhoods, displacing residents, and the result was that black politicians, like white liberals and the Left, were often on the defensive in the 1980s. Accordingly, some of the decade's most potent African American political expressions originated outside of mainstream politics, at the grassroots level of community activism and in the cultural realm.

The Association of Community Organizations for Reform Now (ACORN) started in Little Rock, Arkansas, in 1970. Building on the National Welfare Rights Organization's work, it helped welfare recipients attain basic needs and made strategic alliances with the working poor. ACORN continued to grow under challenging conditions, expanding into a national organization with chapters in twenty-six states. By the 1980s it encompassed such initiatives as affordable housing, voter registration, and resisting intrusive urban renewal projects, as well as concerns over crime, police, and neighborhood safety. Though ACORN explicitly avoided a racial focus, opting to frame issues along lines of economic interests that could unite poor and working-class people regardless of race, its emphasis on the urban poor nevertheless ensured a large black constituency. This ultimately included significant representation of people of color among its leadership. Though in the 1980s ACORN ventured into electoral politics, establishing political action committees and adding a potent "insider game" to its repertoire, it remained able and willing to mobilize more militant direct action tactics. These included a widespread urban squatting campaign and the establishment of "Reagan ranches" that protested the administration's heavy military budget and paltry social spending and symbolized rampant homelessness. ACORN also pursued alliances with like-minded organizations and movements, joining Jackson's Rainbow Coalition and assisting his campaign, and forging links with opponents of Central American intervention and with the disarmament movement.[31]

If ACORN represented community organizing's potential as a national political force, Boston's Dudley Street Neighborhood Initiative (DSNI) illustrated the local impact of neighborhood-based grassroots activism. Unlike ACORN, the multicultural DSNI embraced racial and ethnic identity, providing for adequate representation in its governance for all the neighborhood's major groups: black, white, Latino, and Cape Verdean. Beginning in the mid-1980s with a Don't Dump on Us campaign to clean up the neighborhood's thirteen hundred vacant lots, remove abandoned vehicles, and eradicate putrid illegal trash transfer stations, the still active DSNI galvanized community support and spirit and achieved a major highlight that demonstrated the potency of bottom-up organizing, crafting a comprehensive plan for neighborhood revitalization that was subsequently adopted by the city. The organization's Sarah Flint enthusiastically touted community activism's efficacy as compared with simply voting for representative officials: "It is something to be a registered voter. But when you actually exercise those rights . . . and get things done you find out, yes, there is definitely something to doing advocacy work." And she added, "You don't know unless you try if you can accomplish anything." At its most effective, local, issue-oriented community activism led to changes in the mainstream political culture, as in the boisterous direct action protests of Philadelphia's Tenant Action Group, which created a climate of political engagement that contributed to greater representation of African Americans in the city's decision-making positions, including the elections of three black mayors. But amid larger structural forces, community organizing in the 1980s had its limits. Despite some successes in leveraging gains in health care, education, housing, and job training, community groups swam against the frequently overwhelming tides of urban disinvestment and the withdrawal of federal dollars.[32]

For this reason, during the 1980s African Americans seized upon the cultural arena as the most viable place to pursue political claims and to articulate a wide-ranging agenda. The decade's literary scene foregrounded a highly visible collection of women writers, led by Toni Morrison, Alice Walker, Gloria Naylor, and Toni Cade Bambara, whose fiction voiced aspects of black women's experiences that rarely found a wide public forum. Their protagonists journeyed through narratives of historical discrimination, incest, inner-city deterioration, sexual awakening, healing and spirituality, and self-determination. Though it is notoriously difficult to measure the ability of cultural artifacts to transform social and political life, the accomplishments of these writers in terms of commercial success, literary acclaim, and reaching white "crossover" audiences with themes of black history, experience, and struggle undoubtedly enhanced the profile of African Americans. They communicated a subjectivity and complexity about black lives—particularly black women's lives—that was conspicuously absent from the damning tales of welfare queens and the demeaning diatribes of underclass victimization that abounded in the media.

The decade also witnessed the appearance of a pack of black filmmakers airing "authentic" black experience for wider consumption. Whereas the 1970s "blaxploitation" films featured urban antiheroes waging extralegal resistance against racist oppression, in the 1980s, black directors including Spike Lee, John Singleton, and the brothers Albert and Allen Hughes emerged to share their visions. Films like *Boyz n the Hood, New Jack City, Menace II Society,* and *Straight Out of Brooklyn* reached black communities but also capitalized on the voyeuristic cravings of white crossover audiences for a glimpse of life on black urban America's mean streets. These films outstripped commercial expectations, producing high profit-to-cost ratios that pleased the studios responsible for their distribution. To achieve this success, the films widely deployed what one observer termed the "ghettocentric imagination." This was a way of representing the experiences of urban black youths that mobilized familiar elements of the media's underclass frame—drugs, street crime, dislocated families, police oppression, hip-hop music—but inflected them with more complex and personal representations of lived experience in the ghetto.[33] In other words, black filmmakers used these films to represent their constraints and their aspirations in their own voices.

Though sharing elements of the "ghetto action cycle" films, Spike Lee's work stands out for its cinematic sophistication, conversance with black history, and ability to represent diverse perspectives on race and politics. Lee's *Do the Right Thing* (1989) offered a particularly complex and penetrating examination of race relations at decade's end. With this film Lee claimed a place in the black filmmaking tradition alongside the legendary early-twentieth-century director Oscar Micheaux, combining a sense of racial pride with a willingness to expose the less admirable characters within black communities—from Micheaux's preacher con men and traitorous servants to Lee's comically materialistic black nationalists and uncommitted fathers. Drawing creative inspiration from the racially explosive tragedies that were liberally sprinkled through New York City's public life in the 1980s, *Do the Right Thing* explores a landscape of racial tension while remaining deliberately ambiguous about what actually constitutes the "right thing." Tellingly, the film's climax pivots on a clash of cultural politics as the neighborhood's black youths mount a rowdy demonstration, fueled by Public Enemy's "Fight the Power" on a blaring boom box, to protest the lack of African American sports heroes on the Wall of Fame at the white-owned Sal's Pizzeria. With superior acting and a memorable ending featuring racial conflagration and contrasting epigrams from Martin Luther King and Malcolm X, the film offered black viewers competing models for coping with America's racial predicament and warned whites about the persistence of toxic racial sentiments in the post–civil rights era. "What I hoped was that it would provoke everybody, white and black," Lee remarked. Given this agenda, the film garnered generally positive reviews and sparked intense controversy, leaving viewers debating its significance. The *Chicago Tribune*'s Clarence Page testified to the film's value: "Lee may ruffle feathers with this film but he also provides a tremendous public service. With his candid account of interracial issues our society is often too timid to face he offers a powerful [story] about the course we are taking as a society, unless we do the right thing."[34] The warning Page identified in *Do the Right Thing* proved prescient and resonated equally through the era's ghettocentric musical offerings.

No cultural expression emanating from black America in the 1980s detonated as loudly or as contentiously as rap music. Originating in downtrodden 1970s New York City area neighborhoods, and interwoven with a set of distinctive related forms including hip-hop "break beat" DJs, break dancing, and graffiti, by the 1980s rap emerged as hip-hop culture's most pervasive element. Public Enemy pioneered the exploitation of rap's political potential with the seminal albums *It Takes a Nation of Millions to Hold Us Back* and *Fear of a Black Planet*. The group's militant social commentary consciously placed itself in a tradition of black resistance, with lyrics referencing historic figures from Marcus Garvey and Malcolm X to Rosa Parks and Nelson Mandela. In the late 1980s the postindustrial "fortress city" of Los Angeles spawned gangsta rap, a genre that dominated the waning years of the Reagan presidency and the Bush administration. Gangsta rap employed harder rhymes and slower cadences than had earlier rappers, producing a West

Coast feel. Though critics zealously, sometimes accurately, lambasted gangsta rap as glorifying violent "gangbanging," or gang activity, and misogynistic sexuality, often these appraisals assessed the music too hastily and literally, with little reference to its place within black cultural traditions. The cultural historian Robin D. G. Kelley explained, for instance, that the boastfulness of gangsta rap was rooted in long-standing cultural traditions—from the coded sexuality of early-twentieth-century bluesmen to the "baaadmen tales of the late nineteenth century" and the "age-old tradition of signifying," all involving a quintessentially African American "playfulness with language." Gangsta rap's misogyny ranged from combative to casual, from "kids talking dirty after having to be serious in school all day" to the truly chilling. Even *Essence*, while ostensibly lauding hip-hop's vitality as a way to make sense of circumstances for African Americans, conceded the problem of its sexism.[35]

Though family values politicians predictably vilified rap, they bypassed its trenchant critique of postindustrial urban society and the conditions faced by African American youths in the 'hood. Recurrent themes included police oppression, denial of access to the public space, and an assumption of the criminality of black urban youth. Ice T/Body Count's "Cop Killer" and N.W.A.'s "Fuck tha Police" represented the apex of deliberate provocation, sparking public outrage and calls for censorship. Yet both detailed a chronic history of routine police harassment of black youths, racial profiling, and violence for sport that— until the widely broadcast videotaped beating of Rodney King by the Los Angeles police in 1991—had escaped national consciousness outside the black community. To the uninitiated, familiar only with the incendiary titles, the two tracks seemed like riotous incitement to violence, but those who bothered to listen could discern more. "Fuck tha Police" used a framing device consisting of a courtroom trial, with members of N.W.A. providing testimony to create a fantasy where street justice prevails as official law enforcement proves morally bankrupt. Asked in an interview whether "Cop Killer" glorified killing cops, Ice T responded that the record doesn't say "Let's go cop killing . . . Let's put our shit on, let's all go out tonight and do it," arguing instead that the song is about a character, "a psychopath that's had enough." He underscored the song's legitimacy as a cultural expression offering a window into his community's experience of oppressive police treatment, combining a classic free speech argument with a call to social justice: "Why all this protest about a record that *speaks* about killing cops and not protest against the cops killing kids out there in the streets?" When the 1992 Los Angeles riots erupted after an all-white jury acquitted the police officers responsible for King's beating, Ice T expressed vindication for his artistic representations of the attitudes of Los Angeles's South Central neighborhood: "My answer to what happened [in the riots] is 'Refer to album 3, track 5.' What do I think about the police? See album 4, track 2." Though this assessment contradicted his claim that his songs' narrators represented characters rather than his own unfiltered perspective, Ice T's remark exemplified how the era's most potent and politicized statements occurred outside of mainstream politics. Responding to economic constraints, a conservative offensive, and limited gains within electoral politics, African Americans used hip-hop and the cultural realm to thrust ideas and messages into the public consciousness. For those listening carefully enough, these messages contained the pulse of black aspirations talking back to the stereotype of underclass pathology. As Ice T observed, "No one lives in the ghetto by choice. Go to school, build your brain. Escape the killing fields. That's what the whole shit is about."[36]

7

FIGHTING THE BACKLASH
The Many Paths of Feminism

To young women enmeshed in the headiest days of the 1970s women's liberation movement, the future looked bright. A wholesale transformation of American institutions and society toward a fairer, more egalitarian order appeared possible. The National Organization for Women (NOW) and other groups of second-wave feminists enjoyed success in efforts to promote enforcement of the anti-job-discrimination provisions of the Civil Rights Act of 1964. Feminists were broadening social awareness of violence against women, filling the gap in services for the victims by opening rape crisis centers and battered women's shelters. Women appeared in public life in a variety of nontraditional occupations, widening a national discussion of women's appropriate roles and potential achievements. The Supreme Court's landmark 1973 decision in *Roe v. Wade* affirmed that women who chose to seek abortions could avail themselves of a constitutionally protected right to privacy. And though never actually burning bras, as popular accounts professed, the women's liberation movement engaged in a massive cultural project of redefining women's worth beyond postwar society's emphasis on physical appearance and domesticity.

By the early 1990s the landscape had changed. Stagnation and even evidence of backsliding abounded. The Equal Rights Amendment (ERA), favored in the 1970s by a majority of Americans of both sexes, swiftly approved by Congress, and rapidly embraced by enough states to seemingly make eventual ratification a matter of time, was confined to the dead letter office of American public and political life. Accounts surfaced in the morning newspapers, scholarly literature, and mass-circulation periodicals alike, bearing such hand-wringing titles as "The Failure of Feminism," "The Post-Feminist Generation," and "Who Stole Feminism?" It would be difficult to walk into a bookstore without bumping up against a display of Susan Faludi's mega-bestseller *Backlash: The Undeclared War Against American Women*, which chronicled the counterattack on feminism in politics, popular culture, the mainstream media, and fashion. Even high-minded public television took notice: PBS's *Firing Line* aired a debate on the topic "Resolved: That the Women's Movement Has Been Disastrous." On the afternoon drive home, commuters could hear the rising talk radio superstar Rush Limbaugh proclaiming that "feminism was established to allow unattractive women easier access to the mainstream" and raving about "feminazis." This state of affairs left many wondering what became of the bright future and expansive horizons that 1970s feminism and the women's movement promised, and it raised the question "What happened to the movement in the 1980s?"

The complex answer starts with a piece of inescapable historical context. The women's movement was subject to the same conservative forces that pervaded the rest of American life in the 1980s. Time ran out on the ERA as the ten-year ratification period for congressional passage of a proposed constitutional amendment expired under a heavy onslaught of anti-ERA organizing in key states. Conservative state lawmakers diligently chipped away at abortion rights protections, staking out limits on *Roe v. Wade* as the rising influence of Republican appointments to the federal judiciary under Presidents Reagan and Bush asserted itself. These legalistic wranglings took place against an ever more violent backdrop, where pro-life extremists bombed and torched clinics. A potent New Right movement in American politics loudly battled to reverse the gains of feminism, to turn back the tide of sexual liberation and reinforce "traditional" patriarchal households. In this effort, the New Right was abetted by a president it adored and helped elect, whose social mores were rooted in a vision of small-town America that predated the convulsions of the 1960s. A groundswell of journalistic reportage purported to expose the bittersweet ironies and unintended negative consequences of the women's movement, while popular culture dramatized the human costs of these mixed blessings.

Yet despite conservatism's ascendancy in national politics, the women's movement continued to make gains in less-trumpeted strata of American life. Though the ERA breathed its dying gasps at the beginning of the decade, this setback released women's activism to follow a variety of paths. What appeared to media observers—with a varying range of degrees of wishful thinking—as the women's movement's ultimate defeat represented merely its fragmentation. Feminists quickly regrouped and made gains in politics, the workplace, and, more quietly, a wide range of institutions within American life. Where 1970s women's liberationists drew on the 1960s New Left's radicalism and created public spectacles of direct action protest, in the 1980s women's activism tended toward stealth. Incrementally but inexorably, women institutionalized their radicalism, capitalizing on the expanded occupational vistas that the women's movement had opened up to fill the gaps in services for women. Increasingly they worked within mainstream institutions to infuse them with a gender-conscious point of view and advance a feminist agenda. Far from beating a hasty retreat, feminism operated under the radar, using an approach that one feminist scholar christened "unobtrusive mobilization."[1]

Working within male-dominated institutions and dependent on them for funding and for their livelihood, women who used unobtrusive mobilization were constrained to adopt less confrontational methods. They infused public discussions with language and ideas that promoted greater understanding of women's perspectives and worked from within institutions to exert greater influence and open them up to feminist concerns. These subtle challenges to institutional norms rarely made headlines; they were a far cry from women liberationists' crowning a sheep Miss America and disrupting the 1968 pageant. Nevertheless, unobtrusive mobilization helped women wield influence in an array of sectors and on a variety of issues, from politics to religious life, athletics to academe, the military to the judiciary, job discrimination to rape crisis centers, comparable worth to sexual harassment. Given the era's conservative momentum, often this added up not to monumental gains in women's status, but rather to defending the hard-won gains of the previous decade in a gritty war of position. At decade's end, one such defense, the abortion rights campaign, renewed the activist spirit and demonstrated that traditional mass mobilization was not dead, but rather more like a slumbering giant, easily awoken, existing alongside the decade's subtler forms of activism.

Post-ERA = "Postfeminist"?

At the 1980s outset, led by the flagship organization NOW, the ERA fight commanded the bulk of feminist energies. What began in the 1970s as a quest to legalize a seemingly self-evident principle—the full text of the proposed amendment read "Equality of rights under the law shall not be denied or abridged by the United States or by any state on account of sex"—had lost considerable steam with the emergence of a potent and organized opposition that infamously raised the specter of unisex bathrooms and the end of Boy Scouts and Girl Scouts. More seriously, the anti-ERA forces warned of the erosion of traditional protections for women, such as conjugal rights, alimony, and child support, and stoked fears of gay marriage and a military draft for women. Still more damaging, opponents successfully linked the ERA to the highly divisive abortion issue, contending that ratification would lead to compulsory federal funding for abortions. The pushback was led by the charismatic and energetic Phyllis Schlafly, Stop ERA founder and spearhead of the "pro-family" Eagle Forum conservative interest group. Told of feminists' efforts to reintroduce the ERA in Congress upon its 1982 expiration, Schlafly gloated that the proposal was "dead now and forever in this century" and sent out invitations for a victory party. By contrast, NOW's president, Eleanor Smeal, predicted that the setback would make women redouble their efforts and "fuel the continuing fight for women's equality."[2]

Initially, proponents of the defeated amendment devoted energy to reintroducing the ERA and talked loudly about political retribution for opponents. Kathy Wilson, chair of the National Women's Political Caucus, identified a "dirty dozen" legislators, many of whom were Democrats, who blocked ratification at the state level. Smeal was more pointed and partisan, suggesting that it was Republicans who had "deserted women's rights," removing the ERA from their platform in 1980 and leading the charge against it in 1982. Within two weeks congressional supporters reintroduced the measure, with the Democratic senator Edward Kennedy calling its "temporary defeat" a "national disgrace." The Republican senator Bob Packwood waxed philosophical, placing the ERA among a long line of civil liberties measures that make slow but sure marches to fruition, while public opinion polls still registered majority support with the American public. But supporters and detractors alike realized that nothing was likely to happen soon.[3]

In truth, the ERA's momentum had crested before the 1980s even started. Though thirty-five of the necessary thirty-eight states ratified the proposed amendment by 1977, by the 1982 expiration date the measure still fell three states short. Worse yet, a handful of states even repealed their ratification amid negative media coverage and opponents' organizing efforts. Even staunch advocates who immediately reintroduced the ERA conceded that passage would take ten to fifteen years, since convincing state legislators to flip votes loomed difficult amid antifeminist backlash. What really animated supporters was changing the political landscape itself. From the ashes of defeat rose a blueprint for women's political power. In the states that NOW targeted in its failed last-ditch effort for ratification, women's support for the amendment ran more than two-thirds, while a majority of men opposed the measure. In the fifteen states that never ratified the ERA, 79 percent of women legislators but only 39 percent of their male colleagues cast pro-ERA votes.[4] The obvious implication: rather than spending time and energy on arduous campaigns of moral suasion, women ought to dedicate themselves to electing more women candidates whose sympathies were more likely to align with their aspirations. This held true for a range of issues, from the ERA, to reforming discriminatory Social Security statutes and insurance industry practices, to the decade's most contentious issue: abortion rights. Pro-ERA women's soul-searching postmortem produced a conviction that electoral politics represented the next front.

From the dark clouds of the ERA ratification campaign's "disgraceful defeat," feminists seized upon a silver lining. Led by NOW, whose membership boasted a quarter of a million members and a $13 million budget, they had honed a sizable political base. Since state lawmakers were instrumental in the ERA's defeat—often bucking popular sentiment in casting their votes—electing more sympathetic state legislators ranked high on the list of immediate concerns. Lynn Taborsak, a Connecticut NOW coordinator, echoed the sentiments of many, stating bluntly, "We will only back public officials who will give full consideration to our issues." Though those prospective officials theoretically could be male or female, she outlined a plan to "dramatically increase the number of women in elected office" in the hopes of providing extra security that women's issues would receive priority. Characterizing this as a prerequisite for a renewed ERA push, Taborsak and her colleagues laid out a strategy of decentralization, looking toward state judiciaries to remedy sex discrimination. In the wake of the ERA's failed ratification, Koryne Horbal, a founder of the Democratic National Committee's Women's Caucus, returned to grassroots organizing in her home state of Minnesota, right down to the level of the state's four thousand precincts. Horbal's goal was to elect legislators with a feminist stance on the issues, particularly a pro-choice position on abortion. Her vehicle consisted of an educational wing called Project 13 and a political wing called Campaign 13, with thirteen representing the number of states necessary to block a proposed constitutional amendment, such as the proposed antiabortion measure for which conservative forces were mobilizing. Campaign 13 exemplified the defensive mode into which 1980s feminist organizing efforts were often channeled.[5]

New national organizing efforts complemented these grassroots campaigns. Vowing "We'll remember in November," NOW responded to the ERA setback by raising more than $2 million in a fund-raising drive to elect political candidates favorable to feminist issues and to oust opponents. The political action committee (PAC) established itself as NOW's preferred vehicle, unleashing a campaign that created forty-six new PACs in twenty-seven states for a total of more than eighty of these committees nationally by the 1982 elections. At its annual convention NOW outlined a familiar agenda that consisted of protecting reproductive rights and anti-job-discrimination efforts. But it also displayed increasing savvy about the way the Washington game was played. NOW courted controversy by shunning moderate Republican women, even those with pro-women's-rights track records, in races against comparable Democratic men. NOW reasoned that Republican support for Reaganomics drained programs that benefited women, such as affirmative action, women's equity initiatives in education, and various welfare programs.[6]

The growing emphasis on electoral activism radiated far beyond NOW. The National Women's Political Caucus and the National Abortion Rights Action League (NARAL) got into the PAC game as well, with NARAL claiming victory for 70 percent of the 186 candidates it supported, including replacing six anti-choice incumbents in the U.S. House of Representatives with pro-choice Democrats. The political mobilization expanded beyond explicitly feminist groups. Organizations from the Business and Professional Women to the American Nurses Association formed PACs, reflecting what *BusinessWeek* identified as a desire for enhanced clout as women moved up in the professional world's pecking order. A growing contingent of women realized that the mounting professional gains feminism catalyzed were starting to generate the economic resources necessary to leverage political power. One Minnesota businesswoman remarked that in the past, candidates assumed that women "don't give money because we're cheap," but she observed that with swelling ranks of women candidates, "it's a relatively new thing for women to be actively sought." A Pittsburgh women's campaign fund-raiser explained the growing momentum for female candidates: "I don't hear any male candidates today talking about day care or housing ownership for women."[7]

The escalating power of women's political mobilization asserted itself that November. Nineteen eighty-two marked the beginning of feminist women's deepening engagement with mainstream politics, a phenomenon epitomized by the emergence of Emily's List in 1985. Surmising that a critical element in the Missouri Democratic senatorial challenger Harriett Woods's razor-thin 1982 loss to the incumbent, John Danforth, was a lack of money at the campaign's outset, the philanthropist Ellen Malcolm launched a donor network designed to fund pro-choice Democratic women candidates. She called her invention Emily's List, an acronym for her recipe for political success—"Early Money Is Like Yeast." Malcolm crafted a national fund-raising juggernaut, capitalizing on the "missionary zeal" of a growing pool of politically active women. The idea was to become political power brokers, creating a network of donors who, taking advantage of campaign finance loopholes, could write checks directly to recommended candidates, then "bundle" their contributions through Emily's List. To hone and refine the network, women held get-togethers across the country, bringing their address books to add potential new donors in what one described as "the ultimate Tupperware Party." Among Emily's List's notable successes, in 1986 Maryland's Barbara Mikulski received 20 percent of her funds from the network, becoming the first Democratic woman to be elected senator in twenty-six years. Reflecting on women's increasing political potency and strategic sophistication, Mikulski remarked, "You're seeing the maturation of a lot of work. There are no shortcuts to power for us."[8]

"Gerry! Gerry!"

No episode so symbolized women's enhanced role in politics as the groundbreaking 1984 vice presidential bid of Geraldine Ferraro. The three-term Queens, New York, congresswoman from Archie Bunker's district encapsulated feminist political aspirations. Ironically, Ferraro herself, a veteran of Beltway intrigue by the time of her selection, also echoed the skepticism some women voiced about whether the time to grasp power had really arrived. Conferring with colleagues the summer before Walter Mondale offered her the number two spot on the ticket, the subject of a woman Democratic vice presidential nominee arose, and Ferraro opined, "There's no way any presidential candidate is going to choose a woman as a running mate unless he's fifteen points behind in the polls."[9] A year later, a Gallup poll at the time of Ferraro's selection showed Mondale trailing President Reagan by only seven points.

The Ferraro choice sparked feverish media attention. *Time* proclaimed the end of "a political taboo of two centuries' standing" that left a woman "an election away from being a heartbeat away" from the presidency. *Newsweek* ran a twenty-five-page special report documenting all aspects of how Mondale "popped a dramatic question" to the "frosted blond." To be fair, the hokey references to the candidate's sex and the gender anxiety they betokened did not begin and end with the press, but were shared by politicians and the American public. On the campaign trail, digging for southern votes, Ferraro suffered a query from the Mississippi agriculture commissioner about her blueberry muffin baking capabilities. With a shrewd knack for balancing feminism and feminity, Ferraro remarked, "He probably never met a female vice-presidential candidate before." That the "Ferraro Factor" occasioned media frenzy did not hinge solely on the candidate's gender. After all, the 1970s and 1980s witnessed the rise of such prominent women leaders as Great Britain's Margaret Thatcher and

India's Indira Gandhi. But as the feminist icon and *Ms.* magazine founder Gloria Steinem pointed out, no one identified Thatcher or Gandhi as "transforming politics" by "bringing women and women's cultural values into the electoral system."[10] Ferraro's significance revolved around her connection to feminism. Though some feminists questioned the ardor of her commitment to the cause, they also speculated that this represented a conscious political strategy to maintain a public distance from the movement. To most observers at both ends of the political spectrum she coded as feminist on the strength of her pro-equality outlook and her stand on the abortion issue.

An Italian American and a Catholic, forced to articulate her position on a critical and controversial topic, Ferraro underscored her personal opposition to abortion and her public policy support of choice. To support her stance, she often raised the prospect of a rape resulting in pregnancy. Drawing on her real-life experiences of sexual violence in the Special Victims Bureau of the Queens District Attorney's Office, Ferraro had personalized the issue in a congressional vote on loosening restrictions on federal funding for abortion by asking lawmakers, "If your wife or sister or daughter were raped or became pregnant, would you not give her the right to make her own decision?" One formidable institution that answered this question in the negative was the Catholic Church. As a pro-choice woman candidate from a Catholic background, Ferraro aroused special ire. The New York archbishop John O'Connor clashed famously with her over a letter she penned two years previously, which noted that a diversity of positions on abortion existed among Catholics. O'Connor, claiming that Ferraro had suggested that the Catholic Church allowed multiple positions, derided her publicly, almost certainly costing the Democratic ticket votes among Catholics. In addition to what amounted to a stalemate with O'Connor, antiabortion protesters and hecklers consistently accompanied Ferraro's 1984 campaign stops, sometimes with the threat of violence. Despite receiving treatment not encountered by male pro-choice candidates, including Vice President George Bush, who supported abortion rights in certain circumstances, Ferraro resolutely defended the separation of church and state. She responded to attacks on her faith and religion, turning the tables on political opponents by questioning President Reagan's qualifications as a "good Christian" in light of his devastating cuts to health and social programs that benefited women and the poor. Her criticism of a popular president occasioned a minor drubbing in the media, but to many the episode reflected Ferraro's toughness and determination to speak her mind on the campaign trail.[11]

More than her pro-choice credentials linked Ferraro to feminism. Her acceptance speech at the 1984 Democratic National Convention highlighted equal pay, affirmative action, and the ERA as goals worthy of energy and commitment. If Ferraro's candidacy gave wider voice to the feminist agenda, it was also true that the women's movement helped make possible Ferraro the candidate. Her ascent to the vice presidential nomination paralleled women's vast inroads into the professions, including politics, since the 1960s. Concerns about gender and feminism suffused media coverage of Ferraro's every step, epitomized by the brouhaha that erupted over the financial dealings of her husband, John Zaccaro. As Ferraro first promised to release the couple's tax documents, then reneged, media criticism mounted. The conservative columnist George Will wryly suggested that this hesitancy "may mean he has not paid that much in taxes." Confronting Will on *This Week with David Brinkley*, Ferraro assured the public that proper documentation would be released and suggested that Will would have to apologize. When Ferraro proved right, Will sent her a dozen roses and a note: "Has anyone ever told you that you are cute when you are mad?" to which she replied, "Vice Presidents are not cute." Ferraro's forceful yet graceful battle against sexist expectations earned wide admiration. Upon release of her husband's tax information, Ferraro graciously endured a marathon one-and-a-half-hour press conference, delivering a "bravura performance." Her aplomb in patiently answering even the most irritating questions drew the ultimate praise: comparisons to Ronald Reagan's ease with the media. Though some chafed at Ferraro's nasal Queens accent, and President Reagan's chief pollster, Richard Wirthlin, called her "abrasive," he conceded her status as a "historical celebrity," noting that supporters and detractors alike "applaud the fact that one more barrier has been broken."[12]

Ferraro's dual fight, for women in politics and for the Democrats, was again on display in the widely anticipated vice presidential debate with George Bush. Media speculation viewed Ferraro's foreign policy inexperience as a liability, but she managed to hold her own. She lambasted the Reagan administration for its lack of action on arms control and its cuts to spending on the poor. In a key exchange, Bush attempted to distinguish between the Reagan administration's handling of the recent bombing of the U.S. embassy in Lebanon and the Iran hostage crisis under the Democratic president Jimmy Carter. "Let me help you with the difference, Mrs. Ferraro, between Iran and the embassy in Lebanon . . ." Bush began, with what *Time* labeled an "ill-chosen tone of condescension." Ferraro forcefully retorted that she resented Bush's "patronizing attitude that you have to teach me about foreign policy." Though mainstream media scored the overall debate as a draw or a slight Bush victory, the consensus held that this was Ferraro's strongest moment. Bush's subsequent bravado, telling a New Jersey longshoremen's union "We tried to kick a little ass last night," played off the campaign's gender dynamics. Though Bush pointed out that the comment wasn't for public consumption and maintained that "the idea that there's some kind of conspiracy against her and the feminist thing is absolutely absurd," he avoided dissuading his staff from distributing KICK ASS GEORGE buttons. The Reagan campaign manager Edward Rollins commented, "It's a macho game we play," a quip that hinted at an intentional strategy directed at Ferraro.[13]

In the wake of Reagan's mammoth victory, pundits scuttled to assess the meaning of Ferraro's candidacy. Running against an incumbent who had revived the economy and restored a sense of patriotism to many Americans, Mondale sought a game-changer in the electoral calculus: the first woman on a major party ticket. In the end, though, Ferraro's presence amounted to an electoral wash. The flak over her husband's finances and the wrath of antiabortion forces likely cost the Democratic ticket as many votes as were added by the way she energized the electorate. Despite Ferraro's trailblazing, the aphorism that people vote the top of the ticket in presidential politics endured. As a Cleveland policeman gushed, "Ferraro is one hell of a lady. I just wish we could have Reagan with her." This ambivalent comment illustrated the era's growing sense of politics as entertainment, a cult of personality in which Reagan's affability trumped Mondale's lackluster charisma, often regardless of ideology. Ferraro, too, had demonstrated star quality on the campaign trail, regularly outdrawing Mondale and confidently working crowds of admirers who cheered, "Gerry! Gerry!" Though she shattered a potent cultural myth that women could not endure the stress of a national campaign, one woman reporter noted a more specific reaction to her speeches: "It is the feminist lines that win the biggest applause."[14]

The Ferraro moment's significance, as supporters from all fifty states and more than sixty foreign countries testified in letters to the candidate, lay in its impact on individual women. A Republican woman from Alabama not only declared that she could not have been any prouder had Ferraro been the GOP candidate, she compared the vice presidential run to a "first step on the moon" for American women. Furthermore, she explored Ferraro's treatment in the media, claiming that disproportionate attention to the candidate's husband's finances and her views on abortion represented public anxiety about a woman ascending to unattained heights in the male domain of national presidential politics. Proclaiming that Ferraro epitomized what politicians should be, Idahoan women wrote of their pride and admiration for her integrity and intellectual fervor, but also of her "fierce loyalty" and compassion for those who "need the most and have the least" amid Reagan's slashed social spending programs. These comments reveal Ferraro as a new kind of candidate who combined traditional male political attributes with feminine sensibilities and values. Another Idaho woman thanked Ferraro for her pathbreaking contribution and the hope it sparked in American women, contending, "I know now that we will progress much more rapidly in the next decade and others to follow, because with your nomination we finally and firmly have our foot in the door!" The enthusiasm over Ferraro's re-enchantment of politics stretched to the usually Republican plains of Kansas, where women supporters praised her "composure" in the vice presidential debate and the way she handled herself in the campaign generally, which was "better than most of the men running." An insurance agent conceded that although her politics were no longer as liberal as when she campaigned for Eugene McCarthy in the 1960s, her pride at voting for a woman surpassed all other elections. A University of Kansas language professor expressed gratitude to Ferraro for inspiring her to transcend what she had assumed to be the professional limits of her career. "My female colleagues and I never cease to be amazed at how you have altered our perceptions of ourselves," she wrote. "It has never happened in our adult lifetimes that we derive such pride from a public figure."[15]

Internationally, women concurred, sending their appreciation for Ferraro, often laced with their national and global concerns. An Indian woman praised Ferraro's courage and applauded her pioneering spirit, suggesting that her slogan should be "equality for the better half." Then, echoing a common global concern about Reagan-era nuclear escalation, she concluded, "Fair sex rule can give peace to a world which is on the verge of disaster." A Costa Rican woman addressed Ferraro as "Dear Heroine" and implored her to expose the "TRAGIC FALLACY" of Reagan's militarism in Central America and to stop the region's deadly wars. An Iranian woman, distraught about repression by "fanatical fascistic" religious elements in her home country, hailed Ferraro as a "surrogate" of women in the United States and "of the Earth," urging her not to forget "the women of the world."[16]

Despite the Ferraro campaign's wide-ranging appeal, its immediate aftermath yielded only mixed results concerning women's increased role in national politics. Though backlash observers claimed that women were "demoralized by Ferraro's public drubbing," a longer view suggests that this was a temporary phenomenon soon followed by a resumption of women's progress. Between the elections of 1980 and 1992, the election that marked the end of the Reagan-Bush era, the number of women in the U.S. House of Representatives more than doubled, expanding from twenty-one to forty-eight. The tally of woman senators held steady at two throughout the decade, doubling to four in the 1990 election and increasing to seven in 1992, including Carol Moseley-Braun as the first African American woman senator. Moreover, where Democrats and Republicans had been in close parity among women in Congress at the beginning of the 1980s, by 1992 three-quarters of U.S. congresswomen and five out of seven women senators were Democrats. The decade saw the emergence of a trio of California Democratic women who continue to impact national politics—Diane Feinstein, Barbara Boxer, and Nancy Pelosi, who ultimately became the first woman Speaker of the House. The number of women state legislators stood at fewer than 800 nationally in 1980 and rose to 1,270 by decade's end, an increase of 37 percent. In the 1970s two women governors were the first elected who had not followed their husbands to office, and through the election of 1990 six new women governors won election in their states. Such success belies the decade's reputation as an epoch of retreat for women and illustrates women's shifting strategies from the confrontational feminist battles of the 1970s to a quieter, perhaps even more efficacious, focus on "capacity building."[17] This marshaling of resources for the long haul, to create and expand institutions capable of advancing women's goals, surfaced not only in politics but throughout public life.

The Myth of Decline and Unobtrusive Mobilization

If Ferraro's story represented a high point for women in the 1980s, progress usually asserted itself in much quieter ways. The story of efforts to describe, define, and campaign against sexual harassment illustrates how feminist initiatives did not simply wither amid the well-documented backlash, but typically found subtler means to advance the cause. The term "sexual harassment" did not even exist until 1975, when it was coined to promote a "speak-out" about the issue of "sexual exploitation of women on the job." Creating this new language for the unwanted advances that generations of women workers had endured was made possible by the insights of the feminist movement, which ushered in a sea change in rethinking sexual interactions in the workplace through the lens of power. Grassroots feminist groups succeeded in raising awareness in the late 1970s, to the point where the Equal Employment Opportunity Commission (EEOC) adopted a set of guidelines regarding sexual harassment in the workplace. Chaired by Eleanor Holmes Norton, a black feminist who had cut her political teeth with the seminal 1960s civil rights organization the Student Nonviolent Coordinating Committee, the EEOC defined sexual harassment as "unwelcome sexual advances, requests for sexual favors, and other verbal or physical conduct of a sexual nature" that affect the conditions of employment or decisions regarding employment of an individual. Drawing on the feminist-influenced ideas of Lin Farley and Catharine MacKinnon, the EEOC further stated that sexual harassment also exists when such conduct interferes with work performance or creates an "intimidating, hostile, or offensive working environment." Still, as the 1980s opened, sexual harassment was contested social terrain, with a multiplicity of viewpoints in play among the American public. Surveys revealed that sexual harassment in the office was "as common as the coffee break," with anywhere between 42 percent and 70 percent of women reporting having experienced some form of the behavior. Yet the studies also pointed to a chasm between the sexes on the issue. A landmark *Redbook* magazine–*Harvard Business Review* study of two thousand executives presented fourteen scenarios of sexual situations in the workplace, finding men far more likely not to view them as harassment. Many Americans, especially men, subscribed to attitudes such as those of the executive who rationalized that "a compliment in the mind of one person is harassment in that of another," or the bank officer who lamented the EEOC guidelines as "government snoopervision."[18] Comments such as this evoked the threat that men perceived to a deeply embedded form of male play, a prerogative that expressed power and reinforced hierarchy.

The EEOC was ahead of the courts on this issue. The federal judiciary was just starting to address the matter in the late 1970s, its early rulings displaying a distinct "lack of judicial empathy." Sociologists contended that the courts' initial rulings did little to alter the traditional "there's no harm in asking" view toward sexual propositions. Grassroots feminist organizations had begun to make their mark in the movement against sexual harassment by the early 1980s, often through professionalizing their activities. Working Women's Institute, a pioneering group in defining and raising consciousness in the 1970s, partnered with Bell Telephone to develop and institute sexual harassment training programs. Lin Farley, a veteran of radical feminist and lesbian activist groups in the 1970s, wrote *Sexual Shakedown* to publicize the issue and later appeared with the actor Ed Asner (famous as Mary's boss on the 1970s *Mary Tyler Moore Show*) in a documentary film version of her book. A project instituted by NOW's Legal Defense and Education Fund resulted in several programs and publications in American colleges and universities designed to raise awareness of sexual harassment and mediate complaints. Despite growing traction in the broader society, no major legal changes recognized the gravity and scope of the issue. Indeed, sexual harassment was not even established as a form of sexual discrimination under Title VII of the Civil Rights Act of 1964, which protected the careers and economic well-being of working women. It was also unclear whether Title VII arguments would provide the preferred legal strategy by which to pursue sexual harassment claims.[19]

In the 1970s, courts were reluctant to find early sexual harassment cases in violation of Title VII sex discrimination provisions, often regarding plaintiffs as individual victims rather than as a targeted class or group. The courts also tended to view male harassers as individuals rather than as agents of their employers' authority. Beginning in the mid-1970s, however, feminism had succeeded in illuminating realities about the unequal distribution of power between the sexes and women's anemic representation within management positions for the broader culture. A series of federal appeals court rulings began to turn the tide in favor of sexual harassment claims. Moreover, these rulings instituted the idea that in addition to traditional claims of quid pro quo harassment—in which, typically, male supervisors pressured female employees to trade sexual favors for professional advancement—the courts now recognized a new form of harassment: the hostile work environment. In this scenario, typically, women workers were subjected to persistent unwelcome harassment that undermined the terms and conditions of their employment, producing a hostile environment. Despite growing recognition in the lower courts, by the mid-1980s the Supreme Court still had not spoken. Finally, in the 1986 case of *Meritor Savings Bank v. Vinson*, the Supreme Court ruled that sexual harassment constituted a form of Title VII sexual discrimination, applying to both quid pro quo and hostile work environment scenarios. This landmark decision represented a major victory for feminists, one that stemmed in large part from their own strenuous and organized efforts. A diverse range of women's organizations, many of whose work on sexual harassment dated back to 1970s consciousness-raising about the issue, filed amicus curiae briefs on behalf of the plaintiff Mechelle Vinson's suit against her employer. Two of the most important of these efforts were spearheaded by the Working Women's Institute and the Women's Legal Defense Fund, which wrote briefs representing a diverse range of women, from homemakers to the NOW Legal Defense Fund, coal miners to the Sisterhood of Black Single Mothers, and Wider Opportunities for Women to the Puerto Rican Institute for Civil Rights.[20]

Though the *Vinson* case left unanswered questions, such as the terms and extent of employers' liability in sexual harassment cases, it cemented the issue's legitimacy and compelled action from mainstream American institutions. By the end of the 1980s, more than three-quarters of Fortune 500 companies instituted formal policies against sexual harassment. This reflected feminist activists' economic arguments that harassment was bad for business and resulted in low morale, high turnover rates, and diminished productivity—not to mention costly litigation. Explaining his company's efforts to "raise sensitivity to the issue" a Campbell's Soup spokesperson reasoned, "It's in the company's own interest to prevent problems and quickly resolve the ones that do occur." *Good Housekeeping* interviewed a DuPont personnel development manager who described the goal of her company's standard half-day seminar on sexual harassment as making sure that employees know about available in-house resources in case of a problem. The anti-sexual-harassment activist turned human resources consultant Freada Klein elaborated: "Even when there's a policy, some women are afraid to come forward. Companies need to reach out to their employees to say it's okay to speak up." That corporate employers did not always engage in these efforts with the same sense of moral justice as activists did not negate the fact that victims enjoyed expanded opportunities for recourse. The EEOC fielded 34 percent more complaints of sexual harassment by the end of the decade than it heard at the outset. The nonprofit sector displayed mounting attention as colleges and universities established increasingly stringent sexual harassment policies. Many of these reflected feminist insights, such as the notion that even purportedly consensual relationships between students and professors may constitute harassment given their rootedness in "unequal power relationships."[21]

The progress of anti-sexual-harassment activism took place against a backdrop of ever more assertive conservative leadership. In 1981, the newly elected President Reagan replaced the EEOC chair Norton—with her long-standing ties to the feminist and civil rights movements—with the conservative Clarence Thomas, whose antipathy to affirmative action was a matter of public record. Along with this change, in keeping with his administration's mission to deregulate business and industry, Reagan significantly cut the commission's budget, encouraging Thomas to relax, weaken, and even scrap its guidelines. Remarkably, anti-sexual-harassment activists battled valiantly against the prevailing political winds, managing not only to save the guidelines but, through legal victories such as the *Vinson* case, to expand awareness of the issue and the resources available to victims. It is a story of tactical adaptation that saw activists move from direct action and feminist consciousness-raising to educational campaigns, legal action, and working through corporate America and mainstream institutions. Though these initiatives met with a spectrum of public reaction, subsequent events amplified public recognition of sexual harassment. In 1991, nationally televised hearings—highlighted by Anita Hill's testimony alleging sexual harassment—sought to assess whether the very same Clarence Thomas who had headed Reagan's EEOC was fit for confirmation as a Supreme Court justice. Similarly, the Tailhook scandal, in which male naval aviators assaulted their female counterparts at a Las Vegas hotel, served to focus mounting attention on widespread charges of sexual harassment within the military.[22] Through all of this, efforts to expand understanding of the costs of sexual harassment, and to define what kinds of behavior might contain grounds for legal challenges, owed much to a quieter, gentler feminist mobilization within mainstream institutions.

The expansion of rape crisis centers during the 1980s followed a similar path. The effort to define nonconsenting sex as rape and to be clear about what consent entailed dated back to early feminist consciousness-raising sessions of the late 1960s and the 1970s. The common personal experiences of rape that women discovered during these sessions led to the development of ad hoc institutions designed to fill the vacuum in available services for women. Rape crisis centers were an outgrowth of this process. Early on, in the 1970s, the centers tended to be seedbeds of radical feminism staffed by grassroots volunteers who provided nonmedical services and encouraged local hospitals and police to follow protocols that displayed greater sensitivity to rape victims. They also functioned as collectives, pursuing the same concern with consensus-based, nonhierarchical decision making that was endemic in the radical women's liberation movement and the male-dominated New Left. Over time, as they established legitimacy and expertise, the centers and their allies mobilized political pressure that prompted individual states and localities to support their work as part of official human services programs. More resources materialized, often in the form of grant money to hire social workers and mental health professionals. Typically, the prerequisite for such expansion was incorporation as a nonprofit under a traditional board of directors.

The timeline for this new era of professionalization dovetailed closely with the onset of the 1980s. Gone were the twenty-four-hour volunteers on call and the agony of protracted consensus decision making on major policy issues. But neither did this winnowing of radicalism mean that the rape crisis centers no longer advanced feminist ideas and agendas. On the contrary, as the centers institutionalized themselves, feminists worked within the new constraints, often taking advantage of expanded resources and opportunities to mobilize in subtler and usually less disruptive ways than their 1970s sisters. For instance, when the Southern California Rape Crisis Center (SCRCC) adopted its motto "All We Do Comes from Victims," it used victims' experiences to formulate a reform agenda, a testimony to the broader rethinking of rape in terms of its impact on victims. This mobilized radical feminism's signature organizing strategy—"the personal is political"—toward the less confrontational goals of developing model programs for rape exams in hospitals, pressuring for legislative changes to help rape victims, and developing rape awareness programs for high schools. At the same time, the SCRCC used its increased access to mainstream institutions to "occupy and indoctrinate," seizing the opportunity to interject feminist ideas about sexual assault into the police training sessions it operated and into the Hollywood film and television projects on which it consulted. The DC Rape Crisis Center (DCRCC), a pioneering facility run by and for black women, traced a similar trajectory from alternative service to institutionalization during the 1980s. The DCRCC survived economically through a contract with the D.C. school system to teach child-safety awareness, which provided a backdoor opportunity to address issues of sex education and sexual violence more broadly. Carol Lavery, a cofounder of the Pennsylvania Coalition Against Rape, marveled at the transition of the rape crisis services movement from consciousness-raising to an established infrastructure of resources where victims receive crisis intervention, personalized legal assistance in court, and other customized services. Praising this "tremendous accomplishment," she explained the significance of feminist leadership in driving mobilization and funding within bureaucratic, state-sponsored settings: "Unless we set the standards for professionalism within this field, somebody else is going to do it for us."[23]

The political science and women's studies scholar Mary Fainsod Katzenstein coined the term "unobtrusive mobilization" in her study of the transformation of women's roles within the Catholic Church and the military. Katzenstein found that women of both groups pursued changes that incorporated gender consciousness and feminism's egalitarian insights, often in disruptive ways that risked disciplinary action.

Yet substantial differences in goals and strategies surfaced. Military women tended to seek modest reforms toward gender equality within the military. While trying to avoid being dismissed as "not a team player" or labeled "a feminist," women leading these changes attempted to identify and seek redress for sexual abuse within the military, to end sex discrimination in military occupations, and to halt harassment of suspected lesbians. Religious women, on the other hand, as epitomized by Women-Church, a multilingual, multiracial women's group, adopted a more radical tone, calling for a new church that "acknowledges that it is guilty of sexism, heterosexism, racism and classism." With that provocative diagnosis of the traditional church's shortcomings, Women-Church engaged in an array of social justice issues—operating women's homeless shelters, advocating on behalf of women prisoners, exploring the unique challenges of keeping faith for lesbians, and working for the Sanctuary and Central America solidarity movements.[24]

Athletics represented another proving ground for unobtrusive mobilization as sports provided one of the clearest places where opportunities for women expanded in consummately measureable ways, from the sheer number of women athletes to dramatically increased funding for girls' and women's teams. As the decade opened, the 1970s' momentum toward greater opportunities for women and girls in sports, catalyzed by the women's liberation movement and the 1972 passage of Title IX of the Higher Education Act, still proceeded apace. Title IX protections against sex discrimination in federally funded programs sparked tremendous growth at all levels of athletics. In the 1980s, however, maintaining this progress toward a more egalitarian order often involved playing defense. In *Grove City College v. Bell* (1984), the Supreme Court decided that Title IX protections applied only to the specific programs within colleges and universities that received federal funding and not to entire institutions. Since athletic departments typically did not receive federal funding, this effectively gutted Title IX in college athletics, resulting in swift and sizable cuts to women's teams and scholarships. Congress's passage of the 1988 Civil Rights Restoration Act changed this. Overriding President Reagan's veto, the law prohibited discrimination throughout educational institutions receiving federal funds. This triumph entailed some losses along with the restored gains. One unanticipated consequence of Title IX's success was diminishing coaching and administrative opportunities for women, as higher coaching salaries lured male coaches and NCAA oversight of women's athletics saw numerous male administrators displace the female leadership of the Association for Intercollegiate Athletics for Women. Still, though parity with resources allotted to men continued to be elusive, the 1980s emerged as a decade of exponential growth in women's athletics.[25]

At the same time, radical feminism transformed higher education inside the classrooms as well, creating new fields of knowledge. Feminists spurred the growth of women's studies as an academic field in the 1970s, a subject that developed and expanded as a response to the erasure of women's contributions in the history books and their accomplishments as literary and cultural producers. This intellectual ferment generated ideas and theories that were mobilized in campaigns for women's inclusion throughout the academy, from curricular changes to more equitable hiring and promotion. Though not without resistance from the male-dominated administrative ranks, women's studies became firmly entrenched in the United States and internationally during the 1980s. In the United States, women's studies doubled in scope, with close to 50 percent of four-year colleges offering these programs by the end of the decade. With this growth, feminists in academe tended to put rowdy 1970s-style protest behind them, shifting gears to transform their institutions from within. By all accounts, this movement enjoyed considerable success, transforming entire academic disciplines and rethinking the process of social and political change from the ancient era to modern times. History students now studied the challenges of ordinary women and the accomplishments of rediscovered female pioneers alongside the deeds of vaunted dead white men. Literature students reclaimed the traditionally denigrated contributions of female authors who generations of literary scholars had dismissed as a "mob of scribbling women."[26] Of course, women's greater inclusion in the curriculum and the displacement of cherished entries in Western civilization's canon of great works earned women's studies a critical mass of enemies among traditional academicians, cultural conservatives, and the politicians who represented them, making women's studies one of several favorite targets in the "culture wars" that also enveloped black studies and ethnic studies programs in the late 1980s and early 1990s. But women's studies also demonstrated tenacious staying power over these media-amplified objections, its classrooms sparking the interest of a new generation of younger women who by the 1990s were christened "the third wave."

Seeking to make feminism relevant to their own lives, younger women sought to enhance perspectives on sexuality, femininity, ethnic and racial identities, class issues, lesbianism, and a host of other matters that went beyond what they believed second-wave feminism addressed in its heyday. Many of the new concerns revolved around questions of whether women shared a common identity or were defined by multiple intersections of identity—including, among others, race, class, gender, sexual orientation, and age. For their part, older feminists, veterans of the movement's heady days in the 1970s, lamented that this new wave had contracted an acute case of historical amnesia, forgetting that their very freedoms and expanded possibilities were forged on their feminist foremothers' diligent organizing and militant protest. Mainstream media predictably enough picked up this intergenerational feminist strife as a newsworthy development whose centerpiece was a newfound aversion to the "f word," in this case, *f* for "feminist." Polling data revealed that though younger women tended to embrace a full feminist agenda—from pay equity to believing men should share more equally in child rearing—they demonstrated an allergic reaction to the label, opting instead for the disclaimer, "I'm not a feminist but . . ." Despite such protestation, younger feminists emphatically agreed with their elders on one key issue, and they proved willing to mobilize to defend its legal protections.

April 1989

In the 1980s American women's access to safe and legal abortion was under siege, literally. By decade's end, pro-life radicals attacked abortion providers in some three dozen bombings and acts of arson—with many more attempted. In 1984 alone, clinics in Virginia, Maryland, Alabama, Washington, the District of Columbia, Texas, California, Georgia, and Florida were bombed or burned. Add to this the pervasive picketing, vandalism, and harassment of women entering clinics, and a portrait of the pro-life movement's radical wing emerges. But extremists who perpetrated violence against people and property were only part of the picture. Attacks on abortion were among a broader series of developments appearing after the landmark 1973 *Roe v. Wade* decision legalizing abortion, which ended the mid–twentieth century's dominant trend toward the liberalization of sexual behaviors and attitudes and recast women's sexuality in particular. The pro-life movement enjoyed robust support from conservative politicians who courted voters largely on the basis of this one issue, even attracting constituencies whose economic interests clashed with their platforms. It also enjoyed strong rhetorical support from President Reagan, who pledged to right-to-life activists that he would not rest until the ratification of a constitutional human life amendment superseding *Roe v. Wade* and also pledged to withdraw federal funds from facilities that practiced abortion counseling. Yet this proved a tricky issue for Republicans to navigate. While making opposition to abortion a key piece of his social agenda, in truth, Reagan expended little political capital on behalf of the pro-life movement, often averting television cameras when meeting with antiabortion groups. His vice president and successor, George H. W. Bush, only fully converted to "steadfast pro-lifer" status on the campaign trail in 1988, after formerly supporting federal funding for some abortions and opposing a constitutional amendment stating that life begins at conception. This was the state of the nation's most brutally divisive issue in 1989, when the Supreme Court decided to hear *Webster v. Reproductive Health Services*, a case that threatened to reverse *Roe v. Wade*.[27]

Pro-choice forces responded by mobilizing more than three hundred thousand women for a Washington, D.C., rally on a cool April Sunday. The demonstrators urged a Supreme Court that increasingly bore the imprint of Reagan's conservative appointments to "Keep Abortions Safe and Legal." Marchers displayed images of coat hangers—real ones, placards with images, and a three-foot-high replica—evoking the dangers of illegal abortion in the pre-*Roe* era. To underscore the point, women who were veterans of those days offered testimonials of back-alley abortionists operating in unsafe and unsanitary conditions. On the recommendation of NOW, many women wore white, a sartorial link with the women's suffragists of the early 1900s. Media accounts noticed the crowd's diversity and remarked on the plethora of mother-daughter pairings. Jane Fonda and Tom Hayden lent the rally a connection to both 1960s activism and Hollywood star power, which was reinforced by the presence of the prominent actresses Cybill Shepherd,

Morgan Fairchild, Kelly McGillis, and Susan Sarandon. Demonstrators carried signs and banners with messages signifying the mobilization's strategic rationale, including, ungrammatically, WHO DECIDES? YOU OR THEM? and KEEP YOUR LAWS OFF MY BODY, which emphasized the increasing government encroachment on the privacy rights *Roe* established. Pro-choice mothers with children in tow toted MOTHERHOOD BY CHOICE signs, highlighting the position of abortion rights within a range of reproductive concerns. MENOPAUSAL WOMEN, NOSTALGIC FOR CHOICE signs in the hands of older women symbolized intergenerational solidarity and hinted that controlling women's sexuality was also at stake. Even the *National Review* called the march an "impressive spectacle," and observers concurred with the NARAL executive director Kate Michelman's claim that the "sleeping giant" of pro-choice activism had awakened.[28]

The significance of the national media's sudden discovery of the movement's breadth varied depending on the observer's perspective. To the *National Review*, media accounts of the march amounted to "free publicity," a gratuity that would never have been extended to the other side. This proved to be a dubious assertion. Tallying exponentially smaller numbers—*The Boston Globe* estimated hundreds as opposed to hundreds of thousands of pro-choice marchers—pro-life counterdemonstrators took advantage of the dictates of fair journalism. Even coverage displaying obvious pro-choice sympathy devoted disproportionate ink and airtime to reporting pro-life chants of "What About the Babies?" and to the Cemetery of the Innocents that antiabortion activists erected. News outlets also mentioned the much smaller march of sixty-seven thousand that pro-life forces orchestrated that January, noting that unlike the pro-choice crowd, they received a pledge of support from President Bush.[29]

Indeed, the April 1989 demonstration was a microcosm of feminist and pro-choice activism's secret history in the 1980s. Despite polls at the time of the rally indicating that between 63 percent and 74 percent of Americans believed that abortion should be legal and left to a woman and her doctor, antiabortion activists managed to attract a generous share of media attention.[30] Feminists like Meredith Tax hastened to claim majority status for the pro-choice movement: "After this march there can be no doubt who's in the mainstream on this issue. I've never seen so many straight-looking people in one place in my life." The Planned Parenthood president Faye Wattleton described anti-abortion groups as a "fringe element" and explained the process that led media to overstate their strength: "a small group of hard-core organizers . . . come into town and link up with a few people who have been agitators for many years, who have consistently picketed and vandalized abortion and family planning clinics. They can turn out two or three hundred people, and you could say, 'Wow, this massive well-organized movement is growing all over the country.'" Similarly, the pro-life film *The Silent Scream*, which used then brand-new ultrasound technology to purportedly document the fetus's pain and suffering in a twelfth-week abortion, received much wider distribution and publicity than pro-choicers' response film *Abortion for Survival*.[31] Led by Operation Rescue, pro-life groups claimed the upper hand in making nightly news leads and newspaper headlines, but this belied a subtler, less media-arousing story.

Undergirding the April 1989 rally and the Supreme Court's subsequent ruling in *Webster*—upholding a Missouri law stating that life begins at conception and barring public funding and facilities for abortions—was a quiet but persistent story of the pro-choice movement's professionalization and institutionalization. The national media portrayed a dormant pro-choice movement awakened by the threat to abortion rights that *Webster* posed, a view reinforced by a handful of activists who lamented, "We've been asleep at the helm." In reality, at the time of the *Webster* ruling, pro-choice forces had steadily developed and entrenched their operations and expanded their outreach for more than a decade and a half. These efforts not only sustained the grassroots social movement that contributed to making the 1973 *Roe* decision a reality, they enhanced its capacity. Pro-choice institutionalization brought increased financial stability, built more effective coalitions with political allies, and placed the movement in a better position to pursue important lobbying work. As antiabortion demonstrators appropriated tactics of radical street protest from the 1960s Left in addition to their deadlier activities, pro-choice groups like NARAL stole a page from the New Right playbook, initiating direct mail campaigns to increase membership and raise money. Mainstream pro-choice organizations, bolstered by their institutional strength and lobbying capacity, helped block Reagan's 1987 nomination of the conservative Robert Bork to the Supreme Court. Though increasing institutionalization and an emphasis on working within the system meant fewer disruptive protests, the record demonstrates that it sustained rather than smothered the movement.[32]

In *Webster*'s aftermath, conservative states passed new laws that further chipped away at women's access to abortions, especially poor and younger women who were subject to hundreds of restrictive initiatives. This expanded a right-wing strategy prominent for more than a decade since the Hyde Amendment cut off abortion funding for women on welfare, thereby banning the use of federal funding for abortions. But the *Webster* decision and the ensuing restrictive state legislation proved an organizing windfall to the pro-choice movement as many young women became engaged, often at the grassroots level.[33] The story of the 1980s abortion wars emerges as one in which feminist activists battled mightily, amid limited political opportunity and against the conservative tide, to retain the hard-won gains of the 1960s and 1970s. Though only partially successful, this struggle exemplified the quiet determination with which feminists confronted the backlash and mobilized throughout the decade.

8

THE SHOCK TROOPS
OF DIRECT ACTION
ACT UP Confronts the AIDS Crisis

On a March morning in 1987 a group of 250 protesters assembled for a demonstration on New York City's Wall Street, a site selected for its connection to American business and to big pharmaceutical companies particularly. At the time of the protest, Burroughs Wellcome, the manufacturer of AZT, the lone federally approved drug for AIDS treatment, held a monopoly on the drug's patent. This contributed to ballooning prices for AIDS patients, estimated as high as $10,000 annually, that made the drug cost prohibitive for an alarming portion of affected patients already forced to endure a number of harmful side effects associated with AZT. The demonstration featured a direct action protest designed to interrupt business as usual and garner media attention to raise public awareness for the protesters' cause. Ultimately, seventeen demonstrators were arrested and charged with disorderly conduct. A photo in the following day's *New York Times* under the heading "Homosexuals Arrested at AIDS Drug Protest" shows demonstrators lying limp in classic 1960s-era civil disobedience style, with one protester being dragged away by two of New York City's finest.[1] The demonstrators' demands, enumerated on a flyer they distributed, revealed detailed knowledge of which corporations and universities were conducting research on particular AIDS drugs. These demands conveyed the conviction that people with AIDS should play a vital part in the decision making that affected their lives and treatment. The list identified specific individuals and institutions as the "villains" of the

AIDS crisis, seeking to make them publicly accountable. Drug companies were implored to "Curb your greed!" and, underscoring the failure of the Great Communicator to address the epidemic, protesters exhorted, "President Reagan, nobody is in charge!"[2] The AIDS Coalition to Unleash Power (ACT UP) had made its first big splash.

If urban problems, widening economic inequality, and social welfare received callous treatment in Reagan-era America, the AIDS crisis labored to receive any treatment at all. By 1987, what had begun in the early 1980s as a mysterious "gay plague" had claimed an estimated twenty-five thousand lives.[3] Events such as the death of the 1950s and 1960s screen icon Rock Hudson received copious media coverage, but the epidemic had yet to receive serious attention from the federal government. In his public speeches, President Reagan refrained from using the term "AIDS" for the first six years of the crisis.

In response to the worsening epidemic, ACT UP, initially a New York–based group, functioned as the shock troops of AIDS activism. Quickly becoming the movement's radical cutting edge, its anger and intelligence, theatrics and persistence, and creativity and militancy prodded targeted institutions with heightened urgency. Through its street-level presence, media savvy, and visual imagery, ACT UP's direct action protests also battled the larger issues of prejudice and discrimination surrounding the AIDS crisis, from combating myths regarding the disease's transmission, to arguing (often against gay conservatives) for the need to maintain a "sex positive" outlook, to safe sex campaigns and clean needle exchanges. But ACT UP's dramatic public profile told only part of the story. Internally, the group created a palpable sense of community for the activists who participated in and shared its vibrant movement culture. While sometimes drawing, consciously or subconsciously, from the radical activist movements of the 1960s, ACT UP pioneered innovative aesthetic and organizational strategies infused with a gay cultural sensibility to establish its own distinctive brand of activism.

Origins, Antics, and Principles

ACT UP originated from the need to agitate for quicker progress in response to the AIDS crisis. Popular history holds that the playwright Larry Kramer founded ACT UP in 1987 because the Gay Men's Health Crisis (GMHC), also founded by Kramer in 1982, had become too institutionalized, too beholden to its financial underwriters, too cautious politically, and too preoccupied with attending to people who were dying, to meet the necessary challenges of the rapidly expanding AIDS crisis. As Kramer admonished the GMHC, "No longer do you fight for the living; you have become a funeral home."[4] Several ACT UP members have quibbled with this iconic account, citing the GMHC's service to the community of people with AIDS as a vital form of activism in its own right and pointing to the role of activists other than Kramer in ACT UP's founding. What is clear is that while the GMHC stressed a multifaceted approach to the prevention, treatment, and cure of AIDS/HIV, ACT UP's mission explicitly called for direct action protest and public demonstration.

From the very beginning, ACT UP's protests combined direct action and civil disobedience with a heavy dose of theatrics, suggesting that ACT UP principals had gleaned a lesson or two from their forebears about using symbolic politics to raise public awareness and attract media attention. At the initial Wall Street demonstration, the group hung an effigy of the Food and Drug Administration (FDA) commissioner Frank Young. It also staged "die-ins," including one in Chicago that echoed Vietnam War–era theatrical protests such as the Living Theatre's "Plague" piece and the Guerrilla Art Action Group's "Blood Bath." Sometimes ACT UP borrowed from the theater-as-politics playbook of 1960s trickster activists such as the Yippies and Diggers, who mounted such absurdist spectacles as nominating a pig for president and staging a "Death of Money" parade in full funeral regalia in order to dramatize radical critiques of mainstream politics and values. In one episode, ACT UP infiltrated the Republican National Convention using fake badges secured by ingratiating themselves with the Kinko's staff. In another, more elaborate guerrilla theater ruse, ACT UP members invented fake names and posed as Republican women to gain admittance to a Republican Women's Club where Senator Alfonse D'Amato was speaking. Maria Maggenti, for instance, wore a "little red shift and these really cute Pappagallo shoes." Inventing a cover story to explain away her nose ring, a badge of subterranean downtown New York at the time, Maggenti told the guests that her father had served in India during the Nixon administration. When D'Amato began, they stripped away the costumes that facilitated "passing" as Republicans to reveal giant buttons proclaiming LESBIANS FOR BUSH and hoisted up an assortment of ACT UP posters and flyers.[5] Though some ACT UP members

preferred to distance themselves from the radical politics of a generation before or plead ignorance of its vocabulary of activist tactics, many
of the techniques and sensibilities of theatricalized protest had so institutionalized themselves by the late 1980s that ACT UP's activists could
draw from them seamlessly, even as they updated and adapted the repertoire for their own ends.

While Lesbians for Bush demonstrated ACT UP's playful side, the
group was fueled by a sense of outrage and anger over drug company
greed and federal government inaction. ACT UP's official "self-
definition," or mission statement, asserted that its fundamental purpose
was to unite "in anger" to fight AIDS. On the front lines of demonstrations, the group's signature rhythmic chant—"ACT UP! Fight Back!
Fight AIDS!"—seemed a perfectly straightforward accompaniment to
direct action, but on closer inspection it embodied a couple of the
group's core principles. The verb "to act up," as the AIDS activist Jon
Greenberg explained, indicated misbehavior that was "not so severe as
to be morally wrong," but rather "inconvenient" or discomforting, and
that challenged the limits of authority. This kind of "acting up" was
central from the outset: the group had established its militant acronym
before settling on AIDS Coalition to Unleash Power as the words for
which that acronym stood. Its actions provoked authority and confronted the general public's ingrained prejudices. The second part of
the chant, "Fight back!" conveyed the sense of opposition that pervaded the group's actions. ACT UP urged demonstrators and sympathetic bystanders to "fight back" and actively combat authorities and
institutions that inhibited a swift and effective response to the AIDS
crisis. Moreover, the rhetoric of "fighting back" captured the adversarial relationship ACT UP had with the Reagan administration and
the FDA, opponents that had already proven hostile. "To be a movement activist during Reagan/Bush was to work in the Resistance," one
member wrote. It required a daily "war to influence policy and widen
the public space to live as lesbian, gay, and bisexual people."[6]

Targets, Treatments, and a Misstep?

In October 1988 more than a thousand demonstrators disrupted business as usual at the FDA's Rockville, Maryland, headquarters, in an

action called Seize Control of the FDA that resulted in 176 arrests. Activists targeted the FDA as the federal government agency most responsible for testing and approving drugs for AIDS treatment, contending that its laggard approval process was responsible for a mounting cost in the lives of their friends and loved ones. One of ACT UP's defining goals was getting "drugs into bodies" as quickly as possible. When the FDA cited its mission to make sure drugs were safe and effective before appearing on the market, AIDS activists countered that people already dying of AIDS risked little by trying promising experimental drugs. With its action at the FDA headquarters, ACT UP blamed a dysfunctional bureaucracy for the dozens of daily AIDS deaths. ACT UP placards trenchantly featured the skulls of three corpses and bore the inscription TIME *ISN'T* THE ONLY THING THE FDA IS KILLING.[7]

The FDA protest signaled a change within the dynamics of ACT UP. As Gregg Bordowitz observed, it shifted "the group away from a defensive posture to an offensive posture." At the FDA protest, ACT UP abandoned its early program of reacting to conservative cultural attacks on AIDS victims and the gay community and came up with "a vision for the way that health care should be done in this country, the way that drugs should be researched, and sold, and made available."[8] ACT UP's ability to articulate this vision rested on the arduous research efforts of the group's Treatment and Data Committee (T&D), which diligently researched and analyzed myriad complex, technical AIDS-related treatment issues. During the months leading up to the FDA action, the committee educated the group's general membership about the agency's role and functions. T&D produced a detailed *FDA Action Handbook* that explained the nature and history of the FDA, its role in controlling access to AIDS drugs, and its misdeeds in the drug approval process.

ACT UP's Mark Harrington, a spearhead in the handbook's creation, explained the need for this educational effort: "In those days, a lot of people thought that the FDA actually tested the drugs. They didn't understand that they actually just oversee the testing, which is done by NIH or by industry." He continued, "So, there was a whole lot of explaining about an institution, a set of regulations and laws, and some scientific concepts that had to be done in two months, so that everybody in ACT UP could understand it, so that we could get across the message to the American people when we went to the FDA."[9] Harrington's remarks underscore how ACT UP's internal educational process represented a kind of AIDS treatment consciousness-raising designed in turn to promote a media-friendly public message. To this end, ACT UP's Media Committee prepared a detailed press kit that alerted the media to the group's conviction that experimental new AIDS therapies constituted a crucial component of health care and that people with AIDS ought to be entitled to access to these therapies as a right.

Echoing one of the main tenets of 1960s-style participatory democracy—that ordinary citizens ought to be involved in the critical decision making that affects their lives—Bordowitz pointed to ACT UP's placement of people with AIDS at the forefront of public discussion as one of the group's major accomplishments. Prior to ACT UP, discussion of AIDS treatment had been dominated by the technical jargon of the scientific/medical community, bureaucratic health-care institutions, and politicians revving up homophobic, socially conservative constituencies by calling for mandatory testing. Within a year after the protest, the FDA and NIH increasingly allowed people with AIDS to take part in discussions surrounding the drug approval process and even came to seek their participation. ACT UP, Bordowitz explained, had "wrested control" of the AIDS discussion from the "hands of the right wing" and steered it toward the control of "people with the disease itself." Rather than simply "making statements that responded to assaults from the right," ACT UP sought to seize control of the FDA and, in Bordowitz's words, "run the fucking thing ourselves." "We knew we weren't actually going to do that," he explained, "but . . . it was incredibly important to stay on point with that rhetoric."[10] What Bordowitz meant by this reflected ACT UP's desire to transform the language surrounding the AIDS epidemic.

While the 1988 FDA protest addressed AIDS on a national stage, ACT UP confronted the crisis militantly at the grass roots as well. The group's original New York chapter focused attention on Mayor Edward Koch's administration and its negligence on a variety of interrelated urban health issues connected with AIDS. Prior to its March 1989 Target City Hall action, ACT UP recruited numerous new protestors who were similarly concerned about the state of health care in New York City. The group then used the momentum of this expanded outreach to mount its largest demonstration to date. *The New York Times* reported that three thousand demonstrators ringed City Hall, calling for additional health-care funding, the expansion of overcrowded hospitals, and increased housing for homeless people with AIDS.[11] ACT UP crafted a handbook similar to the one it had made for the FDA action, which educated demonstrators about the complex of interrelated public health issues they wanted the Koch administration to address. Demonstrators carried placards laden with clever, incisive double entendres, such as SINCE THE CITY CUT AIDS EDUCATION, MORE KIDS GET TO LEAVE SCHOOL EARLY and FOR MANY BLACKS AND LATINOS UNABLE TO AFFORD AIDS CARE THE COST OF LIVING IS TOO HIGH.[12] Even though the New York City government was ostensibly the focus of Target City Hall, by addressing a range of public health issues, ACT UP highlighted systemic issues of social and economic inequality pervasive in the 1980s, such as homelessness and lack of affordable health care, thus indicting Reagan-era national priorities as well.

Target City Hall, like Seize Control of the FDA, demonstrated a surprising potential for activism to convey complex messages about socioeconomic inequality, municipal governance, and an alarming health-care crisis. At the street level, however, it remained a direct action protest that disrupted the public space with noise, blocked traffic, and paraded banners to dramatize the cause. In December 1989, ACT UP turned up the volume on theatrical protest with a 4,500-strong rally and demonstration at New York's St. Patrick's Cathedral that, despite the unprecedented turnout, yielded mixed results. The Stop the Church action targeted the Catholic Church for its attempts to influence government policy on AIDS and a number of related public health issues.[13] The group charged that the church, led by Cardinal John O'Connor in New York City, endangered lives by blocking safe sex education, reasserting its position against contraception, fanning the flames of homophobia, and obstructing access to safe and legal abortions. The presence of the abortion rights group WHAM! (Women's Health and Action Mobilization) at this event as cosponsors indicated a redoubled effort to practice the coalition politics referenced in ACT UP's title. The group singled out O'Connor for his influence in reversing the National Conference of Catholic Bishops' exception to a ban on contraceptives in the face of the AIDS crisis. They also cited O'Connor's long-standing record of antagonism toward gays and lesbians and claimed that the shadow of his influence in New York extended beyond the Catholics within his domain and into municipal policy.

The protest, staged to disrupt Sunday Mass, aimed to publicize the Catholic Church's culpability in perpetuating the epidemic. It began with a legal picket outside St. Patrick's, climaxing in a "die-in" designed to symbolize the epidemic's quickly mounting death toll. Inside the church, smaller affinity groups lay down in the aisles, threw condoms, and chained themselves to the pews. *Time* magazine reported that one protester screamed "You bigot, O'Connor, you're killing us" during the sermon. In a widely reported incident that became the iconic media image of Stop the Church, one of the demonstrators threw a Communion wafer to the floor, causing *Time* to dub the protest a "sacrilegious scene." O'Connor responded by leading his parishioners in a prayer designed to rise above the clamor of the protest. In the end, the police arrested 111 protesters, many of whom were carried out on stretchers after they refused to stand up. ACT UP charged the police, many of whom were Catholic, with brutality in responding to the protests. Though some observers have pointed out that O'Connor probably had prior knowledge of the demonstration and orchestrated his parishioners' outrage, ACT UP lost the public relations ground war on that particular day. The mainstream media sensationalized the group's direct action tactics, focusing on their desecration of church property and disruption of a religious ceremony, and highlighted issues of religion while largely ignoring the Catholic Church's role in the AIDS crisis.

Within ACT UP, debate roiled in the aftermath of Stop the Church. Some members defended the action's tactics. Maxine Wolfe contended that Stop the Church succeeded at eroding the Catholic Church's considerable influence over New York City's municipal life. Michael Petrelis concurred, offering perspective on the thrown Communion wafer and the charges that Stop the Church was blasphemous: "Oh, please, you can get another wafer; you can't bring your friends back from the dead." On the other hand, members like Michael Nesline criticized Stop the Church because "it didn't feel like it was about AIDS, it felt like it was about lapsed Catholics" within ACT UP who were "acting out their disappointment and rage at the Catholic Church." Indeed,

Nesline traced his personal disengagement with ACT UP to this incident. Similarly, Bordowitz "started getting alienated from ACT UP" around this time and opined that there was not much to gain from the action, explaining that the church "is not a body that makes policy about AIDS that I have to live under" and citing his preference for focusing on health care.[14]

Though Stop the Church represented a rare instance when ACT UP proved unable to project its intended message coherently to the media, the visual images accompanying the protest delivered pointed perspectives about accountability for the epidemic. Among the most arresting was the KNOW YOUR SCUMBAGS poster which juxtaposed images of O'Connor and a condom whose shape bore a striking likeness to the cardinal's headpiece. Below the condom, in smaller lettering than the poster's headline, the caption read "This One Prevents AIDS." Dramatic, clever, and innovative visuals emerged as a hallmark of ACT UP's approach.

Silence, Death, and Kissing: AIDS Activist Visuals

Many of the most memorable images associated with AIDS activism emanated from Gran Fury, a collective associated with ACT UP who were committed to making "guerrilla art" to raise public awareness of issues affecting people living with AIDS. Though Gran Fury took its name from the Plymouth model widely used as an undercover police cruiser in New York City, the name also evoked the cathartic anger that the ACT UP acronym embodied. The collaboration of some of its artists predated the name Gran Fury and even the establishment of ACT UP itself. In 1986 several artists who later became Gran Fury designed a poster that eventually became the iconic image of AIDS activism. It showed a pink triangle, referencing the Nazi symbol for homosexual prisoners, with SILENCE = DEATH written in large white capital letters underneath, all against a black background. Below the "Silence = Death" message, in smaller white lettering, the fine print detailed the rationale for this equation: "Why is Reagan silent about AIDS? What is really going on at the Centers for Disease Control, the Federal Drug Administration, and the Vatican? Gays and lesbians are not expendable . . . Use your power . . . Vote . . . Boycott . . . Defend yourselves . . . Turn anger, fear, grief into action."[15] The poster used the postmodern art technique of appropriating recognizable symbols and juxtaposing them with written language to produce fresh meanings. Silence = Death came to emblematize AIDS activism, appearing on T-shirts, buttons, and stickers. It was adapted and redeployed prodigiously for demonstrations and actions, shining a bright light on individuals and institutions criticized as "silent."

After ACT UP's 1987 founding, members of what later became Gran Fury coalesced around an installation called *Let the Record Show*. The ACT UP member and New Museum of Contemporary Art curator Bill Olander initiated this project, offering ACT UP space in the museum's window to create an artwork about AIDS. The ensuing project mobilized the diverse skills of an array of artists. One component involved gathering AIDS statistics from news media sources to quantify the dimensions of the crisis. These statistics, displayed on an LED sign in the style of the renowned 1980s deconstruction artist Jenny Holzer, revealed the inadequate government funding for AIDS research and education, the disproportionate correlation of incidences of AIDS to racial minorities such as blacks and Hispanics, and the epidemic's rising death toll, implicitly indicting the Reagan administration's inactivity. The artists and activists also collected a selection of "horrific" quotes from cultural and political conservatives whom AIDS activists viewed as the opposition and whom they wished to implicate publicly. The project took comments—such as the Moral Majority founder Jerry Falwell's opinion that "AIDS is God's judgment of a society that does not live by His rules" and Senator Jesse Helms's remark that "the logical outcome of testing is a quarantine of those infected"— and literally cast them in concrete slabs for the historical record the installation's title referenced. Ronald Reagan was also represented, but the concrete slab underneath his photographic image was left intentionally blank to symbolize his crime as one of silence. The Silence = Death graphic reinforced this point, displayed in full neon signage above the rest of the installation. The artists concluded that the best way to hold these figures accountable was to metaphorically put them on trial, and so, continuing Silence = Death's appropriation of Holocaust imagery, *Let the Record Show* employed a photomural of the Nuremberg trials as a backdrop to suggest a connection between the fatal implications of the Reagan administration's lack of an AIDS policy, the callousness of American society at large, especially on the part of conservatives, and Nazi war criminals.[16]

The *Let the Record Show* artists developed a creative process that both drew on and transcended examples of activist visual art of the Vietnam War era. In the 1960s the Art Workers' Coalition (AWC) voiced its political opposition to the war with a special focus on the war's effect on the art world milieu in which its members operated. Like the AWC, the *Let the Record Show* collaborators sought to create "non-commodifiable" art that could deliver a political and social message and resist commercial co-optation. As Gran Fury's Michael Nesline remarked, "There's not going to be any art product at the end of it that can be resold and could accumulate in value."[17] Their aesthetic drew from art but always gave politics precedence. The group's style eschewed the modernist artistic emphasis on originality, giving priority to the need to "try to arrest the viewer to stop and look at stuff." Marlene McCarty explained, "We never, ever, ever, came together and said, 'We're going to make art.'" Rather, she claimed that Gran Fury's goal was to deliver messages to the mainstream world in the most "raw and rambunctious" way possible.[18] Though the precedence of political commitment over aesthetics echoed the art world activists of the 1960s, the *Let the Record Show* artists and later Gran Fury succeeded in mobilizing a far wider visual vocabulary in the service of AIDS activism.

Gran Fury created several visuals to accompany the nationwide Nine Days of Protest campaign during the spring of 1988. One of the most striking of these, epitomizing the group's aesthetic and rhetorical style, showed the logo of the medical profession, two serpents intertwining around a staff, on a plain white background. This image, juxtaposed with the statement "All People with AIDS Are Innocent," challenged the mainstream media's suggestion that people with AIDS usually belonged to one or more marginalized and presumably "deviant" groups—including homosexuals, IV drug users, and prostitutes—that implicitly bore greater culpability for their disease than "innocent" victims of AIDS such as children, hemophiliacs, and heterosexuals.[19] It also held the medical community responsible for offering the best possible treatment to all people living with AIDS, regardless of social position. At the very bottom line of the poster, in elegant yet understated cursive lettering, the group placed its own signature.

Gran Fury developed a vocabulary of what one member called "snappy one-liners":[20] pointed, brief, often double-entendre-crammed barbs to counter homophobic, unenlightened, and misguidedly apathetic views that it aimed to overturn. The SEXISM REARS ITS UNPROTECTED HEAD poster contained one of Gran Fury's most notorious images, featuring an erect penis with the provocative admonition MEN: USE CONDOMS OR BEAT IT to counter the media stereotype of AIDS as a prohibitively gay male disease. The message AIDS KILLS WOMEN highlighted that point at the bottom of the poster.

Another Gran Fury poster positioned a bloody red handprint between the broad agitprop accusation THE GOVERNMENT HAS BLOOD ON ITS HANDS at the top of the poster and a factoid highlighting the crisis's severity—ONE AIDS DEATH EVERY HALF HOUR—at the bottom. Appearing originally in poster form, "The Government Has Blood on Its Hands" was then reproduced in diverse formats, such as on T-shirts and stickers that were sold in an ACT UP gift shop.[21] Gran Fury excerpted the "Men: Use Condoms or Beat It" line from "Sexism Rears Its Unprotected Head" and created a popular and highly visible sticker with this catchy barb. So while Gran Fury eschewed making commodifiable art, its members were not averse to making commodifiable paraphernalia to bankroll AIDS activism and disseminate its ideas to a wider audience.

Considering the art critic Lucy Lippard's observation that artists "are by nature unequipped for group thinking or action,"[22] Gran Fury enjoyed a relatively lengthy career, spanning half a dozen years in the late 1980s and early 1990s. Oral history interviews with Gran Fury artists suggest that members' shared enthusiasm for working collectively played a vital role in this longevity. "It was amazing," Gran Fury's Marlene McCarty remembered, "to be able to come together with these eleven people, and just like, everybody was in there throwing out their two bits. Some of the comments were completely out in left field, but everything was processed and processed. And you saw how eleven people were better than one." While McCarty describes the collaborative creative process at its best, even Gran Fury artists who acknowledged its frustrations concurred that it was ultimately deeply rewarding. Robert Vasquez-Pacheco, who came to Gran Fury with a painting background and had never worked in a collective, recalled, "We would sit down and bring ideas to the table and say yes, no, reject them, change them. That was something totally new for me. I had never had that experience for someone to say, 'No, we're not going to do it that way. We're going to it this way.'" Ultimately, however, Vasquez-Pacheco concluded that despite the fact that individual artistic vision was subject to collective revision, "It was good, it was fun." The secret to collective fun trumping personal artistic disappointment and frustration in Gran Fury lay in the precedence of activism over art. As Marlene McCarty explained, "We were not like, 'Let's do something that's never been done,' we were just, 'Oh, that works, let's do that.'" McCarty's comment illuminates Gran Fury's process of appropriation from the wide palette of postmodern art. The group drew eclectically from such sources as Barbara Kruger's deconstruction art, Jenny Holzer's pioneering incorporation of language and text in works of art, and the commercial aesthetics of modern advertising. Whatever visual elements might most effectively serve the cause made it into Gran Fury's work. The goal, in McCarty's words, was not about being in a "rarefied, contemplative environment," but rather "to be outside, where people might read some of these texts or images who would not necessarily go into an art gallery."[23]

Gran Fury's strategy of deploying imagery in public venues to reach new audiences outside the art world was epitomized by the 1989 Kissing Doesn't Kill campaign. The group installed panels on buses in cities including New York, Chicago, San Francisco, and Washington, D.C. The panels' design borrowed substantially from modern advertising, particularly the United Colors of Benetton campaign that famously featured groups of children and young adults representing a multicultural array of backgrounds to sell its sweaters, scarves, hats, and other vestments. Kissing Doesn't Kill foregrounded three multiethnic couples kissing to evoke the Benetton ads, but Gran Fury added a new twist—two of the three couples were same-sex couples. Above the male-female, male-male, and female-female couples, Gran Fury placed the heading KISSING DOESN'T KILL: GREED AND INDIFFERENCE DO.[24] Smaller text targeted specific sectors of American society that ACT UP deemed responsible: "Corporate Greed, Government Inaction, and Public Indifference Make AIDS a Political Crisis." Kissing Doesn't Kill displayed the full range of Gran Fury's graphic and rhetorical skill. It featured a quintessential snappy one-liner that repudiated public misinformation about how AIDS was transmitted, it redirected accountability toward powerful institutions and away from victims, and by adopting the visual feel of hip advertising, it broached new audiences, enticing them to decipher its juxtaposition of image and text. Moreover, it sexualized AIDS activism by affirming that sexuality and pleasure themselves hung in the balance. In ACT UP's language, Kissing Doesn't Kill was "sex positive."

Staying Sex Positive: ACT UP Movement Culture

From the beginnings of the AIDS epidemic, tensions arose over how sexual expression would be redefined in the context of the crisis, both within the gay community and the larger American public. One branch of the gay community avoided challenging and even reinforced the mainstream media characterization of AIDS as the result of a culture of promiscuity inherent in the gay lifestyle. In this vein, Randy Shilts's seminal tome, *And the Band Played On*, chronicles public and institutional inaction during the epidemic's early years, while reinforcing the idea that promiscuity was in part to blame. The story follows a male flight attendant, dubbed "Patient Zero," whose licentious philandering is implicated in a disproportionate number of early cases of infection. Shilts moralistically positions Patient Zero among the "arch villains" of the crisis, alongside governmental and health-care bureaucracies. For many gay activists, such sentiments reflected how the gay community had internalized the opinions of homophobes such as the Moral Majority's Jerry Falwell, who viewed AIDS as a divine judgment on sexual mores gone awry. Shilts and other gay conservatives hoped to win public sympathy and resources for treatment through publicly admitting complicity in the crisis and pledging more conservative sexual behavior going forward.

ACT UP's movement culture sought to combat this climate of sexual conservatism. While Gran Fury's Kissing Doesn't Kill and other graphics sexualized AIDS activism publicly, within ACT UP, members carved out a safe place for sexual expression amid a mainstream response to AIDS that rendered American sexual culture more conservative by the minute. ACT UP's weekly meetings emerged as one place where a safe haven existed. Gregg Bordowitz described the overlapping political and sexual energies of the meetings—"There is all kinds of cruising going on on the sides, and eye catching and chattiness"—praising the group's remarkable mixture of intellectual ferment and passion and "erotic energy." Though some ACT UP-ers, such as Gedalia Braverman, focused exclusively on activism, citing a need "to attend to it as business" and explaining that this "wasn't a place for sexual exploits and to get laid all the time and meet cute guys," oral history interviews indicate that this compartmentalization of politics and sexuality was a minority position within ACT UP. As Jean Carlomusto put it, "We were negotiating with these issues of sexual attraction between the group all the time, and it crossed boundaries . . . The men were having sex with the men, the women were having sex with the women, men and women were having sex with each other. It came down to the Emma Goldman saying: 'If I can't dance, I don't want your revolution.' If we can't fuck, what are we doing here?" This vision of sexuality as an integral part of a political and social movement echoed the 1960s counterculture's emphasis on sexual revolution as a vital aspect of the overall cultural transformation it sought. But where counterculturalists sought sexual liberation, ACT UP's expressions of sexuality during the AIDS epidemic took on a different tenor as many of their friends and lovers were dying of a sexually transmitted disease and as the mainstream media popularized conservatives' calls to abstinence and monogamy. In their call for sexual freedom and openness, ACT UP aimed not so much at unleashing unbridled sexuality, but rather at making the post-AIDS world safe for sexual expression—particularly gay sexual expression.

Safe sex education was a vital part of this effort. The Testing the Limits Collective and DIVA TV were ACT UP–related video production groups that focused on raising awareness about safe sex. DIVA stood for Damned Interfering Video Activists. The "interfering" part called attention to its opposition to mainstream media coverage of the AIDS crisis and its attempts to undermine it. Both DIVA TV and Testing the Limits furthered ACT UP's two main public education goals: to "increase public awareness about modes of AIDS transmission and preventative measures" and to "alleviate irrational fears."[25] To accomplish the latter, they hoped to debunk widespread homophobic stereotypes and to explain that AIDS threatened all people, not just a small gay male subculture. During the summer of 1988, in an effort to bring these messages to a more working-class and decidedly heterosexual audience, ACT UP traveled to Shea Stadium, home of baseball's New York Mets. Banners bore messages that linked AIDS with baseball and heterosexual sex, such as MEN WEAR CONDOMS, AIDS KILLS WOMEN, and NO GLOVE, NO LOVE. Jean Carlomusto praised it for successfully making "a distinctly male space into a medium for a message" that would not usually be conveyed there.[26] ACT UP also staged numerous "Kiss-Ins" that similarly commandeered public space to perform a "positive, loving and affirming action" while also challenging misconceptions about how AIDS is transmitted.[27]

Many ACT UP veterans cite the moral clarity of the group's early days as a key part of its appeal—knowing "the right thing to do, or the wrong thing to do," according to one. But for many participants there was also a social, fun side to ACT UP, a side of partying, drinking, revelry, and flirtation charged with sexual attraction, even amid tremendous anger and grief. At one gay pride party during a stiflingly hot summer evening, several ACT UP partygoers spontaneously jumped into the baby pool at nearby Tompkins Square Park. They returned to the party "half naked and dripping wet." Henceforth, this "bunch of boys" became famously known as the "Swim Team" within ACT UP. Tom Kalin referred to the Swim Team as a "micro-culture" within ACT UP, noting that they were "considered to be physically attractive boys—almost exclusively white, almost exclusively symmetrical in muscle, almost exclusively with versions of the '50s rockabilly haircut . . . who knew how to wear, with exact perfection, the black wide belts and the torn jeans and the combat boots and the T-shirts." "They were the collective object of desire in the room," Kalin continued, adding that the Swim Team represented a "buff kind of gorgeous" that contributed to a public image of ACT UP as a sexy group.[28]

Far from a quaint sidebar of ACT UP's movement culture, such sex-positive affirmations infused the group's public politics with vital energy. This rebutted the conservative and homophobic elements within the 1980s cultural and political climate, which encouraged an "easy slippage" from the reality that many gay men were getting sick with AIDS to indicting gay sexual culture as a whole. ACT UP's Kendall Thomas saw this as reflecting the tendency to "move toward moralism" in public discussions of gay sexuality amid the epidemic. ACT UP assaulted this moralism—which reflected the Christian Right's rising influence in public life during the Reagan-Bush years—with a unique cultural politics that embraced sexual pleasure and sexual play. Thomas also credited ACT UP's sexualized cultural politics as integral to personal survival: "The sex-positive, gay affirmative, politically empowering force that was in that room and in the streets of New York or DC at

ACT UP actions—I do feel it saved my life. And there was some great sex that came out of it too."[29]

Many ACT UP activists locate the group's most important achievements in its "drugs into bodies" initiative: the successful pressure to reform the FDA's practices for the testing, approval, and availability of new medications; the impact on the health-care bureaucracy; and changing the course of public debate surrounding AIDS. Yet these considerable accomplishments represent only part of the group's legacy. ACT UP also raised the public visibility of the AIDS epidemic and improved the image of gay men and lesbians at a time when more hostile responses roiled just beneath and sometimes above the surface. Carlomusto observed, "It did an enormous amount to really shake people up about their homophobia: 'Are you so homophobic that you're really glad these folks are dying?'"[30] Moreover, ACT UP re-enchanted activism itself, pioneering innovations in political art, video documentation of activism, organizational strategy, sexual politics, and approaches to the media. This provided a powerful object lesson in the value of activism, educating "a whole generation of people" with "the sense that activism works." Michael Nesline observed that ACT UP "became a vehicle for younger people to get a sense of what it means to be politically active" and to presume "some power that they can impact the political life of our culture."[31] Mark Harrington concurred, citing his own experience: "Before ACT UP I didn't have any faith in mass political action—in any political action. I thought politics was the realm of hypocrisy and shallow platitudes." By contrast, Harrington remarked on what impressed him about ACT UP: "I was in a room full of young people who didn't subscribe to the media's view that our generation was apolitical, careerist and materialistic. And anybody could speak, anybody could run for office—it was like ancient Athens."[32] That ACT UP managed such an achievement at a time when the nation's mainstream political culture was overwhelmingly arrayed against them testifies to the group's remarkable efficacy.

EPILOGUE
The Other Eighties in the Age of Obama

Looking backward from the early twenty-first century, the eighties loom ever more distinctive. The immediate aftermath of this period witnessed the end of the Cold War and a brief moment of speculation during the Clinton years about how the nation should use the "peace dividend"—that is, how it should redirect billions of dollars of accustomed military spending to domestic social purposes—a national discussion that would have been inconceivable without the 1980s critique of Reagan militarism. The recession that doomed Republican rule at the end of the Reagan-Bush era soon gave way to the new, buoyant economy of the 1990s, based on high-tech innovation, the ever-crystallizing reality of globalization, and, of course, the Internet. Domestic politics in the 1990s were marked by a shift from the defensive posture of the 1980s to a new politics of compromise, from Clinton's infamous "Don't ask, don't tell" deal regarding gay service in the military to the Democratic endorsement of welfare reform, free trade, balanced budget measures, and legislation that favored big business, such as the 1996 Telecommunications Act—all of which were more likely to warm the hearts of conservatives than liberals.

In part, such accommodation represented a political necessity given the dismal failure of the Clinton administration's central domestic initiative: national health-care reform. This culture of centrism was joined during the Clinton years, somewhat paradoxically, by intensifying partisan conflict, with the most dynamic voices coming from the political Right. Led by Newt Gingrich's Contract with America, this "Republican Revolution" allowed the GOP to gain control of both houses of Congress in the wake of the 1994 elections. That this surging conservative movement, faced with a beleaguered President Clinton, proved unable to dismantle any of the major government social spending dominions it targeted testifies to the persistent strength the opposition to conservative initiatives had maintained over the Reagan-Bush years. Further Republican efforts to thwart big government proved even more catastrophic, as a 1995 government shutdown left the GOP with egg on its face in the court of public opinion. Partisan squabbling persisted during Clinton's second term, with the impeachment proceedings arising from his extramarital dalliances with the intern Monica Lewinsky providing the highlight—or lowlight.

This polarization continued through the unprecedentedly close, contested, and—by some accounts—corrupt presidential election in 2000 that ushered in the era of George W. Bush, a two-term presidency defined by the terrorist attacks of September 11, 2001, and his administration's response. From the acrimonious debate over the Iraq War, to concerns regarding the detention of terrorist suspects in legal and constitutional limbo in the Guantánamo Bay prison facility, to objections to the Patriot Act's civil liberties incursions, to the public outcry over the torture and humiliation of Iraqi prisoners in the Abu Ghraib prison, to pushback over the CIA's practice of waterboarding terrorist suspects, continuity with 1980s opposition to zealous national defense initiatives and human rights transgressions proved consistent. The 2008 financial crisis at the end of the Bush presidency confronted the historic Obama administration from the opening gun, the moment characterized by passionate debate about the proper role of government amid such a catastrophe. Significantly, President Obama's attempts to rescue corporations that were "too big to fail," to restructure the banking industry, to breathe life into a dying auto industry by revamping it to produce more cars for a new century with scarcer petroleum resources, and, most of all, to pass a substantial stimulus package that provided the largest government-driven job creation engine since the New Deal weren't simply rejected out of hand by opponents clinging to the Reagan-era ideal of smaller government and private sector solutions. The subsequent passage of national health-care reform provided further confirmation that the Reagan Revolution was not as decisive as advertised.

Though from the perspectives of liberals, leftists, and progressives this new era is fraught with its own set of discontents, in many ways the oppositional politics and culture of the 1980s made possible the age of Obama. Despite the emergence of new actors harboring nuclear ambitions on the world stage, the momentum for disarmament that the freeze movement helped generate, and to which Ronald Reagan ultimately contributed, continues among the nuclear principals, reducing the risk of accident and making the world a safer place. The new foreign policy ethic of responsibly managing rather than aggressively undermining leftist political expressions in Latin America is difficult to imagine without the intellectual and moral legacy of the 1980s campaign against Central American interventions. Despite media images of an apathetic generation, the 1980s divestment movement kept the flame of campus student activism alive and enhanced its transnational awareness, a trend recently on view in campus movements for internationally minded causes, from fair labor in the college-logo apparel industry to the campaign against genocide in Darfur.

In the cultural realm, pioneering 1980s mega-events such as Live Aid have institutionalized themselves as a de rigueur response to humanitarian crises from Hurricane Katrina to the earthquake in Haiti—the spirit of which is amply on display in the decidedly mainstream "Idol Gives Back" mega-fund-raisers that the *American Idol* crew mount each season. Critics who once questioned the motives of pop star performers in such events have lost steam in the face of the enormous economic resources and public consciousness these performers have demonstrated an unparalleled capacity to raise. Post-punk music and its sensibilities continue to haunt young musicians even as the music industry itself struggles to find a viable business model. Mobilizing the do-it-yourself punk aesthetic and new media to promote their music, they frequently appeal to shared social and political values to cultivate and engage a fan base.

It is particularly difficult to imagine Barack Obama's thrilling 2008 electoral triumph, breaking the color barrier in presidential politics—with stunning victories in the heretofore red state strongholds Indiana and North Carolina—without Jesse Jackson's pathbreaking ventures of 1984 and 1988 and the momentum of black political mobilization they catalyzed. A similar point might be made about Nancy Pelosi's ascendancy as the first woman Speaker of the House, and how the discomforts of Geraldine Ferraro's unprecedented 1984 vice presidential bid paved the way for the nation to feel comfortable with women at the highest levels of national politics. More broadly, though, feminism's perseverance through the 1980s backlash has preserved a vital force for social progress on issues from pay equity to fostering transnational solidarity with women in the developing world. The fact that ACT UP succeeded in remaining sex positive and maintaining an affirmative public profile amid the duress of the AIDS crisis and the antigay cultural attacks it provoked helped keep alive a progressive trend toward wider acceptance of gay culture and lifestyles during the darkest moment, setting the stage for further integration into the social fabric, as witnessed by the recent halting successes of the marriage equality movement.

These reverberations of 1980s opposition attest to the idea that a given decade contains a far more complex array of forces than media shorthand and popular history can neatly encompass. The 1980s are thus more than simply the decade of Reagan's America or the triumph of a nostalgic, flag-wrapped conservatism. Beneath the surface, there were countless individuals, activists, and organizations that rejected an attitude of supine surrender, opting instead to fight against the grain for what they believed was right, their sense of justice cutting in a fundamentally contradictory direction from those who held the reins of power. To fail to tell their story would be to obscure the value of their commitment, their diligent labors, and their painstaking toil at times when the outlook appeared bleak for those who shared their values. The political and cultural terrain we inhabit is shaped by their strivings.

NOTES

ACKNOWLEDGMENTS

INDEX

NOTES

PREFACE

1. My remarks on presidential popularity are drawn from analysis of figures in the comprehensive statistical table "Presidential Popularity Over Time," which is part of the American Presidency Project, www.presidency.ucsb.edu/data/popularity.php (accessed Nov. 24, 2009).

2. The most thoughtful and provocative examples of this scholarship include Gil Troy, *Morning in America: How Ronald Reagan Invented the 1980s* (Princeton, NJ: Princeton University Press, 2005); Robert Collins, *Transforming America: Politics and Culture in the Reagan Years* (New York: Columbia University Press, 2007); Sean Wilentz, *The Age of Reagan: A History, 1974–2008* (New York: Harper Perennial, 2008); and John Ehrman, *The Eighties: America in the Age of Reagan* (New Haven, CT: Yale University Press, 2005). See also James T. Patterson, *Restless Giant: The United States from Watergate to* Bush v. Gore (New York: Oxford University Press, 2005), and Godfrey Hodgson, *More Equal Than Others: America from Nixon to the New Century* (Princeton, NJ: Princeton University Press, 2004), both of which examine a wider swath that encompasses the last quarter of the twentieth century but nevertheless contain important insights about the 1980s along the way.

3. Bruce Schulman, *The Seventies: The Great Shift in American Culture, Society, and Politics* (New York: The Free Press, 2001), 218–20.

4. "1980 Presidential General Election Results," *Atlas of U.S. Presidential Elections*, www.uselectionatlas.org/RESULTS/index.html (accessed Nov. 24, 2009); "1984 Presidential General Election Results," *Atlas of U.S. Presidential Elections*, www .uselectionatlas.org/RESULTS/index.html (accessed Nov. 24, 2009).

5. David Greenberg, "The Reorientation of Liberalism in the 1980s," in Gil Troy and Vincent Cannato, eds., *Living in the Eighties* (New York: Oxford University Press,

2009), 51–69; Steven Gillon, *The Democrats' Dilemma: Walter F. Mondale and the Liberal Legacy* (New York: Columbia University Press, 1992), 397–99; Wilentz, *The Age of Reagan*, 270–73.

6. For a salient example of this process of self-education and professionalization see Jeffrey Escoffier, "Fabulous Politics: Gay, Lesbian, and Queer Movements, 1969–1999," in Van Gosse and Richard Moser, eds., *The World the 60s Made: Politics and Culture in Recent America* (Philadelphia: Temple University Press, 2003), 207–208.

7. The articles in Gosse and Moser's *The World the 60s Made* constitute the most thorough and effective scholarly documentation of this point to date, and I owe much to their insights.

1: CALLING TO HALT

1. Paul L. Montgomery, "Throngs Fill Manhattan to Protest Nuclear Weapons," *New York Times*, June 13, 1982, 1, 43; Robert McFadden, "A Spectrum of Humanity Represented at the Rally," *New York Times*, June 13, 1982, 42.

2. Pam Solo, *From Protest to Policy: Beyond the Freeze to Common Security* (Cambridge, MA: Ballinger Publishing Company, 1988).

3. Fox Butterfield, "Anatomy of the Nuclear Protest," *New York Times*, July 11, 1982, SM14.

4. Lawrence Wittner, *Toward Nuclear Abolition: A History of the World Disarmament Movement, 1971–Present* (Stanford, CA: Stanford University Press, 2003), 75–76; Solo, *From Protest to Policy*, 44–46; David S. Meyer, *A Winter of Discontent: The Nuclear Freeze and American Politics* (New York: Praeger, 1990), 157, 160.

5. *Freeze It! A Citizen's Guide to Reversing the Nuclear Arms Race* (Norwich, VT: Norwich Peace Center, 1982), 23, in Swarthmore College Peace Collection (hereafter cited as SCPC), Freeze Campaigns [state and local] Records, 1980s, box 2; Meyer, *A Winter of Discontent*, 98–99, 157; Butterfield, "Anatomy," SM14; Solo, *From Protest to Policy*, 47–48.

6. S. Duncan Harp, "Local Option," *The Nation*, Dec. 6, 1980, 596–97; Edward Quill, "Mass. Voters Favor Antinuke Questions," *Boston Globe*, Nov. 6, 1980; Solo, *From Protest to Policy*, 49–50; Judith Miller, "72% in Poll Back Nuclear Halt If Soviet Union Doesn't Gain," *New York Times*, May 30, 1982, 1; Meyer, *A Winter of Discontent*, 173–75.

7. Melinda Fine cited Forsberg's often voiced comment about the freeze as "small enough to be achievable . . . etc.," in an interview September 11, 2008. Forsberg's other comments appear in Wittner, *Toward Nuclear Abolition*, 175–77. See also Solo, *From Protest to Policy*, 57–62; Meyer, *A Winter of Discontent*, 176–77.

8. Mary Ellen Donovan, "Plainfield, N.H., 1981: Against the Arms Race," *New York Times*, Mar. 28, 1981, 23.

9. Nicholas V. Seidita, letter to Norman Hunt, Aug. 2, 1993, Farley Wheelwright Papers (hereafter cited as FWP), bMS 673, box 4, Harvard Divinity School; Jeff

Snyder, "Couple's Nuclear Freeze Plan Grows," *Los Angeles Daily News*, Nov. 29, 1981, 14, in FWP, bMS 673, box 4.

10. Meyer, *A Winter of Discontent*, 111–13; interview with Randy Kehler, August 26, 2008.

11. "Town Meeting," *New Yorker*, Mar. 15, 1982, 35–37; "Vermont Bans the Bomb," *Time*, Mar. 15, 1982, 16; "A Vote for Nuclear Freeze," *Newsweek*, Mar. 15, 1982, 23. The 159 out of 180 figure for the freeze resolution is taken from Wittner, *Toward Nuclear Abolition*, 176, which bases the figure on Judith Miller, "139 in Congress Urge Nuclear Arms Freeze by U.S. and Moscow," *New York Times*, Mar. 11, 1982, A1, A12. Though there are several variations on the figures of the March 1982 freeze resolutions, due in large part to the fact that fourteen towns had approved a freeze measure the previous year, the percentage of Vermont towns approving the freeze falls into the 83.8–91.1 range in each of these sets of numbers.

12. "Cornwall Town Meeting 1982," agenda and minutes, Mar. 2, 1982, Town Clerk File, Cornwall, Vermont.

13. "Town Meeting," 35–37; "Vermont Bans the Bomb," 16; "Vermonters Call for a Freeze on Nuclear Weapons," *New York Times*, Mar. 4, 1982, A16.

14. Susan L. Cutter, H. Briavel Holcomb, and Dianne Shatin, "Spatial Patterns of Support for a Nuclear Weapons Freeze," *Professional Geographer* 38(1) (1986): 42–52.

15. "Nebraska Nuclear Weapons Freeze Campaign (Lincoln)," in SCPC, Freeze Campaigns [state and local] Records, 1980s, box 1; "Omaha Freeze," in SCPC, Freeze Campaigns, box 1; "Oklahoma Nuclear Weapons Freeze Campaign (Oklahoma City)" in SCPC, Freeze Campaigns, box 2.

16. The West Virginia Nuclear Weapons Freeze Campaign, "The West Virginia Jobs with Peace Budget," in SCPC, Freeze Campaigns [state and local] Records, 1980s, box 2; *Don't Blow It: It's the Only One We've Got*, pamphlet of the Alabama Freeze Coalition, in SCPC, Freeze Campaigns [state and local] Records, 1980s, box 1; Margaret Roach and Allen Tullos, "The Freeze Down South," *Southern Changes*, vol. 5, no. 4 (1983): 11–14.

17. Jerry Elmer, *Felon for Peace: The Memoir of a Vietnam-Era Draft Resister* (Nashville: Vanderbilt University Press, 2005), 168.

18. Richard Halloran, "Weinberger Seeks to Assure Allies on Reagan Remark on Atom War," *New York Times*, Oct. 21, 1981, A1; Bernard Gwertzman, "Allied Contingency Plan Envisions a Warning Atom Blast, Haig Says," *New York Times*, Nov. 5, 1981, A1.

19. Jane Kramer, "Letter from Europe," *New Yorker*, Apr. 5, 1982, 162.

20. Michael Clarke and Marjorie Mowlam, eds., *Debate on Disarmament* (London: Routledge and Kegan Paul, 1982), 15; and Wittner, *Toward Nuclear Abolition*, 131–40, 156–59.

21. Wittner, *Toward Nuclear Abolition*, 131–32.

22. E. P. Thompson, "Appeal for European Disarmament," reprinted in E. P. Thompson and Dan Smith, eds., *Protest and Survive* (New York: Monthly Review Press, 1981), 163–65.

23. Nuclear Weapons Freeze Campaign, Correspondence to Local Organizers, Nov. 1, 1983, in Western Historical Manuscripts Collection, sl 454 National Nuclear Weapons Freeze Campaign Records, 1980–1986, folder 102; Solo, *From Protest to Policy*, 112.

24. Thompson, "Appeal for European Disarmament," 165.

25. Barbara Harford and Sarah Hopkins, eds., *Greenham Common: Women at the Wire* (London: Women's Press, 1984), 33.

26. Interview with Melinda Fine, September 11, 2008; interview with Kehler, August 26, 2008; Wittner, *Toward Nuclear Abolition*, 245–51.

27. Solo, *From Protest to Policy*, 72–74; Wittner, *Toward Nuclear Abolition*, 183–84; Meyer, *A Winter of Discontent*, 223–24; "Very Civil Disobedience," *The Nation*, June 12, 1982, 721; Montgomery, "Throngs Fill Manhattan," 1; Christopher Connelly, "Give Peace a Chance," *Rolling Stone*, July 22, 1982, 12–17.

28. John Herbers, "Widespread Vote Urges Nuclear Freeze," *New York Times*, Nov. 4, 1982, A30; Mark Starr, "A Nuclear Freeze Mandate?" *Newsweek*, Nov. 15, 1982, 51; William Safire, "Freedom Is Unfair," *New York Times*, Nov. 11, 1982, A31; Jonathan Moore, "Reagan's Problem: Thawing on Freeze," *New York Times*, Nov. 11, 1982, A31; Meyer, *A Winter of Discontent*, 227–31.

29. William F. Buckley, Jr., "Reagan's McCarthyism," *National Review*, Dec. 10, 1982, 1572–73; Robert Pear, "Foreign Agents Linked to Freeze, Reagan Says," *New York Times*, Nov. 12, 1982, B7; Judith Miller, "President Says Freeze Proponents May Unwittingly Aid the Russians," *New York Times*, Dec. 11, 1982, 9.

30. Meyer, *A Winter of Discontent*, 231.

31. Moore, "Reagan's Problem," A31; Ronald Reagan, "Address to the Nation on Defense and National Security," Mar. 23, 1983, in *The Public Papers of President Ronald W. Reagan*, Ronald Reagan Presidential Library, www.reagan.utexas.edu/archives/speeches/publicpapers.html (accessed Apr. 16, 2008); Solo, *From Protest to Policy*, 133–35; Meyer, *A Winter of Discontent*, 221–22.

32. Wittner, *Toward Nuclear Abolition*, 395–401; David S. Meyer, "Protest Cycles and Political Process: American Peace Movements in the Nuclear Age," *Political Research Quarterly*, vol. 46, issue 3 (Sep. 1993): 451–79; David Cortright, *Peace Works: The Citizen's Role in Ending the Cold War* (Boulder, CO: Westview Press, 1993), 1–12; John Tirman, "How We Ended the Cold War," *The Nation*, Nov. 1, 1999, 13–21; interview with Kehler, August 26, 2008.

2: THE CENTRAL AMERICA SOLIDARITY MOVEMENT

1. Ed Griffin-Nolan, *Witness for Peace: A Story of Resistance* (Louisville, KY: Westminster/John Knox Press, 1991), 24–28; Richard Taylor, "For Penance and Peace," *Sojourners*, Sept. 1983, 14; "The Secret War for Nicaragua," *Newsweek*, Nov. 8, 1982; Joyce Hollyday, "A Shield of Love," *Sojourners*, Nov. 1983, 10; Sharon Erickson Nepstad, *Convictions of the Soul: Religion, Culture, and Agency in the Central America Solidarity Movement* (New York: Oxford University Press, 2004), 70–71.

2. Christian Smith, *Resisting Reagan: The U.S. Central America Peace Movement* (Chicago: University of Chicago Press, 1996), 368–71; Van Gosse, "Unpacking the Vietnam Syndrome: The Coup in Chile and the Rise of Popular Anti-Interventionism," in Gosse and Moser, *The World the Sixties Made*, 100–13; Van Gosse, "El Salvador Is Spanish for Vietnam: A New Immigrant Left and the Politics of Solidarity," in Paul Buhle and Dan Georgakas, eds., *The Immigrant Left in the United States* (Albany, NY: State University of New York Press, 1996), 317–22; Greg Grandin, *Empire's Workshop: Latin America, the United States, and the Rise of the New Imperialism* (New York: Henry Holt, 2006), 96–118; Van Gosse, "Active Engagement: The Legacy of Central America Solidarity," *NACLA: Report on the Americas*, vol. xxviii, no. 5 (Mar./Apr. 1995): 22–29.

3. Walter LaFeber, *Inevitable Revolutions: The United States in Central America* (New York: W. W. Norton & Company, 1983), 36–39.

4. Ibid., 8–18. Since the 1990s, Latin Americanists and economic historians have questioned dependency theory and its corollary, structuralism, which advocated import substitution industrialization as a means to overcome dependency. As an alternative they offered the "New Institutional Economics," which extols the value of free markets and neoliberal economic principles, arguing that the export-based economies that dependency theorists viewed as pernicious actually promoted growth. The NIE school's insights have traditionally been applied to larger South American nations and have been increasingly challenged as a result of twenty-first-century economic difficulties. As a result, the field's leading scholars agree that "it may be too soon to proclaim the demise of structuralist thought" and the dependency theory on which it is based. See Jonathan Brown, "From Structuralism to the New Institutional Economics: A Half Century of Latin American Economic Historiography," *Latin American Research Review*, vol. 40, no. 3 (Oct. 2005): 97–99.

5. Smith, *Resisting Reagan*, 33–56; Grandin, *Empire's Workshop*, 89–102, 108–110; Gosse, "Active Engagement," 26.

6. These ideas draw heavily from the recent scholarship of Hector Perla, Jr., "'Si Nicaragua Venció, El Salvador Vencerá': Central American Agency in the Creation of the U.S.-Central American Peace and Solidarity Movement," *Latin American Research Review*, vol. 43, no. 2 (2008): 136–58; Gosse, "El Salvador Is Spanish," 303.

7. Renny Golden and Michael McConnell, *Sanctuary: The New Underground Railroad* (Maryknoll, NY: Orbis Books, 1986), 37–48; Smith, *Resisting Reagan*, 60–68.

8. Golden and McConnell, *Sanctuary*, 42–46; Susan Bibler Coutin, *The Culture of Protest: Religious Activism and the U.S. Sanctuary Movement* (Boulder, CO: Westview Press, 1993), 26–30; Nepstad, *Convictions*, 95–103, 128–35; Smith, *Resisting Reagan*, 65–66; Harry Mattison, Susan Meiselas, Fae Rubenstein, eds., *El Salvador: Work of Thirty Photographers* (New York: Writers and Readers Publishing Cooperative, 1983), 30–33, 63.

9. Smith, *Resisting Reagan*, 60–68; Golden and McConnell, *Sanctuary*, 46–54; Susan Gzesh, "Central Americans and Asylum Policy in the Reagan Era," Migration Information Source, Apr. 2006, www.migrationinformation.org/feature/display.cfm

(accessed June 10, 2008). A table in Smith, *Resisting Reagan*, 185, and based on data compiled for the Chicago Religious Task Force directory in 1987 provides the most definitive tally of groups that served as sanctuaries.

10. Golden and McConnell, *Sanctuary*, 49–54; Coutin, *Culture of Protest*, 5–12; "Guatemalan Family Reaches Refuge," *New York Times*, Mar. 25, 1984, 18.

11. Juan's story is recounted in Golden and McConnell, *Sanctuary*, 49–51. Perla elucidates the idea of the signal flare strategy in "'Si Nicaragua Venció,'" 142–43. In 1999 Rigoberta Menchú became a subject of controversy upon publication of a study by the anthropologist David Stoll, who claimed that she had misrepresented events in her village and inaccurately presented them as representative of Guatemalan indigenous villages as a whole. Yet Stoll's main contention was with scholarly accuracy, and he conceded the merit of her portrait of the Guatemalan military's atrocities and her worthiness as a Nobel laureate.

12. Perla, "'Si Nicaragua Venció,'" 148–51; Gosse, "El Salvador Is Spanish," 320–21; Gosse, "Active Engagement," 26–27; Van Gosse, "'The North American Front': Central American Solidarity in the Reagan Era," in Mike Davis and Michael Sprinker, eds., *Reshaping the U.S. Left: Popular Struggles in the 1980s* (New York: Verso, 1988), 22–28; "The FBI and CISPES: A Special Report," Swarthmore College Peace Collection, CISPES collection, 1988; "In 50 States CISPES Is Working to End U.S. Intervention in Central America," map, SCPC, CISPES collection, 1985. SHARE and New El Salvador Today later merged and still exist as the SHARE Foundation.

13. CISPES, "March 27: At the Crossroads," flyer for March 27, 1982, Washington, D.C., protest, SCPC.

14. CISPES, "March 27"; Caryle Murphy, "Protest: 23,000 Demonstrate Against Role of U.S. in El Salvador," *Washington Post*, Mar. 28, 1982, A1; Martin Tolchin, "Thousands in Washington March to Protest U.S. Policy in El Salvador," *New York Times*, Mar. 28, 1982, Sect.1, 18.

15. CISPES, "Healing the Wounds of War: Healthcare for the People of El Salvador," SCPC, 1985; Angela Sambrano, National Referendum to End the War in Central America letter, SCPC, 1987; author's correspondence with Van Gosse, Apr. 3, 2009; CISPES press releaase, "Reagan Scores Public Relation Coup in Duarte Election," 1985, SCPC; CISPES, "Nicaragua Update," Jan. 1984, SCPC; Gosse, "El Salvador Is Spanish," 320–21; Perla "'Si Nicaragua Venció,'" 148–51; Gosse, "Active Engagement," 29.

16. Letter to Mid-Atlantic CISPES committees, April 1, 1986, CISPES-1986 Mid-Atlantic Regional Conference folder, SCPC; Mervyn Dymally, "Dear Fellow American Citizen," letter, 1986, CISPES collection, SCPC; Angela Sambrano and Barbara Wein, "Dear Concerned Friends," letter, Mar. 1, 1986, CISPES collection, SCPC. The "bitter prospect" comment is from Ron Dellums, "Dear Friend," letter, 1983, CISPES collection, SCPC.

17. "The FBI and CISPES"; Smith, *Resisting Reagan*, 286–93; Steve Milligan, letter to the editor, *Washington Post*, July 27, 1989, A22; Ross Gelbspan, "Documents Appear to Contradict Sessions on Probe," *Boston Globe*, Nov. 29, 1988, 11; Ross

Gelbspan, "FBI Altered Lie Test Result, Papers Show," *Boston Globe*, Dec. 29, 1988, 1; "FBI Report Critical of Surveillance of Reagan Policy Foes," *San Francisco Chronicle*, June 14, 1988, A15; Ronald Ostrow, "Inquiry Targeted Foes of Latin Policy: 6 FBI Officials Disciplined for Broad Terrorism Probe," *Los Angeles Times*, Sep. 15, 1988, 26; Hugh Byrne, letter to the editor, *Washington Post*, Jul. 27, 1989, A22; Ruth Marcus, "Dissident Group Seeks to Seal Records of 3-Year FBI Probe," *Washington Post*, Nov. 30, 1988, A5.

18. "A Promise of Resistance," *Sojourners*, Dec. 1983, 6; Jim Wallis, "A Pledge of Resistance: A Contingency Plan in the Event of a U.S. Invasion of Nicaragua," *Sojourners*, Aug. 1984, 10–11; Smith, *Resisting Reagan*, 78–79, 401n10.

19. Wallis, "A Pledge of Resistance," 10–11; Smith, *Resisting Reagan*, 81, 401n11, 401n12.

20. Emergency Response Network, *Basta! No Mandate for War: A Pledge of Resistance Handbook* (Philadelphia: New Society Publishers, 1986). The King quote is from 81; Ken Butigan, "The Pledge of Resistance," http://pacebene.org/nvns/essays-nonviolence/pledge-resistance (accessed Feb. 6, 2009) 1–13; Smith, *Resisting Reagan*, 79–81.

21. Butigan, "The Pledge of Resistance," 7; Smith, *Resisting Reagan*, 81–86; Gosse, "Active Engagement," 23; Dee Norton, "Contra-Aid Foes Tie Up Traffic on First Avenue," *Seattle Times*, Oct. 24, 1986," 1; Andrea Schwarzmann, "100 Fast for a Day to Protest U.S. Policy in Central America," *Orange County Register*, Oct. 11, 1986, B7; Mariann Hansen, "Activists 'Dump' U.S. Trade Policy Against Nicaragua," *L.A. Times* (Orange County Edition) July 10, 1988, II, 3; "Peace Groups to Protest U.S. War in Central America with August 22 Action at Arlington Heights Military Base," press release, Aug. 13, 1987, Pledge of Resistance (POR) collection, SCPC; Victor Volland, "8 Activists Arrested at Union Station," *St. Louis Post-Dispatch*, May 16, 1989, in POR collection, SCPC; "Suspenseful Message," photo in *Washington Times*, May 17, 1989, in POR collection, SCPC. For a detailed discussion of 1960s-era public performances, see Bradford Martin, *The Theater Is in the Street: Politics and Public Performance in Sixties America* (Amherst, MA: University of Massachusetts Press, 2004).

22. Gosse, "El Salvador Is Spanish," 322; Mario Lungo Uclés, *El Salvador in the Eighties: Counterinsurgency and Revolution* (Philadelphia: Temple University Press, 1986), 178–79; Smith, *Resisting Reagan*, 78–86.

23. My concluding thoughts on the Central America solidarity movement draw most heavily from Gosse, "Active Engagement," 22–29; Smith, *Resisting Reagan*, 367–70; and Butigan, "The Pledge of Resistance," 10–13. Jackson Browne's *Lives in the Balance* (Asylum, 1986); the Clash's *Sandinista!* (Epic, 1980), especially "Washington Bullets"; U2's "Mothers of the Disappeared" on *The Joshua Tree* (Island Records, 1987); and Oliver Stone's film *Salvador* are just a few of the noteworthy 1980s expressions of popular culture that reference the injustices in Central America that the solidarity movement tried to expose and prevent. Quoted material on the faith-based movement appears in Jeffrey L. Sheler, "Out of the Pulpit, into the Streets: Church Activists Are on the March," *U.S. News*

and World Report, Apr. 21, 1986, 16. For instructive insight into the persistence and transformation of Witness for Peace and CISPES since the 1980s, see their websites, www.witnessforpeace.org/ (accessed Feb. 11, 2009) and www.cispes .org (accessed Feb. 11, 2009).

3: "UNSIGHTLY HUTS"

1. In a sociological study of the shanties as a divestment movement tactic, Sarah A. Soule, "The Student Divestment Movement in the United States and Tactical Diffusion: The Shantytown Protest," *Social Forces* 75 (3) (Mar. 1997): 855–83, the author concludes that media attention to early shantytown protests encouraged the tactic to spread, especially among northeastern colleges and universities with similarly high levels of prestige. Soule effectively conceives a model for the diffusion of the shanties as a tactic among the elite schools, yet as I will argue, the shanties became a wider phenomenon that transcended their origins in elite institutions, ultimately appearing in nonelite institutions as well.
2. Jurgen Habermas, *The Structural Transformation of the Public Sphere: An Inquiry into a Category of Bourgeois Society* (Cambridge, MA: MIT Press, 2001).
3. See, for instance: Lynn Staeheli, "Publicity, Privacy, and Women's Political Action," *Environment and Planning D: Society and Space*, XIV (1996): 601–19; and Margaret Kohn, *Brave New Neighborhoods: The Privatization of Public Space* (New York: Routledge, 2004), 9–14.
4. Interview with Michael Morand, May 18, 2005.
5. Interview with David Lyons, June 15, 2005; correspondence with David Lyons, June 2, 2006; interview with Anne Evens, May 23, 2005.
6. Interview with Rajiv Menon, May 25, 2005.
7. Interviews with Tom Burke, July 6, 2005, and Prexy Nesbitt, May 19, 2005; correspondence with Tom Burke, June 2, 2006, David Leitch, June 2, 2006, and Prexy Nesbitt, June 2, 2006.
8. Eric L. Hirsch, "Sacrifice for the Cause: Group Processes, Recruitment, and Commitment in a Student Social Movement," *American Sociological Review*, vol. 55, issue 2 (April 1990): 243–54, is a study of the spring 1985 protest at Columbia that argues that divestment protests met the criteria for powerful collective empowerment in that they were highly visible, dramatic, and disrupted normal institutional routines. Hirsch also points out the involvement of off-campus groups, such as Harlem community groups, churches, unions, the African National Congress, and the United Nations. Significantly, the Columbia protest he examines occurred before the emergence of the shanties, which only tended to enhance the collective empowerment and outsider participation to which he alludes.
9. A. Bartlett Giammati, *A Free and Ordered Space: The Real World of the University* (New York: W. W. Norton & Company, 1988).
10. Don Mitchell, *The Right to the City: Social Justice and the Fight for Public Space* (New York: Guilford Press, 2003), 35–36; Henri Lefebvre, "The Right to the City," in *Writing on Cities* (Oxford: Blackwell Publishers, 1996), 63–181; "The

right to a particular space" and "the where of protest," are drawn from Mitchell, *The Right to the City*, 102–103.

11. Though shanties were innovative in the sense that they were not used as a tactic in the student protests of the preceding 1960s generation, protest encampments did have some precedent in the United States, perhaps most notoriously in the Depression-era Bonus Army incident.

12. David M. Gross, "Proceeding with Caution," *Time*, July 16, 1990, 56–62; Mitchell, *The Right to the City*, 102–105, insightfully discusses the spatial aspects of the Berkeley Free Speech Movement. The first and the third quoted phrases are from the author's interview with Mark Lurie, May 12, 2005. The second is from the author's interview with Morand, May 18, 2005.

13. Taylor Branch, *Pillar of Fire: America in the King Years, 1963–1965* (New York: Simon and Schuster, 1998), 156, 460, 508, 547; Christopher A. Coons, *The Response of Colleges and Universities to Calls for Divestment* (Washington, D.C.: Investor Responsibility Research Center, 1986), 3; Mike Davis, "America's Black Shining Prince," *Socialist Review*, Mar. 2005, 1; John G. Simon, Charles W. Powers, and Jon P. Gunnermann, *The Ethical Investor: Universities and Corporate Responsibility* (New Haven: Yale University Press, 1972), 1–4.

14. Coons, *The Response of Colleges*, 3–4.

15. Ibid., 4.

16. Joseph Berger, "Dr. King Honored by Wide Protests," *New York Times*, Apr. 5, 1985, A4; Tony Vellela, *New Voices: Student Political Activism in the 80's and 90's* (Boston: South End Press, 1988), 20, 24–30; Coons, *The Response of Colleges*, 5–7; Larry Rohter, "Activism at Schools Seems to Be Stirring as Protests Continue," *New York Times*, Apr. 25, 1985, A1, A20; Todd Gitlin, "Divestment Stirs a New Generation," *The Nation*, May 18, 1985, 585–87. Michael Oreskes, "Protests at Columbia: Students and Issues Have Changed Since the 60's," *New York Times*, Apr. 13, 1985, 25.

17. Interviews with Matthew Lyons, May 23, 2005; Morand, May 18, 2005; Menon, May 25, 2005; and Lurie, May 12, 2005. Figures on demonstrations are from Rohter, "Activism at Schools," A1, A20; and Coons, *The Response of Colleges*, 6–7.

18. Hirsch, "Sacrifice for the Cause," 248.

19. Interviews with Nancy Fishman, May 17, 2005; Lyons, May 23, 2005; and Menon, May 25, 2005.

20. Interviews with Nesbitt, May 19, 2005; Lyons, May 23, 2005; Scott Nova, June 7, 2005; and Morand, May 18, 2005.

21. "Use of University Property Form," Apr. 22, 1985, David and Matthew Lyons Cornell Divestment Movement Collection (LCDMC), Division of Rare and Manuscript Collections, Cornell University Library, box 1, Shantytown Documents, 1986–87; Catherine Johnston, "Statement for the University Hearing Board," June 5, 1985, LCDMC; "CU—Shantytown History," LCDMC.

22. Interview with Matthew Lyons, May 23, 2005; interview with Evens, May 23, 2005; "Use of University Property Form," LCDMC.

23. David Lyons used this phrase in an interview with the author on June 15, 2005; Donald A. Downs's monograph on the events at Cornell in the spring of 1969, *Cornell '69: Liberalism and the Crisis of the American University* (Ithaca, NY: Cornell University Press, 1999), 19, argues that the Perkins administration's handling of the black student activists represented "the dangers of not preserving the distinct intellectual integrity of the university as we pursue our thirst for justice."

24. Matthew Lyons, in a May 23, 2005, interview with the author, offered an explanation for the fire that is missing from the documentary evidence: "It was caused by a kerosene heater," he remarked. "It was stupid. Fortunately, nobody was hurt. Things were rebuilt quickly with strict rules"; "CU—Shantytown History"; memo from P. K. Reaves, deputy fire chief, to Gordon Macumber, director, Life Safety, Cornell University, LCDMC; "Shantytown Fire Regulations," May 11, 1985, LCDMC.

25. "EMERGENCY EMERGENCY EMERGENCY MEMO FROM SHANTYTOWN," LCDMC; interviews with Nesbitt, May 19, 2005, Evens, May 23, 2005, and Matthew Lyons, May 23, 2005; memo to Cornell faculty and staff from students in Shantytown, June 24, 1985, LCDMC, box 1, Shantytown Civil Litigation.

26. "Brief in Support of Motion to Vacate Plaintiff Temporary Restraining Order and for a Temporary Restraining Order to Protect Defendants," June 27, 1985, LCDMC; William G. Herbster, "Memo to Residents of 'Shantytown,'" May 17, 1985, LCDMC.

27. "University Statement Issued Friday, May 17, 1985," LCDMC; Leonard O. Green, "Affidavit," July 1, 1985, LCDMC.

28. "Complaint," *Cornell University v. Loreelynn Adamson, et al.*, June 25, 1985, LCDMC, box 1; memo to Cornell faculty and staff, June 24, 1985, LCDMC.

29. Soule, "The Student Divestment Movement in the United States." The quote is from 859.

30. Vellela, *New Voices,* 30; interview with Lurie, May 12, 2005.

31. Interview with Menon, May 25, 2005; Chad Rosenburger, "Student Activism Returns to Ivy League Campuses," *The Dartmouth's Weekend Magazine,* May 17, 1985; Brian Corcoran, "UVM Trustees Decide Against Divestiture," *The Dartmouth,* Oct. 15, 1985, 1; Carolyne Allen, "Students Build Shanty-towns to Show Divestment Concerns," *The Dartmouth,* Nov. 13, 1985, 1, 10; Toby Benis, "Students to Begin Building Shanty-town at Noon Today," *The Dartmouth,* Nov. 15, 1985, 1–2.

32. Benis, "Students to Begin Building," 1–2; John Herrick, "Group Constructs Third Shanty," *The Dartmouth,* Nov. 19, 1985, 1, 10; Adam Seiden, "Speakers Address Crowd of 200," *The Dartmouth,* Nov. 19, 1985, 1, 7; Toby Benis, "Protesters Will Build Third Shanty," *The Dartmouth,* Nov. 18, 1985, 1–2, 10; interviews with Menon, May 25, 2005, Scott Nova, June 7, 2005, and Jerry Hughes, June 23, 2005.

33. The reference to the "physical and emotional center" is from Dartmouth College's official website, www.dartmouth.edu/ (accessed July 5, 2005); John Herrick, "Students Split on Divestment Issue," *The Dartmouth,* Nov. 22, 1985, 16; interview with Evens, May 23, 2005.

34. Herrick, "Students Split," 16; Toby J. Garnett, "Shanty Wins Design Award," *The Dartmouth*, Jan. 25, 1986, 1–2; Lawrence Levine makes this point about parody in his seminal discussion of the role of Shakespeare in the daily lives of nineteenth-century Americans in *Highbrow/Lowbrow: The Emergence of Cultural Hierarchy in America* (Cambridge, MA: Harvard University Press, 1988), 15–16; Jay Fogarty, "Art Imitating Protest," *The Dartmouth*, Feb. 25, 1986, 4; Adam Rabiner, "Shantytown: A Solution to Housing Woes," *The Dartmouth*, Nov. 22, 1985, 13.

35. "Shantyspeak," *The Dartmouth Review*, Dec. 11, 1985, 4; interview with Hughes, June 23, 2005; Robert Mazzarese, "Continue Constructive Engagement," letter to the editor in *The Dartmouth*, Nov. 22, 1985, 13; B. C. Conroy, "Shanties Verge on Martyrdom," *The Dartmouth*, Jan. 14, 1986, 4; Laurie Adams and Bruce Acker, "Shanties Aren't the Only Ugly Thing on Campus," *The Dartmouth*, Jan. 7, 1986.

36. Interview with Hughes, June 23, 2005; Dartmouth Committee to Beautify the Green Before Winter Carnival, letter to President McLaughlin, Jan. 20, 1986, reprinted in *Dartmouth Review*, Jan. 29, 1986, 9.

37. Laura Ingraham's "Counter-Revolution at Dartmouth," *National Review*, Mar. 14, 1986, 20, lists the numerous media outlets that covered the attack on the shanties at Dartmouth and its aftermath; Jon Wiener, "Students, Stocks, and Shanties," *The Nation*, Oct. 11, 1986, 337–40; Eloise Salholz, "Shanties on the Green," *Newsweek*, Feb. 3, 1986, 63; "Shantyism," *Fortune*, June 9, 1986, 156; "The Usual Fiasco at Dartmouth," *National Review*, Feb. 28, 1986, 20–21; "The Shanty Wars Are About Much More," *National Review*, May 9, 1986.

38. Elizabeth Bury, "A Hawaiian Model for Divestment," *The Dartmouth*, Apr. 20, 1987, 4; "Anti-apartheid Shanties Allowed by Federal Judge," *The Circle* (College Press Service), Sep. 25, 1986, 9; Joan O'Brien, "U. of U. to Review Policy on S. Africa Divestment," *Salt Lake Tribune*, Oct. 30, 1993, D4. The material on the University of Illinois draws on the following articles, all of which are included in the University of Illinois Archives, Champaign-Urbana Coalition Against Apartheid, 1964–1991, box 7 and box 8: J. Philip Bloomer, "UI Warns Students to Get Approval for Shanty," *Champaign-Urbana News-Gazette*, Apr. 9, 1986; Dave Olson, "Protesters Tear Down Shantytown," *Daily Illini*, Apr. 14, 1986, 1, 7; Dave Olson, "Quad Shanties Taken Down," *Daily Illini*, Apr. 21, 1986, 1, 7; J. Philip Bloomer, "UI Divestment Vote Was of Little Surprise," *Champaign-Urbana News-Gazette*, Jan. 15, 1987; and interview with Tom Burke, July 6, 2005. Mitchell, *The Right to the City*, 128–29, draws on the work of French social theorist Henri Lefebvre to coin the term "spaces for representation" to signify democratized public spaces open to a range of diverse people and activities.

39. Paul Rogat Loeb, *Generation at the Crossroads: Apathy and Action on the American Campus* (New Brunswick, NJ: Rutgers University Press, 1994), 171–74; Jennifer D. Kibbe, *Divestment on Campus: Update on the Top 50 Schools* (Washington, D.C.: Investor Responsibility Research Center, 1992); Neta C. Crawford and Audie Klotz, eds., *How Sanctions Work: Lessons from South Africa* (New

York: St. Martin's Press, 1999), see especially Crawford, "Trump Card or Theater? An Introduction to Two Sanctions Debates," 3–24, and Meg Vorhees, "The U.S. Divestment Movement," 129–44.

40. Interviews with Nova, June 7, 2005; Burke, July 6, 2005; Lurie, May 12, 2005; Fishman, May 17, 2005; and Lyons, May 23, 2005; "Shantyism," 156.

4: POPULAR CULTURE AND THE CULTURE WARS

1. George Hackett, "Banding Together for Africa," *Newsweek*, July 15, 1985, 52; Robert Hilburn, "Live Aid Aftermath: Rock Goes Good Guy," *San Francisco Chronicle*, July 21, 1985, 33; Samuel G. Freedman, "Live Aid and the Woodstock Nation," *New York Times*, July 18, 1985, C19.

2. "Will 'Live Aid' Really Reach the Hungry?" *U.S. News and World Report*, July 29, 1985, 8; David Breskin, "Bob Geldof: The Rolling Stone Interview," *Rolling Stone*, Dec. 5, 1985, 63–64; David Fricke, "The Man Who Wouldn't Take No for an Answer," *Rolling Stone*, Aug. 15, 1985, 20.

3. Reebee Garofalo, *Rockin' Out: Popular Music in the U.S.A.*, 4th ed. (Upper Saddle River, NJ: Pearson Prentice Hall, 2008), 347–48; Reebee Garofalo, "Understanding Mega-Events: If We Are the World, Then How Do We Change It," in Reebee Garofalo, ed., *Rockin' the Boat: Mass Music and Mass Movements* (Boston: South End Press, 1992), 33; Fricke, "The Man Who Wouldn't," 31–33; Jay Cocks, "Rocking the Global Village," *Time*, July 22, 1985, 66–67; Esther Fein, "Stands and Phone Lines Jammed for Aid Concert," *New York Times*, July 14, 1985, 1; Esther Fein, "'Live Aid' Concert Is Aiming for the Sky," *New York Times*, July 12, 1985, C5.

4. Fein, "Stands and Phone Lines," 1; Samuel Freedman, "Live Aid and the Woodstock Nation," *New York Times*, July 18, 1985, C19; Robert Hilburn, "Ending Hunger: Now That We Can, We Must," *Los Angeles Times*, July 15, 1985, 1.

5. Pete Hamill, "A Day to Remember," *Rolling Stone*, Aug. 29, 1985, 74. Marcus is quoted in Garofalo, "Understanding Mega-Events," 29, to whose analysis of Live Aid and other related events I am indebted in this discussion. The Geldof quote is from Breskin, "Bob Geldof," 63.

6. Garofalo, "Understanding Mega-Events," 29; Cocks, "Rocking the Global Village," 66–67; Mark Coleman, "The Revival of Conscience," *Rolling Stone*, Nov. 15, 1990, 69; Stuart Hall, *The Hard Road to Renewal: Thatcherism and the Crisis of the Left* (London: Verso, 1988), 251–58; David Gates, "Farm Aid: From Merle Haggard to X, They Played to Save the Farm," *Rolling Stone*, Nov. 7, 1985, 24–28, 67–69; www.farmaid.org/site/c.qlI5IhNVJsE/b.2723609/k.C8F1/About_ Us.htm (accessed July 9, 2009); Garofalo, *Rockin' Out*, 351; Neal Ullestad, "Rock and Rebellion: Subversive Effects of Live Aid and 'Sun City,'" *Popular Music*, vol. 6, no. 1 (Jan. 1987): 67–76.

7. Ullestad, "Rock and Rebellion," 67–76; Garofalo, "Understanding Mega-Events," 30–34; Garofalo, *Rockin' Out*, 351; "Music Yearbook 1985—Sun City," *Rolling Stone*, Dec. 19, 1985, 66; Artists United Against Apartheid, *Sun City*, www.you

tube.com/watch?v=OjWENNe29qc (accessed July 9, 2009); "Sun City: Artists United Against Apartheid," www.imdb.com/title/tt0286176/fullcredits (accessed July 9, 2009).

8. David Fricke, "Caravan for Human Rights," *Rolling Stone*, June 19, 1986, 69–60, 96–99; Anthony DeCurtis, "Amnesty Membership Up: Tour Cited," *Rolling Stone*, Apr. 23, 1987, 25; Wayne Robins, "U2, Sting, Fine-Tune Amnesty Concert," *Newsday*, June 17, 1986, 7; Garofalo, *Rockin' Out*, 352–53; Garofalo, "Understanding Mega-Events," 34; Garofalo, *Rockin' Out*, 351.

9. Jon Pareles, "Amnesty Concert in Jersey," *New York Times*, June 16, 1986, C14; Garofalo, *Rockin' Out*, 353; Garofalo, "Understanding Mega-Events," 33; Cathleen McGuigan, "Singing for a Worthy Cause," *Newsweek*, Sep. 12, 1988, 76; Bruce Haring, "Despite Disorganization, Amnesty Show Is Success," *Billboard*, Oct. 1, 1988, 84; Charles Bermant, "Benefit for Amnesty Keeps 'Doors Open'" *The Globe and Mail*, June 6, 1986, C9; Coleman, "The Revival of Conscience," 76. The quote is from Hendrik Hertzberg, "Vox Pop," *New Republic*, Oct. 10, 1988, 14.

10. Bermant, "Benefit for Amnesty," C9; Nick Robertshaw, "U.K. Kicks Off Human Rights Now!" *Billboard*, Sep. 17, 1988, 6. DeCurtis, "Amnesty Membership Up," 25; Ken Tucker, "A Rock Tour to Aid Political Prisoners," *Philadelphia Inquirer*, June 15, 1986, H1; Hertzberg, "Vox Pop," 14; Garofalo, "Understanding Mega-Events," 35; Springsteen, quoted in McGuigan, "Singing for a Worthy Cause," 76.

11. Ronald Reagan, "Remarks at a Reagan-Bush Rally in Hammonton, New Jersey," Sep. 19, 1984, *The Public Papers of President Ronald W. Reagan*, www.reagan .utexas.edu/archives/speeches/1984/91984c.htm (accessed Sep. 2, 2009); Francis Clines, "President Heaps Praise on Voters in Northeast," *New York Times*, Sep. 20, 1984, B20; Robert Santelli, *Greetings from E Street: The Story of Bruce Springsteen and the E Street Band* (San Francisco: Chronicle Books, 2006), 68.

12. Bruce Springsteen, *Born in the U.S.A.* (Columbia Records, 1984); Kurt Loder, "The Rolling Stone Interview: Bruce Springsteen," *Rolling Stone*, Dec. 6, 1984, 21.

13. Jefferson Morley, "The Phenomenon," *Rolling Stone*, Oct. 10, 1985, 35, 72–75; George Will, "Bruce Springsteen's U.S.A.," *Washington Post*, Sep. 13, 1984, A19.

14. Loder, "The Rolling Stone Interview," 21; Dave Marsh, *Glory Days: Bruce Springsteen in the 1980s* (New York: Pantheon Books, 1987), 388–92; Paulo Calvi, "Bruce Springsteen Database—Killing Floor Discography, Lyrics, Setlists, and . . ." www .brucespringsteen.it/Showdx.htm (accessed Sep. 10, 2009).

15. Susan Jeffords, *Hard Bodies: Hollywood Masculinity in the Reagan Era* (New Brunswick, NJ: Rutgers University Press, 1994), 24–28; James William Gibson, *Warrior Dreams: Paramilitary Culture in Post-Vietnam America* (New York: Hill and Wang, 1994), 9–10; John Orman, *Comparing Presidential Behavior: Carter, Reagan, and the Macho Presidential Style* (New York: Greenwood Press, 1987); Richard Schickel, "Danger: Live Moral Issues," *Time*, May 27, 1985, 91; Bernard Weinraub, "Reagan Hails Move," *New York Times*, July 1, 1985, A1; Adam Pertman, "Tass Hits Reagan Rambo Remark, Recalls Bomb Joke," *Boston Globe*, July 2, 1985, 13; Robert Sklar, *Movie-Made America: A Cultural History*

of American Movies, revised and updated ed. (New York: Vintage Books, 1994), 345.

16. Sklar, *Movie-Made America*, 289–90, 339–45; Stephen Prince, *A New Pot of Gold: Hollywood Under the Electronic Rainbow, 1980–1989* (New York: Charles Scribner's Sons, 2000), 1–18; Stephen Prince, ed., *American Cinema of the 1980s: Themes and Variations* (New Brunswick, NJ: Rutgers University Press, 2007), 1–3.

17. Vincent Canby, "Film: The Vietnam War in Stone's 'Platoon,'" *New York Times*, Dec. 19, 1986, C12, uses the phrase "revisionist comic strips"; David Sterritt, "Oliver Stone: Why 'Platoon' Was Made So Harsh," *Christian Science Monitor*, Jan. 9, 1987, 23; Paul Attanasio, "Platoon's Raw Mastery," *Washington Post*, Jan. 16, 1987, B1; Rita Kempley, "'Platoon': Awesome Requiem," *Washington Post*, Jan. 16, 1987, N17, uses the phrase "explodes the *Rambo* myth"; Vincent Canby, "Film View: 'Platoon' Finds New Life in Old War Movie," *New York Times*, Jan. 11, 1987, A21; "Veterans Reactions to 'Platoon' Vary," *Wilmington Morning Star*, Jan. 28, 1987, 17; Sklar, *Movie-Made America*, 360–61; "Platoon Meets Rambo," *New York Times*, Jan. 22, 1987, A26. Frank Beaver, *Oliver Stone: Wakeup Cinema* (New York: Twayne Publishers, 1994), 83–98, also includes an excellent section on *Platoon*, of which my interpretation makes use.

18. Vincent Canby, "Film View: Costa-Gavras's Striking Cinematic Achievement," *New York Times*, Feb. 14, 1982, II: 19; Peter Greenberg, "Art, Lies and Reality: An Interview with Costa Gavras," *Rolling Stone*, May 13, 1982, 15–18, 72–73; Van Gosse, "Unpacking the Vietnam Syndrome: The Coup in Chile and the Rise of Popular Anti-Interventionism," in Gosse and Moser, *The World the 60s Made*, 100–13; Stuart Taylor, Jr., "Libel Suit Is Filed Against 'Missing,'" *New York Times*, Jan. 11, 1983, C12; "Libel Charges Voided In 'Missing' Dispute," *New York Times*, Feb. 9, 1984, C17.

19. Rita Kempley, "'Under Fire': Underdone, Overblown," *Washington Post*, Oct. 21, 1983, W19; Vincent Canby, "Screen: 'Under Fire,'" *New York Times*, Feb. 14, 1982, C13; Aljean Harmetz, "5 Films with Political Statements Due This Fall," *New York Times*, Sep. 10, 1983, 1; Richard Bernstein, "Issues Raised by 'Under Fire,'" *New York Times*, Oct. 30, 1983, H9; Richard Higgins, "Good Intentions Don't Save 'Romero,'" *Boston Globe*, Nov. 17, 1989, 89; Vincent Canby, "El Salvador's Slain Hero of the Cloth," *New York Times*, Aug. 25, 1989, C15; Prince, *A New Pot of Gold*, 323–28.

20. Prince, *A New Pot of Gold*, 260–61, 272, 323–28; Ben Dickenson, *Hollywood's New Radicalism: War, Globalisation and the Movies from Reagan to George W. Bush* (London: I. B. Taurus, 2006), 23–24; Marc Cooper, "Postcards from the Left," *The Nation*, Apr. 5/12, 1999, 21–26; Leger Grindon, "1986: Movies and Fissures in Reagan's America," in Prince, *American Cinema of the 1980s*, 146; Jack Kroll, "Hell at Close Range," *Newsweek*, Mar. 17, 1986, 81; Gene Siskel, "As Political Film, 'Salvador' More Insult Than Message," *Chicago Tribune*, Apr. 25, 1986, A.

21. Beaver, *Oliver Stone: Wakeup Cinema*, 99–112; Alison Cowan, "Making 'Wall Street' Look Like Wall Street," *New York Times*, Dec. 30, 1987, C16; John Si-

mon, "Death and Soul-Death," *National Review*, Jan. 22, 1988, 64–66; Vincent Canby, "Film: Stone's 'Wall Street,'" *New York Times*, Dec. 11, 1987, C3; Geraldine Fabrikant, "Wall Street Reviews 'Wall Street,'" *New York Times*, Dec. 10, 1987, D1; Maureen Orth, "Talking to Oliver Stone," *Vogue*, Dec. 1987, 166, 172.

22. *Roger and Me*, Dog Eat Dog Productions/Warner Bros., 1989; Gleen Collins, "A Self-Taught Film Maker Creates a Comic Hit," *New York Times*, Sep. 28, 1989, C15; Harlan Jacobson, "Michael and Me," *Film Comment*, Nov.–Dec. 1989, 16–26; William Winters, "'Roger and Me': Truth in Packaging?" [letter], *New York Times*, July 8, 1990, A3; Pauline Kael, "The Current Cinema," *New Yorker*, Jan. 8, 1990, 90–92; Richard Corliss, "Michael & Roger & Phil & Flint: Roger & Me," *Time*, Feb. 12, 1990, 58. Prince, *A New Pot of Gold*, 386–88, includes insightful discussion of the Jacobson and Kael criticisms of *Roger and Me*, concluding that though filmmakers have long ago rejected cinema verité notions that documentary filmmaking should represent the "unmanipulated" truth, making the counterargument that the form is by its nature a creative act, the public and many critics have been slow to accept this idea. Prince also refers to Moore as having arranged his material in "the tidy narrative structure of a Hollywood movie." New York *Newsday* interview with Michael Moore, *Newsday*, Jan. 25, 1990, 65; Hal Hinson, "'Roger: Rage and Irreverence," *Washington Post*, Jan. 12, 1990, D1; Roger Ebert, "The Cheapest Shots: Attacks on 'Roger & Me' Completely Miss Point of Film," *Chicago Sun-Times*, Feb. 11, 1990, 5.

23. Peter Bart, "Red Dawn: Shooting It the McVeigh Way," *Variety*, June 16, 1997, 34; Rhonda Hammer and Douglas Kellner, "1984: Movies and Battles Over Reaganite Conservatism," in Prince, *American Cinema of the 1980s*, 114–17; Prince, *A New Pot of Gold*, 318–21; Dickenson, *Hollywood's New Radicalism*, 25–26.

24. Dickenson, *Hollywood's New Radicalism*, 12–14; Cooper, "Postcards from the Left," 21–26; Bill Roeder, "Ed Asner's 'Aid For El Salvador,'" *Newsweek*, Sep. 21, 1981, 25; "Heston Awaits Asner's Reaction to Protest," *New York Times*, Feb. 23, 1982, C15; Aljean Harmetz, "Screen Actors Panel Stands by Asner," *New York Times*, Feb. 26, 1982, C11; Leslie Berger, "The Actor as Activist: Ed Asner Takes on a Political Role for El Salvador," *Washington Post*, Feb. 16, 1982, B1; Bob Lardine, "Lou Grant Goes Out Kicking," *Boston Globe*, May 22, 1982, 1.

25. Cooper, "Postcards from the Left," 21–26; Dickenson, *Hollywood's New Radicalism*, 27, 78–80; Eric Alterman, "The Hollywood Campaign," *Atlantic Monthly*, Sep. 2004, 74; "Ms. Smith Goes to Hollywood," *Economist*, Nov. 3, 1990, 36; Betsy Streisand, "Committing Political Suicide," *U.S. News & World Report*, Apr. 28, 1997, 10; "Women's Political Group Disbands in Hollywood," *New York Times*, Apr. 14, 1997, 15; Brent Bozell, "Ultra-Feminists Abort Liberal Show-Biz PAC," *Human Events*, May 16, 1997, 10; Harold Meyerson, "Can Liberalism Survive Clinton?" *Dissent*, Fall 1997, 27; Mollie Gregory, *Women Who Run the Show: How a Brilliant and Creative New Generation of Women Stormed Hollywood* (New York: St. Martin's Press, 2002), 121–22.

26. Allan Bloom, *The Closing of the American Mind: How Higher Education Has Failed Democracy and Impoverished the Souls of Today's Students* (New York:

Simon and Schuster, 1987), 74–75; Ezra Bowen, "Are Student Heads Full of Emptiness?" *Time*, Aug. 17, 1987, 56–57. The conservative commentator Dinesh D'Souza coined the sobriquet "Visigoths in Tweed." Paul Berman, ed., *Debating P.C.: The Controversy Over Political Correctness on College Campuses* (New York: Dell Publishing, 1992), 1–3; George Will, "Radical English," *Washington Post*, Sep. 16, 1990, B7.

27. See, for instance, Van Gosse, "Postmodern America: A New Democratic Order in the Second Gilded Age," in Gosse and Moser, *The World the 60s Made*, 1–36.

28. Roger Kimball, *Tenured Radicals: How Politics Has Corrupted Our Higher Education* (New York: Harper and Row, 1990); Liz McMillen, "Foundations Are Being Drawn into Colleges' Debate Over Cultural Diversity in the Curriculum," *Chronicle of Higher Education*, Apr. 26, 1989, A25–27.

29. Kimball, *Tenured Radicals*, 11–12. For a range of primary source perspective on the arts controversies of the late 1980s and early 1990s, see Richard Bolton, ed., *Culture Wars: Documents from the Recent Controversies in the Arts* (New York: New Press, 1992); Senator Jesse Helms, "It's the Job of Congress to Define What's Art," *USA Today*, Sep. 8, 1989, reprinted in Bolton, *Culture Wars*, 100–101; Robert Hughes, "Whose Art Is It, Anyway?" *Time*, June 4, 1990, 46–47; Robert Hughes, *Culture of Complaint: The Fraying of America* (New York: Oxford University Press, 1993), 163–64.

30. C. Carr, "Artful Dodging: The NEA Funds the Defunded Four," *Village Voice*, June 15, 1993, 30–31; John Frohnmayer, *Leaving Town Alive: Confessions of an Arts Warrior* (New York: Houghton Mifflin, 1993), 174–77; "Supreme Court on Decency in the Arts," http://0-library.cqpress.com.helin.uri.edu/historicdocuments/document.php?id=hsdc98-0000037411&type=hitlist&num=0 (accessed Oct. 29, 2009); David Schlossman, *Actors and Activists: Politics, Performance, and Exchange Among Social Worlds* (New York: Routledge, 2002), 207–208; Hughes, *Culture of Complaint*, 171, 200. The "can of soda" comparison appears in "Enemies of the Arts: The Republicans' Hit Men," *Rolling Stone*, Oct. 19, 1995, 47. NEA budget data appears in "The National Endowment for the Arts, 1965–2000: A Brief Chronology of Federal Support For the Arts," www.nea.gov/about/Chronology/NEAChronWeb.pdf (accessed Oct. 29, 2009).

31. William A. Henry III, "Show Business: You Can Take This Grant and . . . ," *Time*, July 16, 1990, 85; David Finkle, "High Performance: Mounting the NEA Backlash Backlash," *Village Voice*, Jan. 5, 1993, 54; Gray is quoted in Elizabeth Hess, "Bargaining with the Devil: How the NEA Lost Its Soul," *Village Voice*, Jan. 24, 1995, 27; Laura Shapiro, "A One-Woman Tour of Hell," *Newsweek*, Aug. 6, 1990, 60; Steven Dubin, *Arresting Images: Impolitic Art and Uncivil Actions* (New York: Routledge, 1992), 248–51.

5: NOISE FROM UNDERGROUND

1. See, for instance, Steve Chapple and Reebee Garofalo, *Rock 'n' Roll Is Here to Pay: The History and Politics of the Music Industry* (Chicago: University of

Chicago Press, 1977), 300; Simon Frith, *Sound Effects: Youth, Leisure, and the Politics of Rock 'n' Roll* (New York: Pantheon Books, 1981), 158–63; Reebee Garofalo, "How Autonomous Is Relative: Popular Music, the Social Formation and Cultural Struggle," *Popular Music* 6:1 (1987): 77–91.

2. The letters to the editor in *Maximumrocknroll* (hereafter cited as *MRR*) 23 (1985) are representative of fans' debates surrounding the issue of American intervention in Nicaragua. Vic Bondi, "Feeding the Noise Back into the System: Hardcore, Hip Hop, and Heavy Metal," New England American Studies Association Conference Paper (May 1993): 2–25, for instance, ascribes political opposition to Reagan conservatism to a "small group of marginalized young people."

3. Dick Hebdige's "Style as Homology and Signifying Practice," in Simon Frith and Andrew Goodwin, eds., *On Record: Rock, Pop, and the Written Word* (New York: Pantheon Books, 1990), 56–65, is a seminal essay on British punk style.

4. Greil Marcus, *Ranters & Crowd Pleasers: Punk in Pop Music, 1977–92* (New York: Doubleday, 1993), 91–92.

5. "Ian MacKaye + Jeff Nelson Interview," *Flipside* 29 (1981).

6. Jim Macnie, "Riffs: Sonic Youth," *Down Beat*, Mar. 1987, 14; Tom Carson, "America's Most Conceptual Bar Band," *Village Voice*, Nov. 6, 1984, 81.

7. Gina Arnold's *Route 666: On the Road to Nirvana* (New York: St. Martin's Press, 1993) provides a personal memoir of her experience as a fan of American indie rock. She includes a discussion of R.E.M.'s influence on the genre's trajectory toward commercial success, which concludes, "Ultimately, you can lay it all at R.E.M.'s feet" (58–59).

8. Frith, *Sound Effects*, 158–63. For indispensable discussions of 1970s punk, see also Jon Savage, *England's Dreaming: Anarchy, Sex Pistols, Punk Rock, and Beyond* (New York: St. Martin's Press, 1992); Clinton Heylin, *From the Velvets to the Voidoids: A Pre-Punk History for a Post-Punk World* (New York: Penguin Books, 1993); and Dave Laing, *One Chord Wonders: Power and Meaning in Punk Rock* (Philadelphia: Open University Press, 1985).

9. "Econo" was the Minutemen's favorite term for describing the do-it-yourself production ethic, which was designed to keep production costs low and authenticity high. This contrasted with high-budget, major-studio-produced music, which many post-punk fans and performers viewed as inauthentic and/or insincere. The Frith quote is from *Sound Effects*, 159. Garofalo, *Rockin' Out*, 367, and Barry Shank, *Dissonant Identities: The Rock 'n' Roll Scene in Austin, Texas* (Hanover, NH: Wesleyan University Press/University Press of New England, 1994), 218–23, offer contrasting viewpoints on the function and meaning of independent record labels. *Flipside* 52 (1987).

10. *MRR* 58 (1988); *Flipside* 52.

11. Garofalo, "How Autonomous," 78; *MRR* 62 (1988). My discussion of how fans experienced post-punk in ways that transcended record industry control takes its cue from Shank, *Dissonant Identities*, 204, which criticizes analyses of popular music that depict an all-powerful recording industry and tend to "reduce the human performance of musical sound to the practices of the recording industry."

He contends that this often conflates "the production of music with the production of records," lamenting that "too often the study of the recording industry has stood in for the study of popular music."

12. Schwartz is interviewed in Daniel Sinker, ed., *We Owe You Nothing: Punk Planet: The Collected Interviews* (New York: Akashic Books, 2001), 109–18.

13. Marcus, *Ranters*, 3, 21; Heylin, *From the Velvets*, 166. Bondi discusses noise as "cacophony" and as a rite of passage in "Feeding the Noise."

14. On punk transgression, see Laing, *One Chord Wonders*, 48–50, 91–94; and Savage, *England's Dreaming*, 66–68, 92–103. Sonic Youth's recurring thematic exploration of the Manson killings remains open to multiple interpretations, but the most insightful commentary has interpreted these songs as critiques of violence in American culture. See Rosemary Passantino, "Sonic Youth '85," *Village Voice*, June 11, 1985, 78; Peter Watrous, "Sonic Youth: California Dreaming," *Village Voice*, July 1, 1986, 85; Alec Foege, *Confusion Is Next: The Sonic Youth Story* (New York: St. Martin's Press, 1994), 119–23.

15. Laing, *One Chord Wonders*, 82. The quote appears in *Flipside* 29. On Minor Threat and the X mark, see "Ian MacKaye + Jeff Nelson Interview" and Bondi, "Feeding the Noise," 6.

16. Savage, *England's Dreaming*, 280–81. The survey is discussed in greater detail in Bradford Martin, "'. . . And You Voted for That Guy': 1980s Post-Punk and Oppositional Politics," *Journal of Popular Music Studies* 16:2 (2004): 142–74. Robert Walser, *Running with the Devil: Power, Gender, and Madness in Heavy Metal Music* (Hanover, NH: University Press of New England, 1993), 18, 175–77.

17. Martin, "'. . . And You Voted,'" 142–74.

18. Ibid.; Shank, *Dissonant Identities*, xiii–xiv, 146–60, 250; *Flipside* 29.

19. My interpretation of post-punk culture as replete with everyday forms of resistance owes a substantial debt to Robin D. G. Kelley's work, see especially *Race Rebels: Culture, Politics, and the Black Working Class* (New York: The Free Press, 1994), 8–9.

20. Bondi, "Feeding the Noise," 10–12; James William Gibson, *Warrior Dreams: Paramilitary Culture in Post-Vietnam America* (New York: Hill and Wang, 1994), 6–10, 39–40; *MRR* 34 (1986).

21. Bondi, "Feeding the Noise," 5, 11; Hüsker Dü, *Land Speed Record*, SST, 1981; Minutemen, *Ballot Result*, SST, 1986.

22. Bondi, "Feeding the Noise," 11, 18; Robert Seidenberg, "Revolt into Convention," *Village Voice*, June 4, 1985, 74; *MRR* 62; *Flipside* 51 (1986).

23. Martin, "'. . . And You Voted,'" 142–74; David M. Gross, "Proceeding with Caution," *Time*, July 16, 1990, 56–62.

24. Martin, "'. . . And You Voted,'" 142–74; Hebdige, "Style as Homology," 56–57.

25. Rachel Felder, *Manic Pop Thrill* (Hopewell, NJ: Ecco Press, 1993), 59–83, and Arnold, *Route 666*, each contain extensive surveys of this music, both indicating strikingly limited participation by African American musicians. My survey of *Flipside* and *Maximumrocknroll* overwhelmingly corroborates this point.

26. *MRR* 23.

27. *Flipside* 57 (1988).

28. Robert Palmer, "Hot Band: Sonic Youth's Thrash Pop May Be the Sound of Young America in the Nineties," *Rolling Stone*, May 18, 1989, 97–100, 179.

29. *MRR* 33 (1986).

30. Frith, *Sound Effects*, 215, 267.

31. *MRR* 23.

32. *MRR* 40 (1986); Arnold, *Route 666*, 52; Neil Strauss, "Exploding Tickets: Pearl Jam Wage an Anti-Trust War Against Ticketmaster on Capitol Hill," *Rolling Stone*, Aug. 11, 1994, 30.

33. *MRR* 62 (1988).

34. Felder, *Manic Pop Thrill*, 87.

35. *MRR* 62.

36. This argument echoes Angela McRobbie's feminist critique in "Settling Accounts with Subcultures," in Frith and Goodwin, *On Record*, 66–80, in which she argues that cultural analysts such as Hebdige in "Style as Homology" had constructed the punk subculture as exclusively male terrain.

37. *MRR* 40.

38. Felder, *Manic Pop Thrill*, 77–80.

39. *Flipside* 57. For a critical view of Lita Ford's representation of femininity see Sut Jhally's documentary *Dreamworlds* (1990).

40. Susan Faludi's section on sexism in popular culture in *Backlash: The Undeclared War Against American Women* (New York: Doubleday, 1991), 75–226, thoroughly documents the tendency of 1980s popular culture to turn back the clock on the feminist advances of the 1960s and 1970s and thereby buttress patriarchy.

41. Foege, *Confusion Is Next*, 219–20; Arnold, *Route 666*, 4–5; John Sullivan, "Alternative to What? From Beer to Cars to Radio, Angst-Rock Surfs the Latest Wave to the Mainstream," *Boston Globe*, Apr. 2, 1995, B1, 26–27; Jon Pareles, "Is Lollapalooza Losing Its Outsider Status?" *New York Times*, June 27, 1993, II: 26. In *Manic Pop Thrill*, 2–4, Felder advances the parallel between British punk circa 1977 and Nirvana's 1991 breakthrough in the United States.

42. Foege refers to the 1980s as "rock's most fertile decade" in *Confusion Is Next*, 2–3. For debate on the significance of Hüsker Dü's signing to Warner Bros., see *MRR* 33 and *MRR* 34.

43. Macnie, "Riffs: Sonic Youth," *DownBeat*, Mar. 1987, 14; Felder, *Manic Pop Thrill*, 74–77; Foege, *Confusion Is Next*, 207.

44. Michael Azerrad, *Come As You Are: The Story of Nirvana* (New York: Doubleday, 1994), 162; Foege, *Confusion Is Next*, 218–19; *MRR* 23.

45. *MRR* 23; *MRR* 33; Ted Drozdowski, "X Marks the Time: How Grunge and Its Champions Worked a Desperate Generation," *Providence Phoenix*, Feb. 18, 1994, II: 12–14. The comment about trading love beads for three-piece suits was a tacit reference to the Yippie founder Jerry Rubin, whose abandonment of radicalism for a new career on Wall Street emblematized 1960s activism's demise in the popular media.

46. Quotes are from Simon Reynolds, "Pop Music: A Woodstock for the Lost Generation," *New York Times*, Aug. 4, 1991, and D. Fricke, "Lollapalooza," *Rolling Stone*, Sep. 19, 1991. Pareles, "Is Lollapalooza Losing," II: 26; Peter Watrous, "Good Things Happen to Lollapalooza," *New York Times*, Aug. 5, 1992, C13–15; Jon Pareles, "Lollapalooza, Tattoos and All," *New York Times*, June 21, 1993, C13, 18; Jon Pareles, "Lollapalooza, a Day Full of Sound and Fury," *New York Times*, Aug. 11, 1992, C11–12; Steve Pond, "The Trick Is to Be Loved but Not Embraced," *New York Times*, June 26, 1994, II: 28; John Leland, "A Woodstock for Post-Punks: Lollapalooza Tests Out a Freaky-Deaky World Order," *Newsweek*, Aug. 17, 1992, 55; Jon Pareles, "Lollapalooza '94 Opens in Las Vegas," *New York Times*, July 9, 1994, I: 13, 17; Christopher John Farley, "Latter-Day Grunge," *Time*, July 12, 1993, 17.

47. Arnold, *Route 666*, 164–66; Jon Garelick, "Rock's Body Politic: The Music Is Still Bigger Than the Message," *Providence Phoenix*, Dec. 9, 1994, 2: 16. The comment about Bush not being reelected appears in Arnold, *Route 666*, 5.

6: FIGHTING THE POWER

1. Ronald Reagan, "Address Before a Joint Session of the Congress Reporting on the State of the Union," Jan. 26, 1982, *The Public Papers of President Ronald W. Reagan*, www.reagan.utexas.edu/archives/speeches/1982 (accessed May 11, 2009); "Reagan's Concept of Party Hurts America, Packwood Says," *New York Times*, Mar. 2, 1982, D22; David Alpern, "The GOP's Family Feud," *Newsweek*, Mar. 15, 1982, 24; Robert Pear, "Reagan Unverified on Fraud Stories, *New York Times*, Mar. 25, 1982, A20.

2. Reagan, "Address." James Berger, in *After the End: Representations of the Post-Apocalypse* (Minneapolis: University of Minnesota Press, 1999), 193, discusses how the then assistant secretary of labor, Daniel Moynihan, borrowed the phrase "tangle of pathology" from the sociologist Kenneth Clark in 1965 to describe a similar complex of conditions to the one journalists and social scientists dwelled upon in the 1980s. In particular, an emphasis on the "weakness" of the black family structure characterized the Moynihan Report. On race as a metaphor for poverty, see Ida Susser, "Poverty and Homelessness in U.S. Cities," in Ida Susser and Thomas Patterson, eds., *Cultural Diversity in the United States: A Critical Reader* (Malden, MA: Blackwell Publishers, 2001), 239; Thomas Edsall with Mary Edsall, *Chain Reaction: The Impact of Race, Rights, and Taxes on American Politics* (New York: W. W. Norton & Company, 1991), 232–35; and Robin D. G. Kelley, *Yo' Mama's DisFUNKtional! Fighting the Culture Wars in Urban America* (Boston: Beacon Press, 1997), 2–8. On the paradox of limited upward mobility for the black middle class amid deteriorating conditions for the majority of black Americans, see the Preface to Manning Marable, *Race Reform and Rebellion: The Second Reconstruction in Black America, 1945–1990*, 2nd ed. (Jackson, MS: University Press of Mississippi, 1991), ix–xi.

3. *The State of Black America, 1985* (National Urban League, 1985), 186–89.

4. Kelley, *Yo' Mama's DisFUNKtional!* 8; Kevin Phillips, *The Politics of Rich and Poor: Wealth and the American Electorate in the Reagan Aftermath* (New York: Random House, 1990), 86–87; David Stoesz, "Poor Policy: The Legacy of the Kerner Commission for Social Welfare," in John Boger and Judith Wegner, eds., *Race, Poverty ,and American Cities* (Chapel Hill, NC: University of North Carolina Press, 1996), 495; Charles Murray, *Losing Ground: American Social Policy, 1950–1980* (New York: Basic Books, 1984); "The Undeserving Poor," *National Review*, Mar. 4, 1983, 231–32.

5. William Julius Wilson, *The Truly Disadvantaged: The Inner City, the Underclass, and Public Policy* (Chicago: University of Chicago Press, 1987).

6. Thomas Sugrue, *The Origins of the Urban Crisis: Race and Inequality in Postwar Detroit* (Princeton, NJ: Princeton University Press, 1996); Kelley, *Yo' Mama's DisFUNKtional!* 92–94; George Galster, "Polarization, Place, and Race," in Boger and Wegner, *Race, Poverty, and American Cities*, 197–200; Douglas Massey and Nancy Denton, *American Apartheid: Segregation and the Making of the Underclass* (Cambridge, MA: Harvard University Press, 1993), viii. George Clinton, "Chocolate City," *Chocolate City* (Casablanca, 1975).

7. Kelley, *Yo' Mama's DisFUNKtional!* 92–94; Melvin Oliver and Thomas Shapiro, *Black Wealth/White Wealth: A New Perspective on Racial Inequality* (New York: Routledge, 1995), 109; Bruce Schulman, *The Seventies: The Great Shift in American Culture, Society, and Politics* (New York: Free Press, 2001), 56–58; John Boger, "Race and the American City: The Kerner Commission Report in Retrospect," in Boger and Wegner, *Race, Poverty, and American Cities*, 22.

8. Statistics on black media representation are from Samuel Adams, "Blackening in Media: The State of Black in the Press," in *The State of Black America, 1985*, 65–103.

9. "Power! (1966–1968)," *Eyes on the Prize II*, Episode 3 (Blackside, 1990). The figures on the elections of black mayors appear in David Colburn, "Running for Office: African-American Mayors from 1967 to 1996," in David Colburn and Jeffrey Adler, eds., *African-American Mayors: Race, Politics, and the American City* (Urbana, IL: University of Illinois Press, 2001); Jeffrey Adler, Introduction to Colburn and Adler, *African-American Mayors*, 8–9.

10. Milton Coleman, "Marion Barry: The Activist Denies He's Changed," *Washington Post*, Jan. 2, 1979, A1; Howard Gilette, Jr., "Protest and Power in Washington, D.C.: The Troubled Legacy of Marion Barry," in Colburn and Adler, *African-American Mayors*, 200–222.

11. "Marion Barry for Mayor," *Washington Post*, Aug. 30, 1978, A14; Tracy Thompson and Elsa Walsh, "Jurors View Videotape of Barry Drug Arrest," *Washington Post*, June 29, 1990, A1.

12. "Marion Barry, One Year Later," *Washington Post*, Jan. 10, 1980, A18; "Marion Barry for Mayor," *Washington Post*, Nov. 2, 1986, C6; "The Next Mayor," *Washington Post*, Sep. 10, 1982, A26; Athelia Knight, "Police Handling of Allegations Stirs Dispute," *Washington Post*, Mar. 13, 1983, A1; Juan Williams, "A Dream Deferred: A Black Mayor Betrays the Faith," *Washington Monthly*, July–Aug.

1986, 24–39; Mitchell Brown, "Power, Identity, and the Limits of Agency," *Du-Bois Review* 5:2 (2008): 369–86.

13. Paul Kleppner, *Chicago Divided: The Making of a Black Mayor* (DeKalb, IL: Northern Illinois University Press, 1985), 10; Arnold Hirsch, "Harold and Dutch Revisited: A Comparative Look at the First Black Mayors of Chicago and New Orleans," in Colburn and Adler, *African-American Mayors*, 110–11.

14. Gary Rivlin, *Fire on the Prairie: Chicago's Harold Washington and the Politics of Race* (New York: Henry Holt & Co., 1992), 55–59, 94–98; William Grimshaw, "Harold Washington: The Enigma of the Black Political Tradition," in Paul Green and Melvin Holli, eds., *The Mayors: The Chicago Political Tradition*, 3rd ed. (Carbondale, IL: Southern Illinois University Press, 2005), 193; Hirsch, "Harold and Dutch," 111; "Harold Washington: Representative, 1981–1983, Democrat from Illinois," in *Black Americans in Congress*, http://baic.house.gov/member -profiles/profile.html (accessed May 26, 2009).

15. Quotes on the debate are from Rivlin, *Fire on the Prairie*, 140–41, 158, and "Harold," *This American Life* 84, Chicago Public Radio, Nov. 9, 2007 (originially aired Nov. 21, 1997) www.thisamericanlife.org/Radio_Episode (accessed May 27, 2009); Hirsch, "Harold and Dutch," 113; Robert Starks and Michael Preston, "Harold Washington and the Politics of Reform in Chicago: 1983–1987," in Rufus Browning, Dale Marshall, and David Tabb, eds., *Racial Politics in American Cities* (White Plains, NY: Longman, 1990), 97.

16. Rivlin, *Fire on the Prairie*, 169, 176, 180, 186–89; Starks and Preston, "Harold Washington and the Politics of Reform," 97; Tom Morganthau, "Chicago's Ugly Election," *Newsweek*, Apr. 11, 1983, 18; Bill Peterson, "Mondale and Washington Booed by Angry Whites," *Washington Post*, Mar. 28, 1983, A1; Nathaniel Sheppard, Jr., "Mayoral Candidate Faces Angry Crowd at Chicago Church," *New York Times*, Mar. 28, 1983, A13. Washington's tax troubles dated back to the 1960s and consisted of a failure to file rather than a failure to pay.

17. Rivlin, *Fire on the Prairie*, 170. Election figures are from Richard Keiser, *Subordination or Empowerment? African-American Leadership and the Struggle for Urban Political Power* (New York: Oxford University Press, 1997), 58; Green and Holli, *The Mayors*, 201; Kleppner, *Chicago Divided*, 249; Hirsch, "Harold and Dutch," 115–18; Gary Rivlin, "In Chicago a Machine Dies," *The Nation*, Apr. 4, 1987, 424–26.

18. Hirsch, "Harold and Dutch," 115–18, 122; Rivlin, "In Chicago," 424; "Harold Washington's Chicago," *New York Times*, Nov. 26, 1987, A30. Palmer's comments are from "Harold," *This American Life* 84.

19. Doug Gills, "Chicago Politics and Community Development: A Social Movement Perspective," in Pierre Clavel and Wim Wiewel, eds., *Harold Washington and the Neighborhoods: Progressive City Government in Chicago, 1983–1987* (New Brunswick, NJ: Rutgers University Press, 1991), 34–63. Foster is quoted in Rivlin, "In Chicago," 425; "Harold Washington's Chicago," A30; Jim Carl, "Harold Washington and Chicago's Schools Between Civil Rights and the Decline of the New Deal Consensus, 1955–1987," *History of Education Quarterly* 41, no. 3 (Autumn 2001): 311–43.

20. Vernon Jarrett, quoted in "Harold," *This American Life* 84.

21. John Coyne, Jr., "Rewriting the Script in Chicago, *National Review*, May 13, 1983, 560–61.

22. Marshall Frady, *Jesse: The Life and Pilgrimage of Jesse Jackson* (New York: Random House, 1996), 305–306; Ronald Walters, "The Emergent Mobilization of the Black Community in the Jackson Campaign for President," in Lucius Barker and Ronald Walters, eds., *Jesse Jackson's 1984 Presidential Campaign: Challenge and Change in American Politics* (Urbana, IL: University of Illinois Press, 1989), 42–46. The political scientist Adolph Reed casts a critical eye toward Jackson's impact on black voter registration in *The Jesse Jackson Phenomenon: The Crisis of Purpose in Afro-American Politics* (New Haven: Yale University Press, 1986), 17–19, but his critique is largely designed to sketch out possible limits on the degree of Jackson's influence.

23. Frady, *Jesse*, 228–52; E. R. Shipp, "Chicagoans Can't Be Neutral About Jackson," *New York Times*, Mar. 20, 1984, B13.

24. Frady, *Jesse*, 309; Evan Thomas, "Pride and Prejudice," *Time*, May 7, 1984, 30–40; Ronald Smothers, "Jackson's 'Rainbow' May Lack Some of Spectrum," *New York Times*, Feb. 12, 1984, 34; Jesse Jackson, "1984 Democratic National Convention Keynote Address," www.americanrhetoric.com/speeches/jessejackson1984 dnc.htm (accessed Dec. 11, 2007).

25. Barry Commoner, "Jackson's Historic Campaign," *New York Times*, July 10, 1984, A23; Frady, *Jesse*, 357–59; Thomas, "Pride and Prejudice," 30–40; Ed Magnuson, "Stirring Up New Storms," *Time*, July 9, 1984; 8–10. Hatcher is quoted in Frady, *Jesse*, 343. He goes on to equate Jackson's "Hymietown"/Farrakhan imbroglio with the affair that is often cited in thwarting Senator Edward Kennedy's aspirations for higher political office, asserting, "It was his Chappaquiddick."

26. Robert Smith, "From Insurgency Toward Inclusion: The Jackson Campaigns of 1984 and 1988," in Lorenzo Morris, ed., *The Social and Political Implications of the 1984 Jesse Jackson Presidential Campaign* (New York: Praeger, 1990), 225–26; Thomas, "Pride and Prejudice," 30–40; Smothers, "Jackson's 'Rainbow,'" 34; George Church, "What Does Jesse Really Want?" *Time*, Apr. 16, 1984, 15–16; Hedrick Smith, "Texas Caucuses: Hispanic Vote Buoyed Mondale and Disappointed Jackson," *New York Times*, May 8, 1984, A27.

27. Danny Collum, "Under the Rainbow," *Sojourners*, Aug. 1984, 4; "Interview with Richard Hatcher," from "The Pilgrimage of Jesse Jackson," *Frontline*, Apr. 30, 1996, www.pbs.org/wgbh/pages/frontline/jesse/interviews/hatcher (accessed June 1, 2009); Smith, "From Insurgency Toward Inclusion," 225–26; Linda Williams and Lorenzo Morris, "The Coalition at the End of the Rainbow," in Barker and Walters, *Jesse Jackson's 1984 Presidential Campaign*, 227–48; E. R. Shipp, "Jackson to Put Energies into Political Coalition," *New York Times*, Nov. 10, 1984, 9; "Jackson Spending Nights with Nation's Poor to Dramatize Their Plight," *Jet*, Apr. 23, 1984, 6–8.

28. "Interview with Andrew Young," from "The Pilgrimage of Jesse Jackson," *Frontline*, Apr. 30, 1996, www.pbs.org/wgbh/pages/frontline/jesse/interviews/young (accessed June 1, 2009); Commoner, "Jackson's Historic Campaign," A23;

Thomas, "Pride and Prejudice," 30–40; Church, "What Does Jesse Really Want?" 15–16; Robert Pear, "Despite Campaign Oratory, Some Differences Are Subtle," *New York Times*, Mar. 30, 1984, B6; Howell Raines, "Parties Study Jackson Role In Convention," *New York Times*, Apr. 8, 1984, 1, 38; Collum, "Under the Rainbow," 4.

29. Frady, *Jesse*, 400–401; Margaret Carlson, "More Than a Crusade," *Time*, Mar. 7, 1988, 16–17; Gary Wills, "Making History with Silo Sam," *Time*, Mar. 21, 1988, 31–32; Kathryn Dudley, *The End of the Line: Lost Jobs, New Lives in Postindustrial America* (Chicago: University of Chicago Press, 1994), 143–47; Jesse Jackson, "1988 Democratic National Convention Keynote Address," www.americanrhetoric.com/speeches/jessejackson1988dnc.htm (accessed Dec. 11, 2007).

30. Frady, *Jesse*, 391–92; Margaret Carlson, "Why Can't Jesse Be Nominated," *Time*, Mar. 21, 1988, 29; Walter Shapiro, "Taking Jesse Seriously," *Time*, Apr. 11, 1988, 12–22; Smith, "From Insurgency," 222–24. For a critique from the left of how Jackson sold out African American interests in 1988 "for 'personal' respect" and a "skimpy" payoff, see Adolph Reed, *Stirrings in the Jug: Black Politics in the Post-Segregation Era* (Minneapolis: University of Minnesota Press, 1999), 211–15. The final quote is from the Shapiro article.

31. Gary Delgado, *Organizing the Movement: The Roots and Growth of ACORN* (Philadelphia: Temple University Press, 1986), x–xi, 169, 172, 193–97; ACORN, "The Reagan Era, 1980–1985," www.acorn.org/index.php?id=12445 (accessed June 9, 2009) and ACORN, "Lessons Learned and Applied, 1985–1990," www.acorn.org/index.php?id=12444 (accessed June 9, 2009).

32. Peter Medoff and Holly Sklar, *Streets of Hope: The Fall and Rise of an Urban Neighborhood* (Boston: South End Press, 1994), 5, 70–74, 81–86, 108–11. Flint is quoted on 85. Ironically, the authors describe how the DSNI butted heads with ACORN over plans for the neighborhood in a battle of bottom-up vs. top-down visions for neighborhood revitalization; see 74–75. Andrew Feffer, "The Land Belongs to the People: Reframing Urban Protest in Post-Sixties Philadelphia," in Gosse and Moser, *The World the Sixties Made*, 67–99; Thomas Sugrue, *Sweet Land of Liberty: The Forgotten Struggle for Civil Rights in the North* (New York: Random House, 2008), 516–17.

33. S. Craig Watkins, *Representing: Hip Hop Culture and the Production of Black Cinema* (Chicago: University of Chicago Press, 1998), 169–231.

34. Ibid., 172–76. The Lee quote is from Michael Kaufman, "In a New Film, Spike Lee Tries to Do the Right Thing," *New York Times*, June 25, 1989, B1; Clarence Page, "Spike Lee's Warning About Race Relations in America," *Chicago Tribune*, June 25, 1989. Both reviews are reprinted in Mark Reid, ed., *Spike Lee's Do the Right Thing* (New York: Cambridge University Press, 1997).

35. Tricia Rose, *Black Noise: Rap Music and Black Culture in Contemporary America* (Middletown, CT: Wesleyan University Press, 1994), 34–61, discusses rap's interconnected development with these other cultural forms. On Los Angeles as a "fortress city" see Mike Davis, "Fortress Los Angeles: The Militarization of

Urban Space," in Michael Sorkin, ed., *Variations on a Theme Park: The New American City and the End of Public Space* (New York: Hill and Wang, 1992), 154–80. Garofalo, *Rockin' Out*, 376–85; Kelley, *Race Rebels*, 187; Alan Light, Review of Ice Cube's *AmeriKKKa's Most Wanted*, *Rolling Stone*, July 12, 1990, 119; Harry Allen, "Hip-Hop Madness," *Essence*, Apr. 1989, 78.

36. Kelley, *Race Rebels*, 185; Alan Light, "Ice T: The Rolling Stone Interview," *Rolling Stone*, Aug. 20, 1992, 29; Alan Light, "Rappers Sounded Warning," *Rolling Stone*, July 9–23, 1992, 15; Alan Light, "Rapper Ice-T Busts a Movie," *Rolling Stone*, May 16, 1991, 83–86.

7: FIGHTING THE BACKLASH

1. Mary Fainsod Katzenstein uses the terms "gender consciousness" and "unobtrusive mobilization" in "Feminism Within American Institutions: Unobtrusive Mobilization in the 1980s," *Signs* 16:1 (Autumn 1990): 27–52; and *Faithful and Fearless: Moving Feminist Protest Inside the Church and the Military* (Princeton, NJ: Princeton University Press, 1998). My argument in this chapter is indebted to her ideas.

2. "The ERA Loses Two More Rounds," *Time*, Feb. 1, 1982, 18; Jane Mansbridge, *Why We Lost the ERA* (Chicago: University of Chicago Press, 1986), 110–14, 122–28; Schulman, *The Seventies*, 168–71; Tom Morganthau, "The ERA: Death Rattle," *Newsweek*, June 14, 1982, 32; Adam Clymer, "Time Runs Out for Proposed Rights Amendment," *New York Times*, July 1, 1982, A12; Lynn Rosselini, "Victory Is Bittersweet for Architect of Amendment's Downfall," *New York Times*, July 1, 1982, A12.

3. Clymer, "Time Runs Out," A12; Lynn Rosselini, "U.S. Equal Rights Measure Is Re-Introduced in Congress," *New York Times*, July 15, 1982, B13.

4. Sara Evans, *Tidal Wave: How Women Changed America at Century's End* (New York: Free Press, 2003), 177; Schulman, *The Seventies*, 169; "Chronology of the Equal Rights Amendment," www.now.org/issues/economic/cea/history.html (accessed Mar. 9, 2009); Mansbridge, *Why We Lost*, 150.

5. "Eleanor Smeal Muses on 5 Years," *New York Times*, Nov. 30, 1982, C10; Elsa Brenner, "E.R.A. Backers See Challenge in Defeat," *New York Times*, July 11, 1982, CN1; Enid Nemy, "Feminist Cause Looks Back to Grass Roots," *New York Times*, Nov. 8, 1982, B10.

6. Clara Germani, "PAC/Woman: New Entrant into the Game of Politics," *Christian Science Monitor*, Sep. 3, 1982, 10; "N.O.W. Opens $3 Million Drive for Candidates," *New York Times*, Aug. 27, 1982, A9; Paul Taylor, "NOW Seeking $3 Million War Chest to Oust ERA Foes, Fight New Right," *Washington Post*, Aug. 27, 1982, A2; "Power, Politics, and Women," *Boston Globe*, Oct. 12, 1982, 1; Nadine Brozan, "NOW Elects New Officers and Plans Future," Oct. 11, 1982, B6; Michael Reese, "Women in Politics: The Gender Gap," *Newsweek*, Nov. 1, 1982, 26; Evans, *Tidal Wave*, 178–81.

7. "Women's Votes Counted Nov. 2," *Off Our Backs: A Women's Newsjournal* 12,

issue 11 (Dec. 31, 1982): 8; "Career Women Push for More Clout in Politics," *Business Week*, Nov. 1, 1982, 83.

8. Kathy Hacker, "Campaigning to Win Power for Women," *Philadelphia Inquirer*, July 20, 1986, 1; Robin Toner, "Female Candidates Are No Longer So Cash Poor," *New York Times*, June 15, 1986, A5; Michele Landsberg, "Gloomy Analysis Ignores Women's Breakthrough in U.S. Vote," *Toronto Globe and Mail*, Nov. 22, 1986, A2; Mikulski's comments appear in Robin Toner, "Gains for Women Predicted in Races for Statewide Office," *New York Times*, May 19, 1986, A1; Evans, *Tidal Wave*, 197–200.

9. Geraldine A. Ferraro, *Ferraro: My Story* (New York: Bantam Books, 1985), 24–26.

10. "Making History: Fritz Picks a Woman," *Newsweek*, July 23, 1984, 3; Tom Morganthau, "Making History," *Newsweek*, July 23, 1984, 16; Evan Thomas, "'Just One of the Guys and a Bit More,'" *Time*, July 23, 1984, 18–20; Janes Kelly, "So Who's That in the Gray Suit?" *Time*, Aug. 13, 1984, 18; Gloria Steinem, "The Ferraro Factor: What Difference Can One Woman Make?," *Ms.*, Oct. 1984, 43–49, 146–48.

11. Alessandra Stanley, "The Rising Star from Queens," *Time*, June 4, 1984, 24–25; Thomas, "'Just One of the Guys,'" 18–20; Ferraro, *Ferraro: My Story*, 135–36, 215–28; Geraldine Ferraro, *Framing a Life: A Family Memoir* (New York: Scribner, 1998), 107–108; Kenneth T. Walsh, "Ferraro: 'A Tough Lady' Draws the Crowds," *U.S. News & World Report*, Sep. 24, 1984, 19.

12. Geraldine Ferraro, "I Proudly Accept Your Nomination," acceptance speech at the Democratic National Convention, July 19, 1984, reprinted in Harriet Sigerman, ed., *The Columbia Documentary History of American Women Since 1941* (New York: Columbia University Press, 2003), 383–85; Steinem, "The Ferraro Factor," 48; Kurt Andersen, "Ripples Throughout Society," *Time*, July 23, 1984, 34–35; Kurt Andersen, "Show and Tell," *Time*, Sep. 3, 1984, 14–18; George Church, "Hoping for a Fresh Start," *Time*, Sep. 3, 1984, 22–23.

13. Kurt Andersen, "Spotlight on the Seconds," *Time*, Oct. 15, 1984, 25–26; William Doerner, "Co-Stars on Center Stage," *Time*, Oct. 22, 1984, 30–31; Ferraro, *Ferraro: My Story*, 240–67; Ken Fireman, "Staff Running with That Remark, Bush Says," *Philadelphia Inquirer*, Oct. 25, 1984, A3; "Bush Denies Trying to Belittle Ferraro," *Boston Globe*, Oct. 25, 1984, 18.

14. Jane O'Reilly, "Our Candidate/Ourselves," *Time*, Oct. 29, 1984, 33; William Doerner, "A Credible Candidacy and Then Some," *Time*, Nov. 19, 1984, 84–85; Melinda Beck, "Ferraro: A World of Options," *Newsweek*, Nov./Dec. 1984 Election Extra, 30; Ferraro, *Ferraro: My Story*, 310–26.

15. This section is based on the following letters to Ferraro that appear in the Geraldine A. Ferraro Papers, Marymount Manhattan College Collection #3: Jackie McGriff, Sep. 19, 1984, box 145, folder: Vice Presidential, Alabama, Sep. 19–27 and undated 1984; Cottie Hood, Nov. 25, 1984, box 158, folder: Vice Presidential, Idaho, Oct. 9–Dec. 2, 1984; Opal Brooten, box 158, folder: Vice Presidential, Idaho, Jul. 13–Sep. undated, 1984; Julie Pendleton, Oct. 18, 1984, box 161, folder: Vice Presidential, Kansas, Oct 15–25 and undated and Nov. 1–6, 1984; Jo Ellen Levy, box 161, folder: Vice Presidential, Kansas, Nov. 7–Dec. 11 and un-

dated, 1984; Mona Keenan, Oct. 19, 1984, box 161, folder: Vice Presidential, Kansas, Oct. 15–25 and undated and Nov. 1–6, 1984; Susan Haudik, Nov. 8, 1984, box 161, folder: Vice Presidential, Kansas, Nov. 7–Dec. 11 and undated, 1984; Gretchen Lonborg, Nov. 6, 1984, box 161, folder: Vice Presidential, Kansas, Oct 15–25 and undated and Nov. 1–6, 1984; Jan Kozma-Southall, Nov. 8, 1984, box 161, folder: Vice Presidential, Kansas, Nov. 7–Dec. 11 and undated, 1984.

16. Ferraro Papers, MMC Collection #3: Karam Singh Panch, July 21, 1984, box 201, folder: Vice Presidential, India, July 6–Aug. 21, 1984; Annabelle Duisberg, Sep. 14, 1984, box 201, folder: Vice Presidential, Costa Rica, Sep. 14, 1984; Hormos Khossoussi, Sep. 6, 1984, box 201, folder: Vice Presidential, Iran, Sep. 6, 1984.

17. The comment about Ferraro's "public drubbing" appears in Faludi, *Backlash*, 270; historical data on women in politics is from womenincongress.house.gov/data/wic-by-congress.html (accessed Mar. 24, 2009); "History of Women in State Legislatures, 1975–2008," Center for American Women and Politics, Eagleton Institute of Politics, Rutgers, the State University of New Jersey, www.cawp.rutgers.edu/fast_facts/levels_of_office/StateLeg-HistoricalInfo.php (accessed March 24, 2009); Evans introduces the idea of "capacity building" in *Tidal Wave*, 197.

18. Carrie N. Baker, "The Emergence of Organized Feminist Resistance to Sexual Harassment in the United States in the 1970s," *Journal of Women's History* 19, no. 3, 161–84; Carrie N. Baker, *The Women's Movement Against Sexual Harassment* (New York: Cambridge University Press, 2008), 115–18; John D'Emilio and Estelle Freedman, *Intimate Matters: A History of Sexuality in America* (New York: Harper and Row, 1988), 314. "Equal Employment Opportunity Commission Guidelines on Discrimination Because of Sex," 1980, reprinted in Laura Stein, ed., *Sexual Harassment in America: A Documentary History* (Westport, CT: Greenwood Press, 1999), 33–34; Dolly Langdon, "A Startling Study Claims That Sexual Harassment in the Office Is as Common as the Coffee Break," *People*, June 8, 1981, 123–24; Claire Safran, "Sexual Harassment: The View from the Top," *Redbook* 156, Mar. 1981, 45–51.

19. Charles Marske, Steven Vago, and Arlene Taich, "Combatting Sexual Harassment: A New Awareness," *USA Today*, Mar. 1980, 45–48; Baker, *The Women's Movement Against Sexual Harassment*, 152–57, 185; Woodrow W. Clark, Jr., "Marketing Documentary Film in the Mass Media," *Society for the Anthropology of Visual Communication Newsletter* 10, no. 1 (1982): 1–5.

20. Augustus B. Cochran, *Sexual Harassment and the Law: The Mechelle Vinson Case* (Lawrence, KS: University Press of Kansas, 2004), 51–55; Baker, *The Women's Movement Against Sexual Harassment*, 166–69.

21. Baker, *The Women's Movement Against Sexual Harassment*, 170–71; M. O'Koon, "Sexual Harassment," *Good Housekeeping*, Jan. 1989, 171.

22. Baker, *The Women's Movement Against Sexual Harassment*, 138, 160, 171; Cochran, *Sexual Harassment and the Law*, 173–80.

23. Sara Evans, "Beyond Declension: Feminist Radicalism in the 1970s and 1980s," in Gosse and Moser, *The World the 60s Made*, 58–59; Evans, *Tidal Wave*, 155;

Frederika E. Schmitt and Patricia Yancey Martin, "Unobtrusive Mobilization by an Institutionalized Rape Crisis Center: 'All We Do Comes From Victims,'" *Gender and Society* 13, no. 3 (Jun. 1999): 364–84; U.S. Department of Justice, Office for Victims of Crime Training and Technical Assistance Center, "Summary of the History of Rape Crisis Centers," www.ovcttac.gov/saact/files/summ_of_history (accessed Mar. 30, 2009), 2–7; Loretta Ross, interview by Joyce Follet for Voices of Feminism Oral History Project, Sophia Smith Collection, Smith College, Northampton, MA, Nov. 3–5, 2004, www.smith.edu/libraries/libs/ssc/vof/vof-narrators.html#Ross (accessed Mar. 30, 2009), 120; Carol Lavery, "An Oral History of the Crime Victim Assistance Field Video and Audio Archive," Apr. 13, 2003, University of Akron, http://vroh.uakron.edu/transcripts/Lavery.php (accessed Mar. 31, 2009), 8–9.

24. Katzenstein, *Faithful and Fearless*; Katzenstein, "Feminism Within American Institutions," 35–53.

25. Linda Jean Carpenter and R. Vivian Acosta, *Title IX* (Champaign, IL: Human Kinetics, 2005), 119–21; Susan Cahn, *Coming On Strong: Gender and Sexuality in Twentieth Century Women's Sport* (Cambridge, MA: Harvard University Press, 1994), 259–61; Robert McG. Thomas, Jr., "Not-So-Equal Coaching," *New York Times*, May 8, 1989, C2; National Coalition for Women and Girls in Education, "Title IX at 30: Report Card on Gender Equity—Athletics C+," in Jean O' Reilly and Susan Cahn, eds., *Women and Sports in the United States: A Documentary Reader* (Boston: Northeastern University Press, 2007), 337–46; Evans, *Tidal Wave*, 192–93.

26. Ann Taylor Allen, "The March Through the Institutions: Women's Studies in the United States and West and East Germany, 1980–1995," *Signs* 22, no. 1 (Autumn 1996): 152–80; Evans, *Tidal Wave*, 200–202.

27. Evans, *Tidal Wave*, 182–83; "The Feminist Chronicles: 1984," Feminist Majority Foundation, www.feminist.org/research/chronicles/fc1984.html, (accessed Feb. 26, 2009); D'Emilio and Freedman, *Intimate Matters*, 345–54; Ronald Reagan, "Remarks at a White House Briefing for Right to Life Activists," July 30, 1987, *The Public Papers of the Presidents*, www.reagan.utexas.edu/archives/speeches/1987/073087a.htm (accessed Apr. 7, 2009); Steven Roberts, "U.S. Proposes Curb on Clinics Giving Abortion Advice," *New York Times*, July 31, 1987, A1; Gil Troy, *Morning in America: How Ronald Reagan Invented the 1980s* (Princeton, NJ: Princeton University Press, 2005), 158–59; Richard Lacayo, "Whose Life Is It," *Time*, May 1, 1989, 20–24.

28. Crowd estimates for the April 9, 1989, march demonstrate how accounts of participation in political demonstrations are notorious for varying dramatically. The 300,000 figure was the park police's estimate, yet event organizers placed the figure at twice that number. Ethan Bronner, "Throngs Rally in D.C. to Keep Abortion Legal," *Boston Globe*, Apr. 10, 1989, 1; Robin Toner, "Right to Abortion Draws Thousands to Capital Rally," *New York Times*, Apr. 10, 1989, A1; James McKinley, "Sad Pasts Live Again on Train to March," *New York Times*, Apr. 10, 1989, B6; Hendrik Hertzberg, "TRB From Washington: People's Choice," *New Republic*, May 1, 1989,

4, 45; Meredith Tax, "March to a Crossroads on Abortion," *Nation*, May 8, 1989, front cover, 631–33; "The First March," *National Review*, May 5, 1989, 9–10; Eloise Salholz, "Pro-Choice: 'A Sleeping Giant' Awakes," *Newsweek*, Apr. 24, 1989, 39.

29. "The First March," 9; Bronner, "Throngs Rally," 1; Toner, "Right to Abortion," A1; "What's News: World-Wide," *Wall Street Journal*, Apr. 10, 1989, A1.

30. Lacayo, "Whose Life Is It," 20–24; Ethan Bronner, "Abortion: An American Divide," *Boston Globe*, Mar. 31, 1989, 1; David Shribman, "Better Paid and Better Educated Are More Apt to Favor Abortion," *Wall Street Journal*, Apr. 26, 1989, A10; Hertzberg, "TRB from Washington," 45. It is also true that polls on abortion varied significantly depending on how the question was worded and according to socioeconomic class and race.

31. Tax, "March to a Crossroads," 631; "Repro Woman: Faye Wattleton Maps Strategy with Marcia Ann Gillespie," *Ms.*, Oct. 1989, 50–53; Salholz, "Pro-Choice," 39.

32. Evans, *Tidal Wave*, 214; Salholz, "Pro-Choice," 39; Lacayo, "Whose Life Is It," 20–24; Bronner, "Throngs Rally," 1. On the professionalization of the pro-choice movement, see Suzanne Staggenborg, *The Pro-Choice Movement: Organization and Activism in the Abortion Conflict* (New York: Oxford University Press, 1991), and Suzanne Staggenborg, "The Consequences of Professionalization and Formalization in the Pro-Choice Movement," in Jo Freeman and Victoria Johnson, eds., *Waves of Protest: Social Movements Since the Sixties* (Lanham, MD: Rowman and Littlefield, 1999), 99–134.

33. William Saletan, *Bearing Right: How Conservatives Won the Abortion War* (Berkeley: University of California Press, 2003); Rickie Solinger, ed., *Abortion Wars: A Half Century of Struggle, 1950–2000* (Berkeley: University of California Press, 2003), xiv; Staggenborg, *The Pro-Choice Movement*, 146; Evans, *Tidal Wave*, 214.

8: THE SHOCK TROOPS OF DIRECT ACTION

1. "Homosexuals Arrested at AIDS Drug Protest," *New York Times*, Mar. 25, 1987.

2. "Massive AIDS Demonstration," flyer for the first ACT UP action, Mar. 24, 1987, Wall Street, New York City, www.actupny.org/documents/1stFlyer.html (accessed Apr. 23, 2007).

3. This figure is cited in Douglas Crimp, "AIDS: Cultural Analysis/Cultural Activism," in Douglas Crimp, ed., *AIDS: Cultural Analysis, Cultural Activism* (Cambridge, MA: MIT Press, 1988), 11.

4. "An Open Letter to Richard Dunne and the Gay Men's Health Crisis," *New York Native*, issue 197, Jan. 26, 1987.

5. Maria Maggenti, interview #010, ACT UP Oral History Project, www.actuporal history.org/interviews/index.html (accessed May 8, 2007), 39–40.

6. Urvashi Vaid, Foreword to Sarah Schulman, *My American History: Lesbian and Gay Life During the Reagan/Bush Years* (New York: Routledge, 1994), xi.

7. Paul Duggan, "1,000 Swarm FDA's Rockville Office to Demand Approval of AIDS Drugs," *Washington Post*, Oct. 12, 1988, B1; "ACTUP Capsule History

1988," www.actupny.org/documents/cron-88.html (accessed May 22, 2007); Douglas Crimp with Adam Rolston, *AIDS Demographics* (Seattle: Bay Press, 1990), 76–83.

8. Gregg Bordowitz, interview #004, ACT UP Oral History Project, www.actuporal history.org/interviews/index.html (accessed May 22, 2007), 31.

9. Mark Harrington, interview #012, ACT UP Oral History Project, www.actuporal history.org/interviews/index.html (accessed May 22, 2007), 13.

10. Bordowitz, interview #004, ACT UP Oral History Project, 32.

11. Bruce Lambert, "3,000 Assailing Policy on AIDS Ring City Hall," *New York Times*, Mar. 29, 1989, B1, B3.

12. Crimp, *AIDS Demographics*, 85–95.

13. Ed Magnuson, "In a Rage Over AIDS," *Time*, Dec. 25, 1989, 33; Crimp, *AIDS Demographics*, 131–40.

14. Michael Petrelis, interview #020, ACT UP Oral History Project, www.actuporal history.org/interviews/index.html (accessed May 22, 2007), 36–38; Maxine Wolfe, interview #043, ACT UP Oral History Project, www.actuporalhistory.org/ interviews/index.html (accessed June 4, 2007), 78; Michael Nesline, interview #014, ACT UP Oral History Project, www.actuporalhistory.org/interviews/index .html (accessed May 22, 2007), 42; Bordowitz, interview #004, ACT UP Oral History Project, 58.

15. Crimp, *AIDS Demographics*, 14–18.

16. Tom Kalin, interview #042, ACT UP Oral History Project, www.actuporalhistory .org/interviews/index.html (accessed June 5, 2007), 31–32; Crimp, "AIDS: Cultural Analysis/Cultural Activism," 7–11; "Gran Fury Talks to Douglas Crimp," *Artforum*, Apr. 2003; Crimp, *AIDS Demographics*, 15–17.

17. Nesline, interview #014, ACT UP Oral History Project, 30.

18. Marlene McCarty, interview #044, ACT UP Oral History Project, www.actuporal history.org/interviews/index.html (accessed June 11, 2007), 18.

19. Crimp, *AIDS Demographics*, 53–55; Richard Meyer, "This Is to Enrage You: Gran Fury and the Graphics of AIDS Activism," in Nina Felshin, ed., *But Is It Art? The Spirit of Art as Activism* (Seattle: Bay Press, 1995) 66, 68.

20. Nesline, interview #014, ACT UP Oral History Project, 33.

21. Crimp, *AIDS Demographics*, 80, 83; Meyer, "This Is to Enrage You," 70–72; Nesline, interview #014, ACT UP Oral History Project, 32–33.

22. Lippard is quoted in the author's *The Theater Is in the Street: Politics and Public Performance in Sixties America* (Amherst: University of Massachusetts Press, 2004), 126.

23. McCarty, interview #044, ACT UP Oral History Project, 38; Robert Vasquez-Pacheco, interview #002, ACT UP Oral History Project, www.actuporalhistory .org/interviews/index.html (accessed May 22, 2007), 19–22, 60.

24. Crimp, *AIDS Demographics*, 18–19; Meyer, "This Is to Enrage You," 51–59.

25. Gregg Bordowitz, "Picture a Coalition," in Crimp, *AIDS: Cultural Analysis/Cultural Activism*, 188–92; AIDS Coalition 3/12/87 meeting minutes, 052, William Bahlman Papers, National Archive of Lesbian and Gay History, box 3, folder 185.

26. Thomas Morgan, "Mainstream Strategy for AIDS Group," *New York Times*, July 22, 1988, B1, B4; Maggenti, interview #010, ACT UP Oral History Project, 13; Carlomusto, interview #005, ACT UP Oral History Project, 24.

27. "Kiss In Feb. 14, 1988," 052, William Bahlman Papers, box 3, folder 179.

28. Maggenti, interview #010, ACT UP Oral History Project, 52, 58; Tom Kalin, interview #042, ACT UP Oral History Project, 79–80.

29. Kendall Thomas, interview #024, ACT UP Oral History Project, 4–9, 20–21.

30. Carlomusto, interview #005, ACT UP Oral History Project, 40.

31. Carlomusto, interview #005, ACT UP Oral History Project, 43; Nesline, interview #014, ACT UP Oral History Project, 45.

32. Harrington is quoted in David Handelman, "ACT UP in Anger," *Rolling Stone*, Mar. 8, 1990, 82.

ACKNOWLEDGMENTS

This book, like many others before it, is the result of a truly cooperative enterprise. Indeed, I have profited from the deft intellect and just plain kindness of many along the way—too many in fact to list here in this roster of those to whom the indebtedness is greatest. To those not mentioned below, my apologies, but please know that you have my heartfelt gratitude.

My home institution, Bryant University, provided crucial support through a timely sabbatical, summer scholarship stipends, and funding for research assistants. At Hill and Wang, I had the pleasure of working with three young and gifted editors, June Kim, Elizabeth Maples, and Dan Crissman, whose advice and suggestions proved especially helpful on a consistent basis. Hill and Wang's publisher, Thomas Le-Bien, was present at the creation and was supportive of the project throughout.

I am most thankful for the unerringly generous mentorship of Bruce Schulman, who helped me conceive of the project and read the full manuscript, and Judith Smith, who contributed insightful comments on multiple chapters. All of the following outstanding colleagues read individual chapters and made valuable suggestions: Paul Lokken, Van Gosse, Antoine Joseph, and Robert Widell. Additionally, New England American Studies Association conferences afforded helpful opportunities to test the ideas of early versions of two of the chapters.

The efforts of a handful of archival and reference experts are particularly noteworthy. Mary Brown, who knew the Geraldine A. Ferraro Papers inside and out, was a gracious host during my time at Marymount Manhattan College. The staff of the Swarthmore College Peace Collection shrewdly helped maximize my productivity during a short stay. And, of course, I cannot bestow enough thanks to Laura Kohl and Maura Keating of Bryant University for their unstinting enthusiasm and diligence on behalf of the cause. Finally, the uniquely competent clerical efforts of Linda Asselin are my Rock of Gibraltar.

The book substantially benefited from the efforts of a group of talented and energetic undergraduate research assistants: Katrin Gorham, Celeste Tennant, Jaclyn Lemieux, and Evan Bartlett, who not only dutifully tracked down the most obscure citations, but who also read and commented substantively on several individual chapters, as did Jerell Smith as part of his Senior Capstone Project. I was also assisted by the thoughtful and surprisingly frank responses students offered in my "History of the U.S. in the 1970s and 1980s" seminar to two of the chapters.

Of course, it is to my family—my wife, Heather, and my children, Jackson, Hazel, Harrison, and Charlie—that I owe the largest debt for their sacrifices in bringing this book to its completion. You give me more inspiration than you can know. Thanks!

INDEX

Abortion for Survival, 169
abortion rights, xii, xiii, 149, 150, 151;
    Catholic Church's position on, 153, 177;
    ERA linked to, 148; George H. W.
    Bush's position on, 153; Geraldine
    Ferraro's support of, 153, 155, 156;
    Hollywood support for, 87, 167–68;
    post-punk support for, 106; public
    support for, 168, 223*n30*; renewed
    activism for, 147–48, 166–70, 222*n28*;
    states' limiting of, 146, 170; Supreme
    Court decision on, 145; *see also* pro-life
    movement
activism, 51–52, 191; ACT UP's impact on,
    187; African American, xvi, 122–23,
    138–39, 218; community, 138–39;
    Hollywood, 86–88, 167–68; nature of,
    xiii, xiv–xv, 11; of 1960s, xiv–xv, 5, 8, 11,
    19, 23, 32, 41, 42, 48, 51, 60, 77, 89–90,
    147, 167, 169, 172, 173, 176; nuclear
    freeze movement's impact on, 23;
    post-1980s legacy of, 189–92;
    professionalization of, xiv; skepticism
    about, 69; youth, xiii, xv; *see also*
    specific movements
Adams, Bryan, 73
affirmative action: access to, 121; in
    municipal government, 124, 131;
    opposition to, 122, 161; for women,
    150, 154

African Americans: in Central America
    solidarity movement, 33; cultural
    activism by, 123, 139–43; direct action
    protests by, 138, 139; in divestment
    movement, 52–53; grassroots activism
    among, 122–23, 138–39, 218*n32*;
    identity politics among, 127; middle
    class, 120, 121, 124; in municipal
    government, xii, xvi, 122, 123–31; in
    music mega-events, 69–70; police
    relations with, 124–25, 127, 130, 131,
    138, 142–43; political imperatives for,
    123–24, 129, 130; in politics, xvi, 122,
    131–38, 139, 157, 191; in post-punk
    music, 212*n25*; stereotyping of, xvi,
    119–21, 122–23, 126, 135, 140, 143,
    214*n2*; urban, 120, 121, 122, 123–31,
    138, 139, 140–43; voter registration
    among, 123, 127–28, 131–32, 138,
    217*n22*; *see also* civil rights movement
African American studies, 89, 90, 165
African National Congress (ANC), 49,
    59, 63
Agnostic Front, 107–108
AIDS activism: in cultural realm, xii, 172;
    direct action in, 171–72, 173–74, 176–79;
    drug protocols as focus of, xiii, xvii,
    174–76, 187; education in, 175–76, 177,
    183, 185–86; politically mobilized
    community in, xvii, 172, 186–87;

Brezhnev, Leonid, 21
Browne, Jackson, 4, 19, 43, 71, 201*n23*
Brutus, Dennis, 59
Buchanan, Patrick, 43
Buckley, William F., 20
Burke, Tom, 64
Burroughs Wellcome, 171
Bush, George H. W., xvii; abortion rights position of, 153, 167, 168; arts funding under, 91; defeat of, 117; Geraldine Ferraro's debate with, 154–55; judicial appointments of, 122, 146; 1988 campaign of, xi; popularity levels of, xviii
Bush, George W., 190
Business Week, 151
Buthelezi, Mangosuthu, 58
Butigan, Ken, 40
Butthole Surfers, 101, 102
Byrne, Jane, 127, 128

California, nuclear freeze movement in, 10–11, 20
"Call to Halt the Nuclear Arms Race, A," 6, 7
Campaign for Nuclear Disarmament (CND), 15, 17
Campbell's Soup, 161
Canby, Vincent, 80
CARE, 69
Caribbean, American intervention in, xviii
Carlomusto, Jean, 185, 187
Carter, Jimmy, x, xvii, 78, 155
Carter administration, European nuclear deployment by, 14
Catch Trout Records, 100
Catholic Church, 153, 163; ACT UP's targeting of, 177–79
CBS, 8, 86–87
Central America: American intervention in, xviii, 28–31, 33, 34, 35, 36, 37, 39, 40, 42, 43, 44, 80–82, 86, 191; civilians targeted in, 30; economic dependence of, 29, 199*n4*; film portrayals of, 80–82; human rights violations in, 27, 28, 30, 34, 36; refugees from, 31–34; *see also* El Salvador; Guatemala; Nicaragua
Central America solidarity movement, xiii, xv, 25–44; ACORN's links with, 138;

civilian witnesses in, 30–31, 33–34, 36; cultural expressions of, 43, 201*n23*; direct action in, 26, 35–36, 39, 40–42; FBI investigation of, 38–39; geographic diversity in, 32–33, 41; grassroots activism in, 37; in Hollywood, 86, 87; impact of, 27–28, 43–44, 191; international cooperation in, 34–35, 36–39, 44; in mainstream politics, 35, 37, 43–44; religion's role in, 27, 31–34, 39–40, 42, 43; secular organizations in, 34–39; symbolic politics in, 34
Central Intelligence Agency (CIA): demonstrations against, 42; Guatemalan coup backed by, 29
Chapman, Tracy, 73
Chase Manhattan Bank, 49
Chevrolet, 70
Chicago, Ill.: political machine in, 126–27, 129–30, 131; racial politics in, 128–29, 130
Chicago Religious Task Force (CRTF), 32
Chile, coup in, 27, 80
Christianity: in Central America solidarity movement, 27, 31–34, 39–40, 42, 43; evangelical, increasing influence of, xiv, 186
Circle Jerks, 101, 105
Civil Rights Act (1964), 145; Title VII of, 159, 160
civil rights movement, 71; apartheid opposition in, 48–49; Jesse Jackson's involvement in, 132, 135; Jews in, 134; legacy of, 121, 125, 158; media strategies of, xv; nonviolent direct action in, 41; student activists in, 52; voter registration following, 125
Civil Rights Restoration Act (1988), 164
Clamshell Alliance, xvii
Clancy, Tom, 104
Clark, Kenneth, 214*n2*
Clash, 43, 96, 201*n23*
Cliff, Jimmy, 71
Clifford, Clark, 7
Clinton, Bill, xvii, xviii, 88, 117, 189, 190
Clinton, George, 71, 121
Clinton, Hillary, 110
Closing of the American Mind, The (Bloom), 88–89
Coffin, William Sloane, 33

Colby, William, 7
Cold War: Democratic politics affected by, 135, 136; end of, xviii, 23, 189; nuclear freeze movement's impact on, 5, 23; politics of, 20; Reagan's invocation of, 4, 14, 25, 78, 82; Third World interventionism during, xviii, 8, 24, 25, 27, 29; *see also* Central America solidarity movement; *see also* Soviet Union
colleges and universities: activism at, 51–52, 54–55, 191, 202; AIDS research at, 171; athletic program sex discrimination at, 164; confrontations at, 54, 56; diversity at, 53; progressive reforms at, xiii, 89–90, 165; public space issue at, 46–48, 51, 53–64, 65; sexual harassment awareness at, 159, 161; shantytowns' aesthetics criticized at, 57–58, 60–62; *see also* divestment movement
Collins, Phil, 68
Columbia Records, 75
Columbia University, divestment movement at, 50–51, 202n8
Committee for a Sane Nuclear Policy (SANE), 3, 40
Committee in Solidarity with the People of El Salvador (CISPES), 34–39, 42, 44
Congress, U.S.: anti-interventionism in, 27, 40, 81; Central America solidarity movement in, 35, 37, 41, 43–44; civil rights legislation in, 164; Equal Rights Amendment in, 145; nuclear freeze movement in, xii, 20, 21, 23; Republican control of, 190; South African sanctions in, 65; *see also* House of Representatives, U.S.; Senate, U.S.
conservatism: activism for, 116, 146; *see also* pro-life movement; anti-welfare position of, 120–21; feminist movement affected by, 146, 147, 150, 161; and homosexuality, 89, 91, 148, 172, 175, 176, 177, 184, 185, 186; impact of, xiv; opposition to, xii, xiii, xvi, xvii, 66, 96, 97, 98, 105, 106, 107, 109–10, 138, 180, 190; in popular culture, xvi, 67, 77–79, 81, 85–86, 109–10, 112; resurgence of, x, 190; *see also* culture wars; Reagan, Ronald Wilson; Republican Party, U.S.

Conspiracy of Hope, 72–73, 74
consumerism, 109–10, 118
Contract with America, 190
contras: attacks by, 25, 28; U.S. support of, 25, 26, 27–28, 30, 34, 41, 44
Coors, 110
Corbett, Jim, 31, 32
Cornell University, divestment movement at, 47, 49, 53–58, 204n23
Cornell University v. Loreelynn Adamson, et al., 57
corporations: AIDS research in, 171, 172, 174; Central American involvement of, 29; film criticism of, 83, 93; media, 68, 78, 82, 85, 93, 96, 100, 101, 103; mega-events sponsorship by, 70; Obama-era legislation concerning, 190; post-punk opposition to, xvi, 110; Reagan's support of, 161; Republican funding by, 133; sexual harassment policies in, 160–61; South African business practices reviewed by, 49–50, 65; *see also* divestment movement
Cosby Show, The, 120
Costa-Gavras, Constantin, 80, 81
counterterrorism, 38
Cristiani, Alfredo, 42
Crucifucks, 101
cultural relativism, 89
culture, xix, 67–94; African American political statements in, 123, 139–43; Central America solidarity movement in, 43, 201n23; conservatism opposed in, xii, xiii, xvi; conservatism reflected in, xvi, 67, 77–79, 81, 85–86, 104–105, 109–10, 112; early 1990s, xviii; feminist backlash in, 146, 213n40; liberal influence on, 89–90; social consciousness in, xii, xvi, 74, 93; *see also* art; film; music; television
culture wars, xiii, xvi, 88–94, 165

Daley, Richard J., 126, 127, 130
Daley, Richard M., 128
D'Amato, Alfonse, 173
Danforth, John, 151
Dartmouth College, divestment movement at, 45, 47, 58–64
Davis, Miles, 71

Ethiopia, famine relief in, 68, 69
Europe: nuclear arms deployed in, 14, 18,
  22; nuclear freeze movement in, xv, 5,
  14–19
European Nuclear Disarmament (END),
  15, 16, 18
Evens, Anne, 54

Fairchild, Morgan, 87, 168
Faludi, Susan, 146, 213*n40*
Falwell, Jerry, 180, 184
Farabundo Martí National Liberation
  Front (FMLN), 30, 34, 42, 43, 82
Farley, Lin, 158, 159
Farm Aid, 71
Farrakhan, Louis, 134, 137
Farrell, Mike, 86
Farrell, Perry, 116
Fatal Attraction, 67
Fear of a Black Planet, 141
Federal Communications Commission, 20
Feinstein, Diane, 157
Fela, 73
Feld, Bernard, 7
Felder, Rachel, 111
Fellowship of Reconciliation, 3, 6
feminism, xvi, 145–71; in art, 91, 93;
  backlash against, xvi, 145–46, 148–49,
  170, 192, 213*n40*; conservatism's impact
  on, 146, 147, 150, 161; direct action in,
  147, 161, 167–68; Geraldine Ferraro's
  identification with, 153, 154, 156;
  grassroots activism in, 150, 158, 159,
  162, 170; institutionalization of,
  147–48, 157–66, 169–70, 192; 1970s,
  145, 147, 158, 160, 162, 165, 166; in
  nuclear freeze movement, 17; third
  wave, 166; *see also* abortion rights;
  Equal Rights Amendment; sexual
  harassment; women
Ferraro, Geraldine, xii, 152–58; feminism
  and, 152–56; legacy of, 156–58, 192;
  media coverage of, 152, 154–55; on
  1984 campaign trail, 152–55
Fife, John, 31, 32
film: action blockbusters in, 78–79;
  African Americans in, 140–41; Central
  America in, 80–82; conglomerates in,
  78, 82, 85, 93; conservative values in,

77–79, 81, 85–86; domestic politics in,
  82–85; liberal community in, 82,
  86–88, 93; marketing in, 79; politics in,
  77–88, 93; self-censorship in, 91; sexual
  assault awareness in, 163; Vietnam War
  in, 78, 79–80
Film Comment, 84
financial crisis of 2008, 190
Finley, Karen, 91, 93
Firehose, 108, 114
Firing Line, 146
Fishman, Nancy, 52, 65
Fleck, John, 91
Flint, Sarah, 139
Flipside, 100, 102, 105, 107
Fogelberg, Dan, 19
Fonda, Jane, 87, 167
Food and Drug Administration (FDA),
  AIDS activism targeting, xiii, 173,
  174–76, 187
Ford, Lita, 112
Ford Foundation, 90
Foreign Agents Registration Act, 38
foreign policy, U.S.: Bruce Springsteen's
  opposition to, 76–77; in Central
  America, xviii, 26, 27, 28, 29–30, 33,
  34, 35, 36, 37, 39, 40, 42, 43, 44, 86,
  191; citizen opposition to, 24, 26–27, 41;
  see also Central America solidarity
  movement; covert, 26, 27, 29–30, 40,
  42, 44; film criticism of, 80–82; film
  support of, 86; leftist critique of, 35;
  nuclear freeze movement's influence on,
  4, 5; post-Cold War, xviii
Forsberg, Randall, 5–6, 8, 9; and Call to
  Halt the Nuclear Arms Race, 6–7
Fortune, 63, 65
Foster, William, 130
Freedom of Information Act, 38
Frith, Simon, 99, 109
Frohnmayer, John, 91
Fugazi, 106, 110
Funes, Mauricio, 43

Gabriel, Peter, 73
Gandhi, Indira, 153
Gardner, Edward, 127
Gardner, Suzi, 112
Garelick, Jon, 117

Garvey, Marcus, 141
Gay Men's Health Crisis (GMHC), 172–73
Geffen, 114
Geldof, Bob, 68, 69–70
General Motors, 65, 84
Ghost Busters, 79
Ghost of Tom Joad, The, 77
Gingrich, Newt, 190
Gitlin, Todd, 51
Glenn, John, 133
Good Housekeeping, 161
Gorbachev, Mikhail, 23
Gordon, Kim, 112
Gosse, Van, 27
Graham, Bill, 70
Gran Fury, xii, 93, 179–84; collective working style of, 181–83; Kissing Doesn't Kill and, 183–84; snappy one-liners and, 182–83
Grant, Bud, 87
Gray, Alexander, 92
Great Britain, nuclear freeze movement in, 15, 16–18
Great Society, 135
Greenberg, Jon, 174
Green Day, 95
Greenham Common, 16–18
Greenpeace, xvii, 116
Grenada, U.S. invasion of, 39
Grove City College v. Bell, 164
grunge rock, 113
Guatemala: CIA-backed coup in, 29; death squads in, 30, 33, 200n11; human rights activism in, 34, 200n11; North American peace activists in, 27; refugees from, 32, 33; U.S. government involvement in, 30, 31, 34
Guerrilla Art Action Group, 173
Guerrilla Girls, 93
guerrilla theater, 42
gun control, 116
Gurowitz, William, 55
Guthrie, Woody, 77

Haig, Alexander, 14, 81, 85
Hall and Oates, 70
Harriman, Averell, 7

Harrington, Mark, 175, 187
Hart, Gary, 134, 136
Harvard Business Review, 159
Hatcher, Richard, 123, 133, 134
Hatfield, Marc, 19
Hawn, Goldie, 87
Hayden, Tom, 167
Healey, Jack, 72
health care, 139, 189; *see also* AIDS activism
Helms, Jesse, 90, 92, 180
Hemdale, 82
Herbster, William, 57
Heston, Charlton, 20, 86
Higher Education Act, 164
Hill, Anita, 162
Hollywood Women's Political Committee, xvi, 87–88
Holzer, Jenny, 180, 183
homosexuality: in art, 90, 91, 92, 93; conservative views on, 89, 91, 148, 172, 175, 176, 177, 184, 185, 186; cultural acceptance of, 192; *see also* AIDS activism; AIDS Coalition to Unleash Power
Honduras, 25, 26, 28
Hopkins, Sarah, 17
Horbal, Koryne, 150
Horman, Charles, 80, 81
Horton, Willie, xi
House of Representatives, U.S.: nuclear freeze resolution in, 19; pro-choice members in, 151; women in, 157
House Un-American Activities Committee, 91
housing, racial inequality in, 121–22, 130, 131, 138, 139
Hudson, Rock, 172
Hughes, Albert and Allen, 140
Hughes, Holly, 91
Hughes, Jerry, 61, 62
Hughes, Robert, 91, 92
human rights: awareness of, 72–73, 74; Bush administration violations of, 190; Central American violations of, 27, 28, 30, 34, 36
Human Rights Now!, 72–73, 77
Humphrey, Hubert, 135
Hüsker Dü, 99, 105, 114
Hyde Amendment, 170